CONTENTS

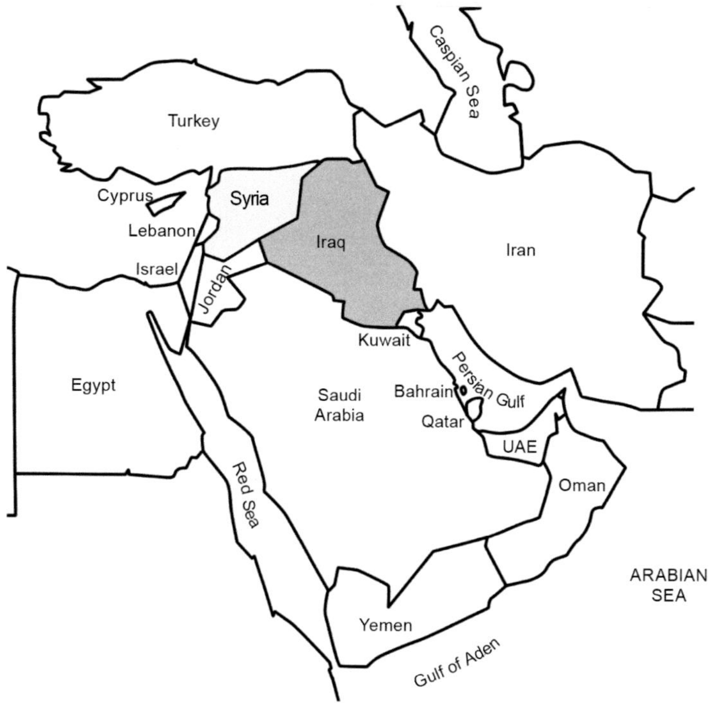

NOTE

In order to simplify the use of this book, all names, locations and geographic designations are as provided in The Times World Atlas, or other traditionally accepted major sources of reference, as of the time of described events. Similarly, Arabic names are romanised and transcripted rather than transliterated. For example: the definite article al- before words starting with 'sun letters' is given as pronounced instead of simply as al- (which is the usual practice for non-Arabic speakers in most English-language literature and media). Instead of using the diacritical marks to represent the letter 'ayn, double a is used, while names like 'Faisal/Feisal' are spelled as 'Faysal'.

Helion & Company Limited
Unit 8 Amherst Business Centre, Budbrooke Road, Warwick CV34 5WE, England
Tel. 01926 499 619
Email: info@helion.co.uk
Website: www.helion.co.uk
Twitter: @helionbooks
Visit our blog http://blog.helion.co.uk/

Designed & typeset by Farr out Publications, Wokingham, Berkshire
Cover design by Paul Hewitt, Battlefield Design (www.battlefield-design.co.uk)
Printed for Helion & Co by Henry Ling Ltd., Dorchester, Dorset

ISBN 978-1-913118-74-7

British Library Cataloguing-in-Publication Data
A catalogue record for this book is available from the British Library

We always welcome receiving book proposals from prospective authors.

ABBREVIATIONS

AAA	anti-aircraft artillery
AAM	air-to-air missile
AB	air base
An	Antonov (the design bureau led by Oleg Antonov)
ASCC	Air Standardisation Coordinating Committee
BAC	British Airspace Corporation (later BAe Warton)
BAe	British Aerospace
BVR	beyond visual range
C3	command, control and communication
CAP	combat air patrol
CAS	close air support
CGS	Chief of General Staff
c/n	construction number
CO	commanding officer
COIN	counterinsurgency
DIA	Defence Intelligence Agency (USA)
DMI	Directorate of Military Industries
FAC	forward air controller
FCS	fire-control system
GMID	General Military Intelligence Directorate (Iraq)
GP	general-purpose (bomb)
HAWK	Homing-All-The-Way-Killer (US-made SAM)
IAP	international airport
IFR	in-flight refuelling
Il	Ilyushin (the design bureau led by Sergey Vladimirovich Ilyushin, also known as OKB-39)
INA	Iraq News Agency
IPC	Iraq Petroleum Company (1929-1961)
IrAAC	Iraq Army Aviation Corps
IrAF	Iraq Air Force (official designation since 1958)
IrAF-ID	Iraq Air Force – Intelligence Department
IRGC	Islamic Revolutionary Guards Corps
Luftwaffe	German Air Force
MANPAD	man-portable air-defence system (shoulder-fired anti-aircraft missile)
MiG	Mikoyan i Gurevich (the design bureau led by Artyom Ivanovich Mikoyan and Mikhail Iosifovich Gurevich)
NATO	North Atlantic Treaty Organisation
nav/attack	navigational and attack (avionics suite)
OCU	Operational Conversion Unit
ONI	Office of Naval Intelligence (US Navy)
OPEC	Organization of Petroleum Exporting Countries
OTU	Operational Training Unit
RAF	Royal Air Force (United Kingdom, since 1918)
Raphael TH	Radar de PHotographie Aérienne Electronique á transmission hertzienne (airborne-photography radar with electronic transmission)
RFC	Royal Flying Corps (predecessor of the RAF, 1912-1918)
RHAW	radar homing and warning (system)
RIrAF	Royal Iraqi Air Force
RSAF	Royal Saudi Air Force
RWR	radar warning receiver
SAM	surface-to-air missile
SEATO	South-East Asia Territory Organisation
Su	Sukhoi (the design bureau led by Pavel Ossipovich Sukhoi)
TPC	Turkish Petroleum Company (1912-1925; subsequently IPC)
UAR	United Arab Republic (Egypt and Syria from 1958 until 1961, and Egypt until 1972)
UARAF	United Arab Republic Air Force (EAF and SyAAF from 1958 until 1961, and EAF until 1972)
USAF	United States Air Force
USN	US Navy
USSR	Union of Soviet Socialist Republics (also 'Soviet Union')

INTRODUCTION AND ACKNOWLEDGEMENTS

The coming-into-being of this volume was protracted and has suffered multiple setbacks. The original idea emerged more than 15 years ago and was rather logical by its nature. The Iraqi Air Force used to play at least an important – and, sporadically, dominant – role in not only the history of Iraq, but that of the entire Middle East, and is also one of the most combat-experienced air forces of the world. While not the first such service in an Arab country, as of the late 1980s and the early 1990s it was considered one of the biggest and most capable air forces in the world.[1] Moreover, since its establishment in 1931, it took part in dozens of violent operations against local uprisings and coups; at least a dozen major campaigns against Kurdish rebellions; three wars with Israel (1948, 1967, and 1973); the long and bitter war with Iran (1980-1988); and four major wars against Great Britain, the USA and their allies (1941, 1991, 1991-2002, and 2003).

For a military flying arm with such extensive combat experience, so much experience from operating dozens of diverse aircraft- and helicopter-types, and rich traditions and heritage, one might expect that its history has been extensively studied and widely published. Surprisingly enough, the situation was diametrically opposite: other than the work of a few enthusiasts that concentrated on the operational history of a small number of British-made aircraft, and excepting the work of Dr. David Nicolle, the history of the Royal Iraqi Air Force (RIrAF) and the Iraqi Air Force (IrAF) largely avoided the attention of historians: indeed, it has avoided attention of even the few Israeli historians that have researched and published on the Arab armed forces over time, regardless of how keen the local armed forces might be to know more. The fewer than a handful of other publications on the subject are almost devoid of primary sources, avoid critical analysis, provide no background and context, and either wildly exaggerate achievements or ignore and explain away failures. Overall, very few more nuanced works on the build-up of the RIrAF/IrAF and its roles and goals as envisaged by various Iraqi statemen and commanders have ever been published in English – it is as if the RIrAF and the IrAF have never mattered in the history of the country they helped to create. Unsurprisingly, our impression is that the Iraqi Air Force was, and remains, one of the poorest-researched and least-known air forces; that, and with the exception of the Syrian Arab Air Force, it is also the branch of the Iraqi – and Arab, in general – armed forces about which there are the most misconceptions and the least understanding available in the public conscience, whether in Iraq or abroad.

All of this is particularly surprising considering the amounts of documentation and photographs that were once available in Iraq, both in official archives and private collections: so much so that, during the mid-2000s, there was still hope that it might become possible to work ourselves through these. The research that led to this volume thus began almost as soon as Brigadier-General Ahmad Sadik contacted one of the authors of this volume in 2004. Sadik used to serve with the little-known IrAF Intelligence Directorate (IrAF-ID) in the early 1980s, before being assigned the position of liaison officer to the French military advisory mission to Iraq. By 1990-1991, he was appointed to one of the top positions of the al-Hussein Project, and in the mid-1990s served as a liaison officer between the Iraqi government and weapons inspectors of the United Nations (UN) in the country.[2] Facing death threats from the notorious Islamic Revolutionary Guards Corps (IRGC) of Iran, he was forced to flee to Syria – which at the time was enjoying a relatively quiet period and one of unprecedented openness towards visitors from the West. Due to his professional background, and as a hobby historian who had already published dozens of related articles in Iraq during the 1990s, Sadik was able to offer unbeatable insights into the inner workings of the IrAF. Unsurprisingly, he followed up with several articles and two books published in Germany, France, and the United States of America (USA) during the 2000s, and then provided a series of extensive interviews – true de-briefs – on the history of both the RIrAF and the IrAF. Moreover, he helped to acquire and translate several related books from Iraq. Tragically, Sadik was incarcerated in Syria in early 2008: nevertheless, his information proved highly reliable and consistent regardless of how often cross-examined and thus of vital importance to this project. For all practical purposes, he is the third co-author of this book.

In more recent times, the work on this project was strongly influenced by engineer Ali Tobchi, a passionate military historian who has collected extensive documentation and almost every single article and book about the Iraqi armed forces ever published in Iraq. Moreover, through his involvement in the al-Hussain project and several others for the development of indigenous weapon systems, he established links to dozens of veteran officers. As well as being a literal 'walking encyclopaedia of the Iraqi armed forces', Tobchi has contributed to this project through extensive translations of several publications available only in Iraq. For us, there is no way to express enough gratitude to either of these two fine gentlemen: we do hope that the results of this project are going to be remembered as a part of their lifetime work.

The third Iraqi national with whom contact proved crucial for this project was late Major-General Arif Abd ar-Razzaq: a British-trained fighter-pilot, commander of the Iraqi Air Force, minister in several governments, and then a prime minister who also became involved in multiple coup attempts undertaken in Iraq during the 1960s. Although he provided only one interview, and doing so years ago, he did manage to offer enough clues, guidance, and information to strongly influence our research into the IrAF.

The reason that our cooperation with Sadik and Tobchi, and that one – yet lengthy – interview with Razzaq are so important is that the official archive of the IrAF has meanwhile been destroyed and looted: indeed, in one of the famous scenes from the invasion of Iraq led by the USA in 2003, US Army troops completely destroyed the memorial room of the IrAF-ID, which contained not only large pieces of several downed Iranian and Israeli aircraft, and the equipment of their crews, but also an extensive archive. Subsequently, not only was a host of documentation from private collections irrecoverably lost due to a manhunt for former IrAF-officers by the IRGC, but even the few aircraft that survived the invasion have meanwhile been reduced to heaps of battered wreckage. Worst of all, former air force officers and other ranks are scattered around the world, some hiding, while others pursue different careers for a living. Yet meanwhile typically for Iraq, vary many other bits and pieces of information presented in this book have been provided by the Iraqis that found refuge in a country destroyed by the wickedness of two big wars in the 20th century, and then in another, destroyed by the worst conflict of the early 21st century.

Additional support – often of crucial importance – has been provided by Dr. David Nicolle and Andy Marden from Great Britain; Martin Smisek from the Czech Republic; Nour Bardai from Egypt; and Ahmed Hassan from Iraq; Jeroen Nijmeijer from The Netherlands; Richard Caruana from Malta; and Goran Sudar from Bosnia and Herzegovina. David's pioneering publications about Arab air forces have proven a source of inspiration for decades, and he has also greatly aided this project through the provision of information and photographs. Martin has been working through the extensive archives in Prague for years and preparing a major work on Czechoslovak military exports to the Middle East from 1945 until 1991 (expected to be published in the Europe@War series in 2021). Nour has proven not only a helping hand with finding very many bits and pieces of information, but also extremely rare photographs from his collection. Last, but not least, Ahmed has selflessly shared additional information and photographs, while Richard, Jeroen, Andy, and Goran have helped with information on the serial numbers and fates of individual aircraft and other details and illustrations.

The final step during the work on this project was provided by a series of publications by the Slovakian Arabist and historian, Dr. Karol Sorby Jr., PhD, from the Institute of Oriental Studies of the Slovak Academy of Sciences; by Dr. Michael Provence, PhD, from the Zentrum Moderner Orient in Berlin, Germany; and by the work of Ibrahim al-Marshi and Samy Salama. After living in Iraq and researching through whatever was left of the local archives and publications, Sorby has authored numerous scientific studies of Iraqi history published in his native Slovak language, as well as in English. Provence has lived and studied in several Middle Eastern countries (particularly Syria and Lebanon from 1998 until 2006) and has authored two ground-breaking books (one of which earned him a Choice Outstanding Academic Title in 2018). Marashi and Salama have published a ground-breaking book on the Iraqi Armed Forces. Their works are precious for providing entirely new, *authentic* insights into the mass of developments from the recent history of the Middle East, and Iraq and Syria in particular – because this is where the contemporary Arab society came into being. Their meticulously researched publications have not only reconstructed largely unknown events from the history of the disintegration of the Ottoman Empire, but especially the artificial division and the contours of the statehoods that have crystallised over time, and – in the case of Marashi and Salama – provide a meticulous reconstruction of the history of the Iraqi Armed Forces.

Wings of Iraq provides not only the history of the RIrAF and the IrAF, but a military-centric point view of Iraq's history. The reason is obvious. Politics dictates the way that armed forces develop their doctrine and strategy and also their tactics. Therefore, and regardless whether for enthusiasts or professionals, it is impossible to understand how, why and when any given nation acquired specific pieces of equipment and weapon systems, how and why its armed forces painted and marked these, and even less so how, why, where and when they deployed them in combat operations without understanding the background and the context of the times. This is even more true for a country like Iraq: a country with a turbulent history dominated by the armed forces originally established with the very purpose of creating the state and then keeping it together; where the armed forces then entered a symbiotic relationship with successive governments, in which – for the lack of historic legacy and native origins – each side needed and used the other; and which then became involved in such important conflicts as that with Iran, and, subsequently, the US-led coalitions.

Without doubt, *Wings of Iraq* is not going to offer precise answers to all of the questions: despite years of cross-examination of collected information it will still contain many (frequently unavoidable) mistakes and a host of points about which many Iraqis – and foreigners – are going to disagree. However, it is the first work to provide a comprehensive – and illustrated – history of the RIrAF and the IrAF in the English language. Our hope is that it might inspire further research and thus not remain the last.

1

THE CRADLE OF CIVILISATION

The territory presently within Iraq includes very diverse terrain. Known as 'al-Jazira', its northern portion is mountainous, with peaks reaching up to 2,100 metres (about 7,000ft) above sea level. The peaks in the north-east, along the border with Iran, are even higher: Mount Ebrahim (Haji Ibrahim) is no less than 3,607m (11,834ft) high. Further south, the country slopes downward to form a broad, central alluvial plain, encompassing the valley of the Euphrates and Tigris Rivers. West of the Euphrates the land gradually rises to meet the Syrian desert. Further south is the vast almost entirely flat and featureless marshy area adjacent to the Persian Gulf.

The climate is mostly continental, with extremes of cold and heat. The mountainous al-Jazira has cool summers and cold winters, often accompanied by snow: the major city in that part of the country, Mosul, has a mean January temperature of 7°C (44°F), and mean July temperature of 32°C (90°F). The lowlands further south have long and hot summers and short and cool winters: the capital Baghdad has a mean January temperature of 10°C (50°F) and 35°C (95°F) in July. The highlands in the north-east enjoy a considerable rainfall from October to May, but there is very little rain further south and especially in the Syrian Desert in the west.

The traditional economy was based on agriculture. Rich in water, up to 50% of the land is arable and – especially along the Euphrates and Tigris – has been heavily cultivated since ancient times. In 1912, the Ottoman Empire granted the first concession for oil exploration to the European-controlled Turkish Petroleum Company (TPC). Entirely unsuccessful at first, and then disrupted by the First World War, the TCP remained operational, and in 1925 obtained a 75-year-concession to explore for oil north of Kirkuk.

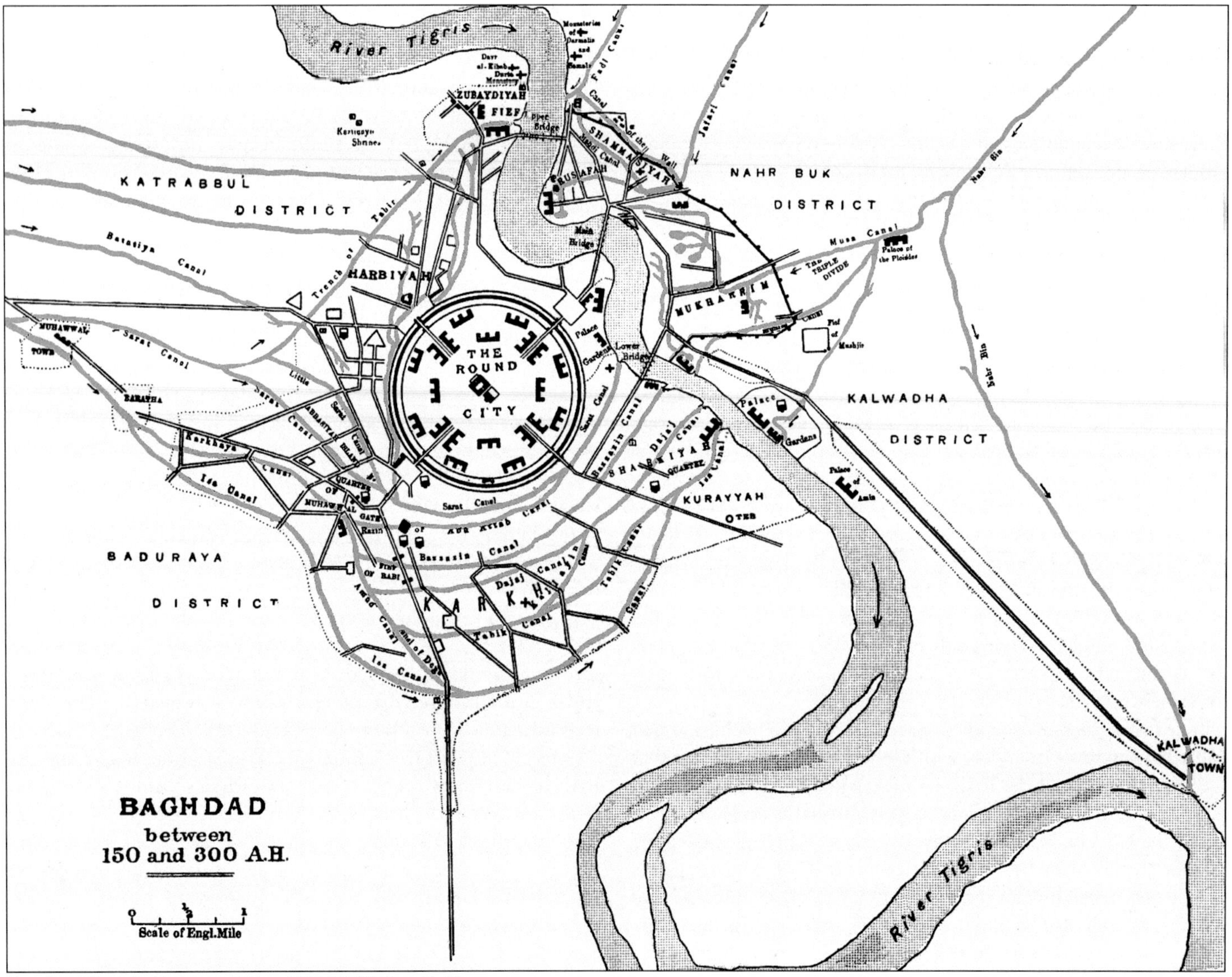

The city of Baghdad between 767 and 912 AD. (William Muir)

This time, the company was highly successful and ever since crude oil and gas have represented the major natural resource of the area and dominate the economy of the region.

The vegetation is meagre through most of the country: the south, south-west, and west are dominated by an empty gravel desert, while the rest of the country has very few trees. Worst of all, the last 40 years of almost uninterrupted wars have badly damaged the environment, polluting land and water, contaminating much of the land and sewing up to 10 million land mines, destroying wildlife and habitats, and neutralising whatever conservation efforts were ever undertaken. Unsurprisingly, wildlife is nearly extinct and consists of just a few gazelle and antelopes, very few cheetahs, jackals, and wolves, and some jerboa and bats. There is still a vivid bird life, including ducks, geese, partridge, and sand grouse, along with vultures, buzzards, ravens, owls and local species of hawk.

HOUSE OF WISDOM

There are plenty of good reasons why Iraqis like to call their country the 'cradle of civilisation': the oldest traces of inhabitation and culture found in this territory date back to times around 65,000 BC. While the Arabic name 'al-Iraq' has been in use since before the 6th century – and means 'deeply rooted', 'well watered', 'fertile', or 'shore of a great river and the grazing land surrounding it' – it is probably of Sumerian origin. Over the last 8,000 years, this area has been the centrepiece, or at least under the control, of such magnificent civilisations as the Sumerian, Akkadian, Assyrian, Canaanite, Amorite, Babylonian, Persian, Hellenic, Roman, Sassanid and Arab. Mesopotamian people invented many technologies, including metal and copper-working, glass- and lamp-making, textile weaving, flood control, irrigation and water storage, and even the first battery. These civilisations developed philosophy, created the first registered religion, and heavily influenced the Abrahamic religions, especially the Hebrew. Based on the sexagesimal (base 60) numeral system, Mesopotamian mathematics and science became the source for the 60-minute hour, the 24-hour day, and the 360-degree circle, while the Sumerian calendar was based on the seven-day week. The last king of the Neo-Babylonian empire dedicated his rule to the excavation and restoration of ancient temples and artefacts that preceded him by almost 1,700 years and he maintained several museums. The powerful Abbasid Caliphate made Baghdad ('The City of Peace', founded in the year 762CE and designed by a Zoroastrian and a Jewish designer) its capital. Only 50 years later, it became the leading metropolis of the Arab and Muslim world, and the capital of one of the richest and proudest empires ever, controlling an area larger in expanse than either that of the Romans, or the one ruled by Alexander the Great. Caliphs ruling from there were as cultured, as passionate and enthusiastic as they were obsessed with science: they developed Baghdad into the leading metropolis of the Arab, Persian, and Muslim world. Open towards other religions and cultures, and insistent on freedom of expression, they attracted scholars from all over the then-known world converting their capital into a place for the Islamic study of Aristotelianism, mathematics (imported from India), arithmetic and its application (for example in the calculation of taxes), and astronomy. Other sciences also flourished, and translator Hunayn ibn Ishaq systematically collected and translated Greek manuscripts, saving them for future generations. Baghdad remained the largest multicultural city of the Middle Ages, and the centre of learning for centuries. The area – including the precious library of Baghdad, the 'House of Wisdom' with countless historical documents and books from every corner of the world, fanatically collected by Caliph Abu Ja'far al-Ma'mun – was then ruined by the repeated Mongol invasions of the 13th century.

THE OTTOMAN EMPIRE[3]

The history of what is modern-day Iraq can be traced back to the 16th and 17th centuries, when the area was gradually incorporated into the Ottoman Empire, which organised it into four provinces. Originally, these were dominated by the military elite of mamluk pashas, taken away as boys from Christian families in Georgia and converted to Islam: they acknowledged the sovereignty of the Ottoman sultan, but gradually moved outside his control. Following two invasions by the Safavid shahs of Persia, the Ottomans recovered the area in the 19th century, and in 1831 imposed their direct control over three provinces from north to south.

According to Western popular culture until this very day, the area widely known as 'Mesopotamia' – stretching from Mosul in the north down the rivers Euphrates and Tigris (the confluence of which is locally known as *Shatt al-Arab* in Arabic or *Arvand Rud* in Persian/Farsi), and ending in the northern Persian Gulf – was supposed to be a 'wasteland': controlled by the 'Sick Man on Europe' or the 'Sick Man on the Bosporus', it was a great sand sea, void of people, with no roads or railways, no electricity or any kind of telecommunications, underdeveloped to a degree where it could not survive on its own. The population of the whole of Mesopotamia was estimated at just three million people at the start of the 20th century, and most of them were supposed to consist of barbaric nomads living in wild tribes, perhaps interested in launching occasional raids further north in the search for loot, and distinguishing themselves from the stone-age era only by using firearms. Created by British and French propaganda of the 19th century, this impression is carefully maintained in popular Western culture until this very day. According to the same 'official version', 'Arabs' also had no modern military traditions before the British and the French began organising and training them between 1915-1918.

Actually, the Ottoman Empire underwent a series of dramatic reforms during the 19th century. In 1876, the young Sultan Abdul Hamid II ascended to the throne and promptly promulgated the constitution and a parliament. The ideas of this 'dangerous reformer' were strongly opposed by Great Britain, France, and Russia: assuming that their civilisation was superior to what they perceived as (and partially were) 'negative attributes' and outright 'barbarity' of the Ottoman Muslims, they conspired to not only destroy the empire but even its legacy, and thus fostered political turmoil and embroiled it in a series of wars. Concluding that the situation threatened the survival of his state, Hamid dissolved the parliament and usurped all the political powers. Recreating an absolutist regime, he decided to bring the disparate population of the empire to a common identity: correspondingly, he adopted a new ideological principle, Pan Islamism, as the means of countering European influence. Nevertheless, he simultaneously introduced sweeping reforms of the economy and education. A large network of carefully maintained roads, and modern railways – the latter spanned more than 10,000 kilometres by 1914 – was constructed over the following years, followed by the largest telegraph network in the world: the latter connected at least every town, and employed a true 'army' of technicians and specialists capable of transmitting messages in at least a dozen languages. Through the early 20th century, all the cities and towns were provided with electricity.

Parallel to this process a huge, state-controlled educational system emerged, based on the construction of schools all over the Ottoman Empire for children of 7 – 18 years of age. Indeed: every village received an elementary school, though the precise schooling available varied based unpon ethnic and cultural lines, and to some extent gender. The economic reforms and improved education resulted not only in a flourishing economy, but also in flourishing journalism: although the press was censored, the journalists introduced ever more advanced ideas from the West, influencing the emergence of multiple political and nationalist movements – including a group of young dissidents organised as the 'Committee of Union & Progress', but colloquially known as the 'Young Turks'. In 1908, the Young Turks forced the Sultan Abdul Hamid II to restore the constitution and parliament, abolish censorship, and release all political prisoners. The new constitution introduced an inclusive governing system in which inhabitants from all ethnic and religious groups elected their municipal and provincial councils. Moreover, it continued cultivating the old and rich tradition of Ottoman citizens addressing their grievances to the state in the form of petitions, in which they could protest everything from official corruption and police brutality to bad service from local officials. Not only the Sultan Abdul Hamid II – who acted as political leader, but also as a caliph, and thus religious leader of the huge Sunni majority of the population – but also the Young Turks, and every provincial governor were conscious enough to always carefully react to every such complaint.

Certainly enough, the reforms and modernisation introduced by Hamid, and then the Young Turks, did not result in a land of milk and honey: far from this, the empire continued to lag behind the Western powers in regards of industrialisation (indeed, as of 1914, it was still lagging behind the Russian Empire). Foremost, the Ottoman Empire had accumulated a huge foreign debt, and was completely dependent on ever more foreign loans for survival. Nevertheless, and while the authorities worked hard on establishing a common Ottoman identity, diverse ethnic and religious groups not only enjoyed their own rights and privileges but had opportunities for their economic prosperity – always based on meritocracy.

THE LATE OTTOMAN MILITARY

Reform of the Ottoman armed forces initially went through a period of French influence. Starting in 1880, when the first German military advisory team led by Lieutenant-Colonel Otto Köhler arrived in Istanbul, it entered a period of close cooperation with the German Empire. Moreover, in 1896, General Colmar Freiherr von der Goltz – already famous as the top military historian and theoretician at home – was contracted to serve as the top instructor for the Ottoman Army. Guided by von der Goltz's ideology of a strong, authoritarian and militant 'nation in arms', the subsequent reform and modernisation of the Ottoman armed forces went hand-in-hand with the build-up of the educational system: indeed, the military educational system grew faster than the civilian. In it, and after obtaining elementary education, the most promising students were – regardless of their ethnic and religious background, and no matter if from Anatolia, the Balkans, modern-day Iraq, Libya, Syria, or Yemen – forwarded to military middle schools such as those in Adana, Baghdad, Beirut, Damascus, Mosul, Salonica, or other provincial capitals, and then military preparatory schools like the one in Baghdad, which was opened before the local civilian schools and had a higher output than that of civilian schools in all three of the Ottoman provinces that made the future Iraq. Finally, the best of the students were sent to the Harbiye Military Academy in Istanbul, where they lived and studied military drills, communication, geography, reconnaissance and surveying, fortifications, and the German, French and Russian languages for three years. Every year, the best 50 amongst them were selected for the pinnacle of the military educational system: General Staff College. The education provided by this system produced entire generations of highly educated and skilled civilian and military officers that grew into self-conscious members of a meritocratic and cosmopolitan elite, perfectly capable of not only commanding armed forces, but also excelling in law, and in international and domestic business and administration.

The result was that the relations of the Ottoman armed forces with their German advisors were far from one-sided: they resembled a partnership. For example, one of Von der Goltz's closest friends in Istanbul was the Baghdad-born Mahmoud Shevket Pasha: like nearly all top Ottoman Army officers of the time, he spent several years in Germany during the 1890s, learned German fluently, and wrote, translated, and published prolifically on military topics including two tactical manuals authored in cooperation with von der Goltz. Shevket Pasha and von der Goltz's military thoughts became the basic textbook not only for subsequent generations of Ottoman Army officers: it was to guide them in forming the Turkish Republic of 1922 and also into attempting to shape the subsequent Iraq in similar fashion.[4]

THE MESOPOTAMIAN CAMPAIGN[5]

Early during the 20th century, the strategic importance of Mesopotamia grew immensely. Not only had the Germans constructed the Baghdad Railway, which shortened the travelling time from Istanbul to Baghdad to 14 days, but the Anglo-Persian Oil Company discovered extensive petroleum deposits throughout the neighbouring Persian Empire, especially in the Abadan area, on the eastern side of the Shatt al-Arab. The British thus deployed a strong military force – centred on the 6th Division of the British Army of India – to protect the rapidly expanding Abadan, right at the start of the First World War in August 1914, and then prepared a contingency plan for an invasion of the Ottoman Empire.

Although voluntarily entering the First World War in alliance with the German and Austro-Hungarian Empires, the Ottoman Empire had no expansive designs in the Middle East: correspondingly, it maintained a defensive stance and had only understrength, poorly equipped and incomplete second grade units stationed in Mesopotamia. While its army of the early 20th century was the first – world-wide – to introduce the triad organisational system (where three platoons formed a company, three companies a battalion, three battalions a regiment, three regiments a division, and three divisions a corps), its two primary units deployed in this area were XII Corps (with the 35th and 36th Divisions) in Mosul, and XIII Corps (with the 37th and 38th Divisions) in Baghdad. The mass of officers and troops in these units were Arabs, or Arabic-speaking people. Further south, the mass of the Ottoman Army consisted of irregular cavalry, all of whom were also Arabic speaking people. The number of regular units was massively reduced as soon as the Ottoman Empire became involved in the First World War on 29 October 1914: the headquarters (HQ) of XIII Corps and the 37th Division were re-deployed to the Caucasus, while the entire XII Corps was sent to Palestine. The situation was thus opportune for the British to invade and conquer Basra in November 1914, with the aim of 'securing oilfields in the Abadan area'. A counterattack by irregular Ottoman cavalry was easily repulsed in April 1915, emboldening the British to start preparing for an advance on Baghdad.

Due to logistics-related issues and other theatres of operations receiving priority, the preparations in question took months. Meanwhile, the Ottomans returned their 35th Division to Mosul,

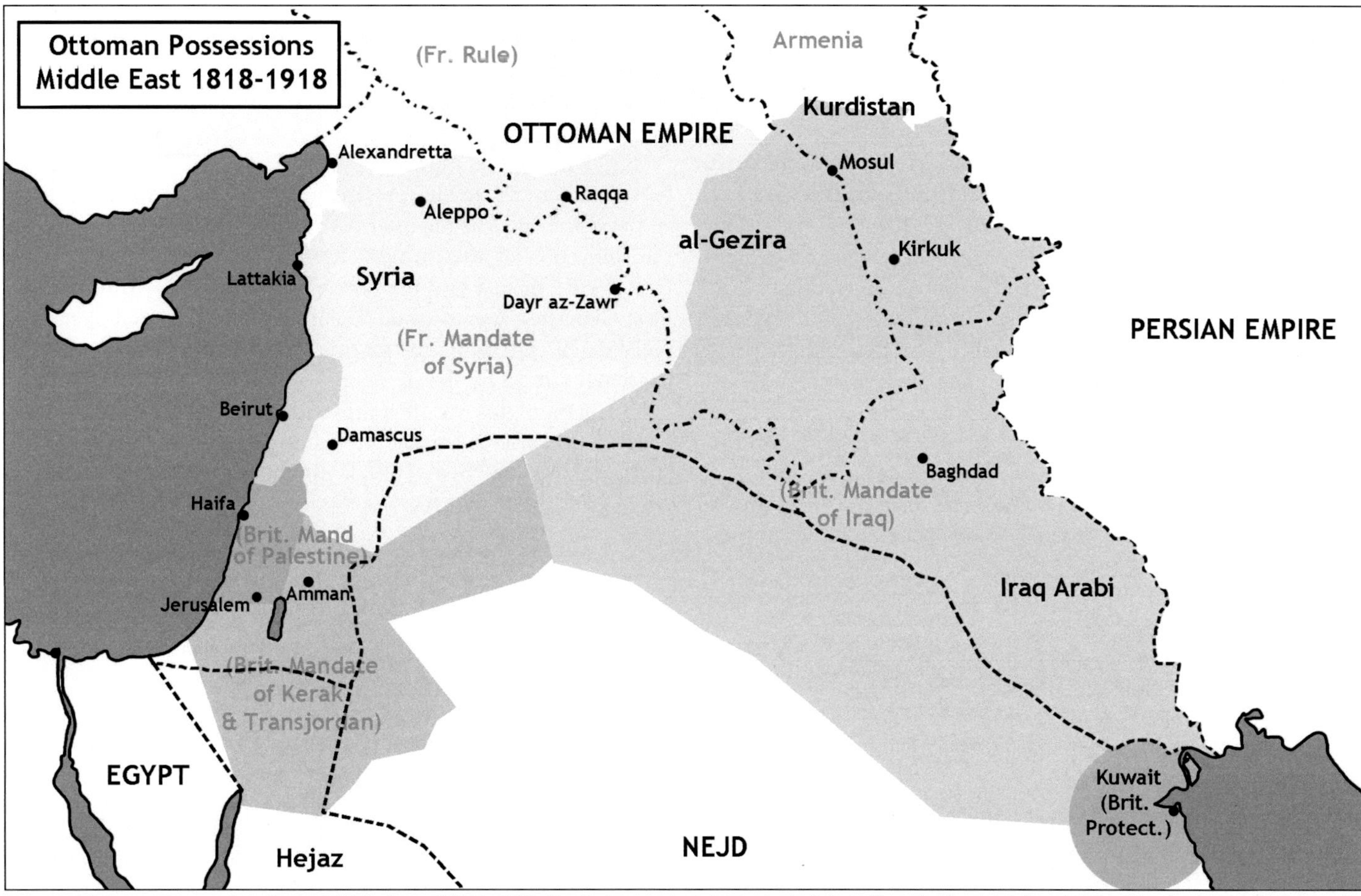

A map of Ottoman Possessions in the Middle East of 1818-1918. Shaded areas depict, (clockwise) Syria (French Mandate), Iraq (British Mandate), Transjordan and Palestine (British Mandates) as carved out by the British and the French on the basis of the Sykes-Picot Treaty and subsequent agreements. (Map by Tom Cooper)

reorganised mounted volunteers into the 1st and 2nd Tribal Cavalry Brigades, reconstituted the 38th Division, and rushed the 45th and 51st divisions to the theatre. With German help, they also established a small flying unit operating a miscellany of aircraft types.[6] It was only in November 1915 that the British Army of India's expeditionary force – consisting of the 6th and 12th Divisions, and one cavalry brigade with a total of about 13,000 troops – launched its advance in the direction of Baghdad: this was stopped cold during the five-day long inconclusive battle of Ctesiphon. The Ottomans then reorganised their armed forces into the Sixth Army, commanded by the 72-year-old von der Goltz, and quickly returned to the battlefield. The Ottoman Army enveloped the British Army of India's corps outside al-Qut (al-Kut) on the Tigris River. After multiple attempts to break out or relive the garrison had all failed, at the cost of up to 23,000 British casualties, al-Qut was kept supplied by transport aircraft. Eventually, the situation of the British forces in al-Qut became critical: not waiting for another relief attempt, on 29 April 1916 the commander of the British garrison capitulated. Out of 13,164 officers and other ranks that went into captivity, over 7,000 – mostly Indian – troops died of starvation, disease, lack of medical attention and brutal indifference on the part of their Ottoman guards over the following months. Occurring shortly after the Gallipoli disaster, this was the second and the most bitter defeat of the British Empire at the hands of the Ottomans.

A new offensive was initiated by the British Army of India more than a year later. On 13 December 1916, its forces advanced up both sides of the Tigris River. They advanced very slowly: it was only on 23 February 1917 that the quantitatively inferior Ottoman defenders of al-Qut gave up and withdrew. Supported by three gunboats and aircraft of the Royal Flying Corps (RFC), the British then moved north, reaching Baghdad on 11 March against the dogged resistance of four depleted divisions – the 35th, 46th, 51st and the 52nd – of the Sixth Army. A counteroffensive by the Ottoman XIII Corps from the direction of Persia was contained, and on 24 April 1917 the British took Samarra, further north. The loss of Baghdad was the first major Ottoman defeat in the First World War.

Subsequently, Mesopotamia assumed a low priority for both sides. After securing Baghdad and Samarra, the British felt that their supply lines were overstretched. Moreover, their efforts in Palestine were considered more important, especially in the wake of the capture of Beersheba on 8 November 1917, and the release of the Balfour Declaration in support of Zionism (originally aimed to gain support for the British war effort within the Jewish populations of the USA, Russia, and Germany). Finally, the British had to divert much of their force for the protection of the oilfields in the Baku area because of the Russian collapse. In turn, the growing crisis in Palestine absorbed most of the Ottoman attention and reinforcements. Ultimately, the war in Mesopotamia ended with the Armistice of Mudros, which officially concluded the hostilities between the Ottomans and the British in the Middle East on 30 October 1918.[7]

THE SYKES-PICOT TREATY[8]

When British forces failed to make any advances in Gallipoli, then were to become stuck during the Battle of the Somme on the Western Front, and experience a defeat in Mesopotamia; London, Paris and Moscow formulated the Sykes-Picot Treaty. Under this, once the Ottoman Empire had been defeated, France was to gain control over all of the eastern Mediterranean coast, and most of what is nowadays southern and eastern Turkey and northern Iraq;

Russia over all of Armenia and eastern Turkey; while the British were to establish themselves in control over nearly everything from Palestine in the west to the Persian border in the east, and the western coast of the Persian Gulf.[9]

The Russian Empire collapsed in 1917, but as soon as the First World War was over, both Great Britain and France rushed to realise their plans. Of course, the realities on the ground at the end of the First World War were 'slightly different' to the seemingly endless tangle of the Sykes-Picot Treaty and various contemporary and subsequent promises, counter-promises, and agreements but, the governments in London and Paris remained loyal to the general idea and considered it more important than any pledges to their Arab, Kurdish, or Armenian allies. Indeed, once in control of the former Ottoman possessions in the Middle East, nothing mattered to the British and French administrators: treating the area as a conquered territory or a colony, they began carving out several dependent quasi-nations: acting as supposed 'tutors' to 'such peoples not yet able to stand by themselves under the strenuous conditions of the modern world'[10], they began inventing 'nationalities' and 'superior races', and 'traditions'; they drew borders where there were none before and imposed what were actually inferior governing arrangements in comparison to those of the Ottomans. Such measures were all aimed to create states ruled by dictatorships of their preference, supposed to be 'easy to control'.

THE MESS

Although the former Ottoman province of Mosul was originally assigned to France, the British not only occupied but also retained that part of the Ottoman Empire. Both the British and the French military occupation authorities promptly abolished the elected municipal councils and – in complete ignorance of the existing situation and demands of the population – began forcefully carving out states organised strictly along hierarchical and authoritarian lines. Indeed, they did their best to ignore and block the findings of the US-run King-Crane Commission, which – after a journey of more than 40 days through what is now Turkey, Syria, Lebanon, Israeli-occupied Golan Heights, Israel, the Israeli-occupied West Bank, Gaza, and Jordan (the British prevented the Americans from entering the future Iraq) – concluded that the vast majority of the local inhabitants (70-80%) preferred the territorial unity of greater Syria and absolute independence. Very few supported any kind of foreign mandates, and fewer than 1% supported Zionism.[11]

The – rather unsurprising – consequences of these actions can be traced directly to the present: insistence on artificial borders and states created in the aftermath of the Sykes-Picot Treaty and the subjection of the former Ottoman provinces to British and French rule, or that of their – or subsequently US – 'hand-picked' local favourites, was to result in continuous unrest and instability, failed states, endless trauma for nearly everybody involved, a *de-facto* perpetual war, and a virtual meltdown in recent years. Iraq became no exception to this rule: together with Palestine (and subsequently Israel), and Syria, it became the centrepiece of this never-ending crisis, and then the 'best' example imaginable.[12]

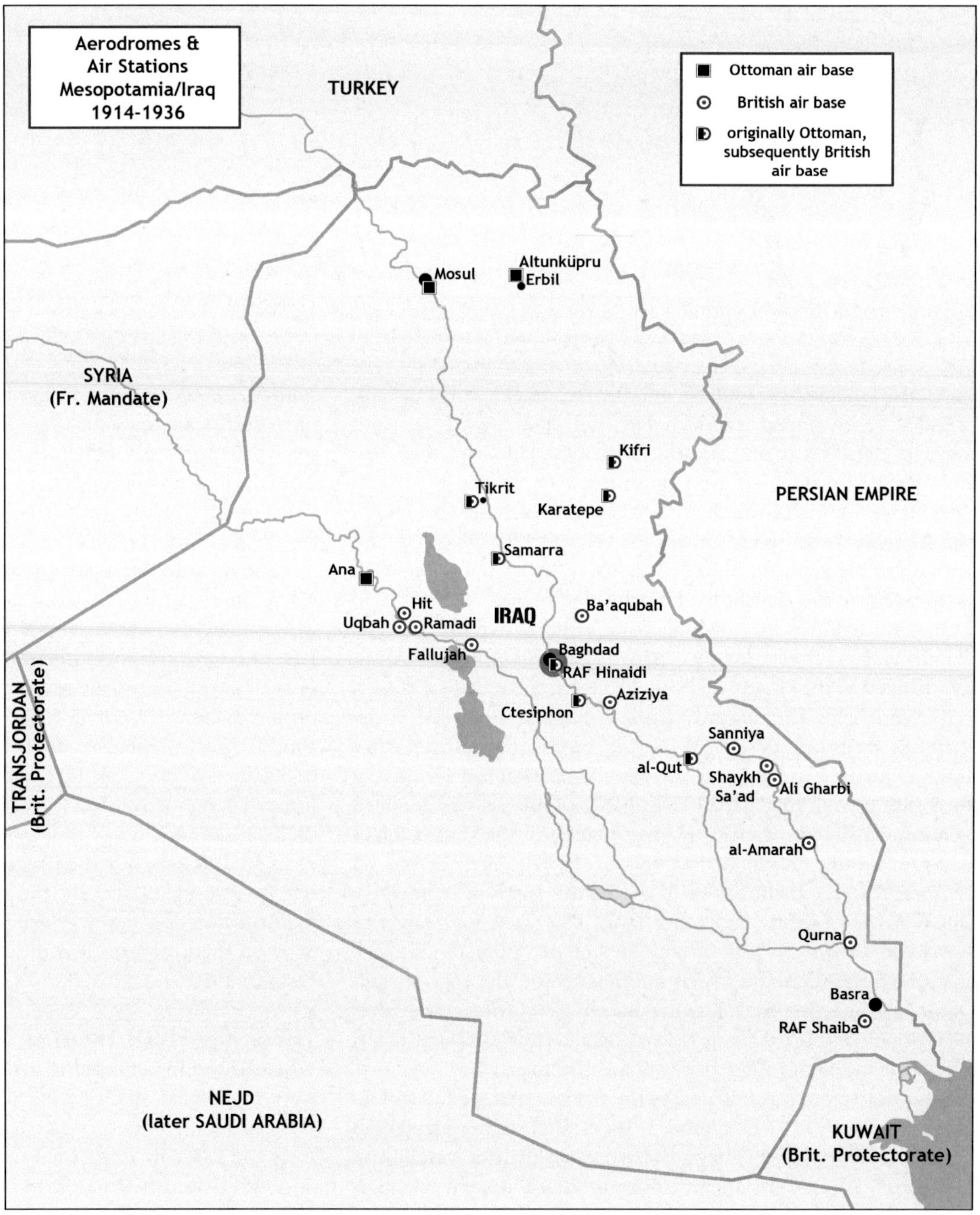

A map of Iraq with aerodromes and air stations constructed by the Ottomans and the British in the period 1914-1931. (Map by Tom Cooper based on research by Dr. David Nicolle)

FIRST UPRISINGS

The population within British-occupied Mesopotamia was not entirely united in regards of how to react to the new authorities. In addition to religion and ethnicity, it was further divided between major tribes and the urban elite, by the geography, by traditions and by language differences. For example, the elites of Basra – mostly merchants in contact with the British since the 19th century – quickly sided with the new rulers; the elites of Baghdad, which had plotted an anti-Ottoman uprising in 1915, gave up not only on this, but also similar pretensions against the British. Worse yet: because their various tribes spoke (and still speak) entirely different versions of their language, the Kurds could rarely find agreement even amongst themselves, let alone with the British or the Arabs.

However, amid an atmosphere dominated by the British military authorities applying collective punishment and atrocities, extra-judicial detention, torture and assassinations against any kind of challenge to their regime, it did not take long for civilian disobedience to turn into armed resistance. The first to rise against the British were the Shia clergy of Najaf and Karbala. Acting 'in defence of Islam', they issued a *fatwa* (religious law) prohibiting any kind of cooperation with the British in early 1918. When the British proved unimpressed by all peaceful forms of protest, on 19 March 1918 a number of armed Shia entered the citadel of Najaf and murdered the local British commander. Although the Punjabi guard then managed to drive them out, they then found themselves besieged by well-armed insurgents. In turn, the British Army of India put the entire town under siege. The insurgents tried to seek help from the nearby tribes, but their messenger was caught while crossing the British lines and executed. From 7 April 1918, the British subjected Najaf to a fierce artillery barrage. After holding out for nearly a month the rebels formally surrendered on 4 May 1918: their leaders were all executed.

The failure of the uprising in Najaf left no lasting impressions upon other local leaders in Mesopotamia. In May 1919, the Kurdish Sheikh Mahmoud Barzani – installed by the British as Governor of Sulaymaniyah – led his combatants into the destruction of the local British garrison and then proclaimed independence. The British force sent against him was repulsed and a larger one, of divisional size had to be dispatched: this was successful in capturing the Sheikh and temporarily pacifying the area, but the atmosphere remained hostile. And still; this and the uprising in Najaf were only the start.

BRITISH MANDATE OF MESOPOTAMIA VERSUS THE ANATOLIAN MODEL

Through 1919 and 1920, popular armed resistance to the British and French occupation became widespread everywhere from Istanbul via Alexandretta and Antioch (present day Iskenderun and Antakya in Turkey, respectively) to Aleppo, the mountains outside Lattakia, Hama, Homs, Damascus and Jerusalem in the west, via Dayr az-Zawr in the northern Syrian Desert, to Sulaymaniyah on the frontier with Persia. The whole of Asia Minor and the Middle East were afire. Nevertheless, London and Paris continued to ignore the demands of the local population. Indeed, on 25 April 1920, during the San Remo Conference, Great Britain was officially awarded the Mandate for Mesopotamia and Palestine by the League of Nations. Abandoned by the British, Arab nationalists in Damascus reacted by effectively repeating the declaration of independence of the Arab Kingdom of Syria: this was a constitutional monarchy ruled by the British ally King Faysal Ibn Hussein of Mecca in 1918-1920. Another declaration called for an independent Iraq, but the mass of officers of the Ottoman Army captured by the British and then convinced to side with Hussein during the Arab Revolt of 1916-1918 rallied in Damascus. They were followed by some former Ottoman Army officers that – repeatedly – rejected invitations to abandon their posts during the First World War, but then found themselves jobless and facing prosecution by the British and French authorities after the armistice. Indeed, two heroes of the Great War, Major-Generals Yusuf al-Azma (born in Damascus) and Yassin al-Hashimi (born in Baghdad) joined Faysal to serve as his Minister of War and Chief of General Staff (CGS), respectively.

Emboldened by the successful resistance put up by their brother-in-arms, Mustafa Kemal – best known as *Atatürk* ('Father of Turks'), who had reorganised large elements of the former Ottoman Army (in which Hashimi's younger brother Taha then served with the CGS in the 1920s) to defeat the French invaders of Anatolia in 1919 – Azma and Hashimi intended to repeat the exercise. Although mistrusting Faysal – indeed, they perceived him as a 'fool' and a 'British puppet' – they quickly organised the Army of the Arab Kingdom of Syria. However, Faysal was no Atatürk: when the British abandoned him and the French invaded Syria in May 1920, he folded, causing disorder in his armed forces. Determined to fight regardless of the circumstances, Azma fell during the Battle of Maysaloon, the decisive clash with the invaders. Hashimi managed to escape to north-eastern Syria.[13]

GREAT IRAQI REVOLUTION

Meanwhile, during early 1920 the Shia clergy of Najaf and Karbala began plotting a new wave of popular protests. Learning lessons from their earlier failure, they took care to cooperate with Sunni and Shia tribal leaders, and with former officers of the Ottoman Army. Mass demonstrations were organised in Baghdad in reaction to the San Remo conference in early May 1920: initially, these were entirely peaceful gatherings at Sunni and Shia mosques. However, when the Deputy Civil Commissioner, Arnold Wilson, dismissed the demands of their representatives, the demonstrators began rioting. Hoping to avoid the spread of unrest, the British arrested notable leaders, but this only provoked violent reaction: by late June 1920, most of Iraq was in arms. The revolt quickly gained momentum and defeated one British garrison after another: by late July 1920 up to 130,000 insurgents controlled the mid-Euphrates region and effectively besieged Baghdad, prompting British commanders to start planning a fighting withdrawal from all of Mesopotamia to the coast of the Persian Gulf.[14]

Amid bitter public critique, the British Army of India's reaction to the Great Iraqi Revolution was severely constrained by London's decision to avoid running a costly counterinsurgency (COIN) campaign. At least initially, the number of available units was barely enough to retain control over the major cities. However, imperial authorities never considered renouncing their control. As the crisis reached its high point, the War Office in London – then presided over by the Secretary of State for War, Winston Churchill – authorised reinforcements in the form of ground troops re-deployed from Persia, and three squadrons of what was since 1 April 1918 officially designated the Royal Air Force (RAF) from Egypt and India. Churchill went as far as to authorise the use of chemical weapons 'against recalcitrant Arabs' even if – primarily due to the slow research and development of suitable bombs – these were never actually deployed. What did happen instead was that the RAF took care to construct – or expand – three major air bases (ABs) in the country: Mosul in the north, Hinaidi near Baghdad in the centre, and Shaibah, 45 kilometres outside Basra, in the south, before going into action.

AIR POLICING

Thanks to air support, by August 1920, the British Army of India did manage to stabilise the situation in the Mandate of Mesopotamia enough to launch a counteroffensive: this consisted of what can be described as 'raids' by ground forces, but was foremost characterised by what became known as 'air policing'. Centred on the use of well-fortified air bases, this strategy consisted of a campaign of widespread and brutal reprisals against the civilian population all around the country. Any town or village identified as 'controlled by terrorists' was surrounded by ground troops (usually by night), and then subjected to sustained, merciless, and highly devastating air attacks. It was during such operations in Iraq that the RAF – amongst others – developed the tactic of using lighter bombs to demolish roofs, and then bombard the same area with incendiary bombs, to set homes on fire. After countless barbarities, including wholesale obliteration of their villages and massacres of their women and children, the leaders of the insurgency in Mesopotamia were forced to the conclusion that any further resistance was pointless. Others were meanwhile bribed into switching sides. The Great Iraqi Revolution thus ended in October 1920 when the last insurgents surrendered Najaf and Karbala to the British.

The ferocity of this first 'air policing' campaign is obvious from known statistics: up to 10,000 Iraqis and around 500 British and Indian soldiers were killed. The fighter-bombers of the RAF flew 4,008 hours, dropped 97 tonnes of bombs and fired 183,861 bullets. In return, they lost 11 aircraft shot down and more than 50 damaged, 10 crewmembers killed and seven wounded. The leadership in London considered this an 'acceptable price' for the overall success. For the first time in the history of warfare, air power led the way to a victory in war. Henceforth air policing was adopted as the standard British strategy for maintaining control over Iraq: in several cases it was 'applied' even against tribes that refused to pay taxes.

2

TUMULTUOUS IRAQ

The ultimate fate of the Ottoman Empire was supposed to be sealed with the Treaty of Sévres of August 1920: western Anatolia was to be given to Greece, south-western to Italy; an Armenian state was to emerge in eastern Anatolia, while the territories further south were to be reorganised into 'mandates' under the Sykes-Picot Treaty and the San Remo conference. Next to nothing of this plan worked – except for the British securing possession of the German-Ottoman concessions for oil resources in Mesopotamia: and the continuous military presence in Mesopotamia was on the verge of turning into a bloody and costly affair. To save its control of the Middle East while drastically reducing the expense, London changed its strategy. Commissioner Wilson was replaced by Churchill, who sought to install an 'indirect' type of administration: in Mesopotamia this meant imposing the Sunni minority over a population that consisted up to 50-60% Shia, 15-20% Kurds, and about 8% Christians, Jews and others. A 'suitable Arab ruler' was found in Faysal Ibn Hussein, still fresh in exile after the French destroyed the Arab Kingdom of Syria. He was appointed the King of Iraq (and his brother Abdullah as the King of Transjordan), quickly confirmed by a rigged referendum and crowned on 21 August 1921. The Mandate for Mesopotamia thus became the British-sponsored Hashemite Kingdom of Iraq.[1]

HASHEMITE KINGDOM OF IRAQ

Once again systematically ignoring thousands of petitions, pleas, and warnings by people from all over the Middle East, the British designed the new state to serve their imperial interests – the mass of which was diametrically opposite to the demands of the locals. Correspondingly, the Hashemite Kingdom of Iraq was styled as a constitutional monarchy with a bicameral chamber: the upper chamber was appointed by the king, the lower was elected by male citizens. The balance of power was in the hands of the king – himself subordinated to the British High Commissioner (as were both chambers of parliament) – who ruled through a government presided over by a British-appointed Prime Minister. The first Iraqi Prime Minister, Abd ar-Rahman al-Kilani, was a religious scholar, but – and in general – all ethnic and religious groups bar the Sunnis were left entirely neglected, outside the loop of governance, and without the means to influence their own future.

Politically, Faysal pursued the ideology of pan-Arab nationalism and sought to improve education in the country. For this purpose, he employed dozens of allies – foremost the entourage of so-called 'Sharifian officers' – that fled with him from the Arab Kingdom of Syria. However, intending to exploit the new situation for their own agendas, the Sharifian officers, and teachers imported from Damascus soon found themselves at odds with almost everybody else: Faysal's rule was thus always at odds with the majority of the population – including not only the Shia and the Kurds, but even those Sunnis amongst which the legacy of the Ottoman Empire was still highly influential.[2] Matters only worsened once the constitution – written by two former Ottoman officers under careful control of a British 'supervisor' – was promulgated in mid-1925: this was far less liberal and less representative than that of the Ottomans from 1908.[3] Overall, the Hashemite Kingdom of Iraq was a patched-up conglomerate of factors entirely at odds with each other: the idea of running this state under British control regardless the cost and consequences was at odds with the demands and expectations of nearly everybody living within its borders: permanent and violent unrest was unavoidable.

THE IRAQ LEVIES

As of 1921, the internal security of Iraq was still in the hands of the British garrison. To reduce the cost of maintaining control over the country, the British began establishing local armed forces. The first regular military force established by them in the Mandate of Mesopotamia were the Assyrian Levies (later Iraq Levies). Developed from the handful of Arabs first enlisted in 1915 and known as the Arab Scouts, from 1919 this was recruited from amongst the Armenians and Assyrian Christians. Later, Kurds, Mandeans and Turkomen were permitted to join, while Arabs were officially excluded from 1922, by when this 6,000-strong, British-officered force of three cavalry regiments, four infantry battalions and an Assyrian pack-battery was paid by the British government. The Iraq Levies were kept strictly outside the control of any kind of local authorities: considered 'local forces of the Imperial garrison', they were subjected to the operational control of the British Army of India. Favoured by the British, who settled some 40,000 Assyrians against the stiff opposition of the Arabs and Kurds, and arrogant towards the local population, they were initially deployed in northern Iraq, until they became a thorny problem due to their involvement in operations against multiple local uprisings, several massacres of civilians, and then a mutiny in May 1922. Reorganised, the Iraq Levies were then re-deployed: bolstered to about 7,500 by the mid-1930s, and organised into six infantry battalions, three cavalry regiments, two mountain regiments, and one field artillery battery, their primary duty became the protection of RAF bases south and west of Baghdad.[4]

OTTOMAN MILITARY INFLUENCE

The process of building up the Armed Forces of Iraq began on 25 October 1920, when Jaafar al-Askari (a former officer of the Ottoman Army and then the Army of the Arab Kingdom of Syria) was appointed the Minister of Defence. Using a nucleus of 10 officers of the same background (including his brother-in-law, Colonel Nouri as-Saad), Askari officially established the Iraqi Army on 6 January 1921. Drawing upon a pool of more than 600 former Ottoman army officers (mostly Arab Sunnis from Baghdad and Mosul), of whom 190 had already served in the Arab Kingdom of Syria – and partly in an attempt to prevent these from becoming a threat to national security – Askari then commissioned 250 of them into the officer corps, on the condition that they would undergo a British training course.[5]

Initial growth of the nascent army was slow, because it was an all-professional service and there was a lack of volunteers and, indeed, a lack of men willing to serve in a British-controlled military service. Therefore, although the government assigned it no less than 25% of its annual budget, and having an authorised strength of 6,000 men, the Army initially numbered only around 2,000. Nevertheless, in a rush to counter the possible return of Yassin al-Hashimi, Askari took care to establish an Officer Training School, three infantry schools and a cavalry school (re-organised as the Royal Iraqi Military College in 1928, and later as the Military Academy), followed by the first two regional commands in late 1921, and then the General Headquarters (GHQ), in early 1922. By the end of the same year, the GHQ included four departments, and controlled a company of Royal Guards, one cavalry regiment, three infantry battalions, and a logistic unit (including a warehouse and workshops), with a total of 2,500 officers and other ranks. Only sustained promotional campaigns in the Iraqi media helped to gradually build-up the Army to about 400 officers and more than 6,800 other ranks by 1924.[6]

From the start, the primary purpose of the Iraqi Army was the protection of the government. The secondary role was the British (less so Iraqi) concern about Turkish pretensions towards northern Iraq: this is why the first two regional commands (which subsequently served the purpose of creating future divisions of the army) came into being in Mosul and Sulaymaniyah, while the third was established in Baghdad. However, while most of the original Iraqi officer cadre were graduates of the Harbiye Military Academy of imperial Istanbul, subsequent generations were educated at the local military schools, where they were indoctrinated by Sati al-Husri's teachings about Iraqi nationalism and pan-Arabist glorifications of an Arab fatherland. Indeed, they were expected to follow an ideology greater than advancing the interests of their ethnic and religious groups, to liberate all Arab states of British and French imperialism, and unite them in one, Prussian-style state created by a strong military.[7]

THE RAF TAKES OVER

Of course, all the activities of the nascent Iraqi Army were carefully monitored by the British imperial garrison and its advisors, which – including the Iraq Levies – numbered about 75,000. The garrison was centred on the RAF Mesopotamian Group, expanded into a full wing of three, and then eight units in 1921 (including Nos. 1, 6, 8, 30, 45, 55, 70 and 84 Squadrons). The Iraq Command officially assumed the responsibility for defence and internal security from the British Army of India in October 1922 and the RAF played the crucial role in the Mandate through practicing air policing at every opportunity. This was the case during the Turkish-supported Kurdish uprising led by Sheikh Massoud Barzani in the Ruwanduz area of northern Iraq of February 1923, when the Iraq Levies and the newly-established Iraqi Army were deployed to counterattack, supported by the RAF. During this operation the commander of No. 45 Squadron, Arthur Harris (the future commander of RAF Bomber Command during the Second World War), developed the practice of deploying transport aircraft as bombers to demolish most of Sulaymaniyah. Ironically, while the town was then quickly secured by the units of the Iraqi Army, and Sheikh Barzani forced to flee with his followers into Persia, the British commanders still sympathised with the Kurds rather than with the Iraqi troops they controlled.[8]

Sheikh Barzani was back in Iraq by June 1923, when he arranged with Baghdad to take charge in Sulaymaniyah again. Nevertheless, another military force had to be sent against him in July 1924, forcing him to flee for the fourth time, and the RAF continued bombing his raiding parties through 1925, repeatedly driving him into Persia. An end to this insurgency was effected only in 1926, when Britain, Iraq, and Turkey signed the Tripartite Agreement that fixed the common frontier between the latter two, enabling Baghdad and Ankara to bring their respective territories under formal control.[9]

THE FIRST ANGLO-IRAQI TREATY

The subsequent build-up of the Iraqi Army went through exactly the same – rather 'tumultuous' – period as that of the entire Hashemite Kingdom. The primary issue was the British presence and influence: the British Military Mission established in 1922 (and some 46 strong), had the final say on the arms, training, size and deployment of all the units, and exercised operational control.[10] Indeed, the British then decided to formalise their privileged status by means of the Anglo-Iraqi Treaty: an 'agreement' designed by the British allowing for 'local self-government', while securing imperial control of all the major affairs of Iraq, the air route connecting Europe with India, telegraphic links, and the RAF's air bases. Its first draft came into being in 1921, and the treaty was quickly signed on behalf of the British by the High Commissioner for Iraq, Sir Percy Cox, on 10 October 1922. However, this treaty became a matter of years-long dispute in Baghdad.

Understanding the true nature of the agreement and the resulting quasi-national rule, the population of what was now the Hashemite Kingdom of Iraq fiercely opposed not only the colonial mandate, but *any* British influence. Unsurprisingly, relatively 'minor' raids against local garrisons of the British Army of India never ceased, even for years after the Great Iraqi Uprising was put down. Moreover, not only Faysal, but successive British commissioners for Iraq had their hands full with public and political resistance. Eventually, Faysal was forced to appoint one of his most outspoken critics and biggest rivals, Abd al-Muhsin as-Saydoon as Prime Minister. A former Ottoman army officer and elected Ottoman parliamentary deputy, Saydoon was, like many other Iraqis, 'still looking north': hoping for a return of the Ottomans. Much to their disappointment, however, Mustafa Kemal decided against such a move. While defeating the British-sponsored Greeks in eastern Thrace, and the French in Cilicia, and thus successfully concluding the Turkish War of Independence, he played a crucial role in the decision of the Grand National Assembly (the Turkish parliament in Ankara) to abolish the Ottoman Sultanate on 2 November 1922: the last sultan was declared a traitor of his people *and of Islam* and sent into exile. This act sent shockwaves all through the Middle East: the vast majority of the population thus lost their top religious leader, and with this single blow the centrepiece of the struggle for the future of the region shifted away from Turkey. This was another factor that was to change only almost a century later.

A Westland Wapiti of the RAF dropping bombs during an air policing operation against Sheikh Barzani's insurgency in northern Iraq during late 1930 or early 1931. (Albert Grandolini Collection)

THE KING'S PARTY AND THE OPPOSITION

Although disappointed by Atatürk's decision, Saydoon continued to refuse ratifying the Anglo-Iraqi Treaty. In 1923, Faysal replaced him with the fiercest opponent of the Mandate: Yasin al-Hashimi.[11] With this act, Faysal introduced the strategy of appointing Hashimi whenever in need of satisfying nationalist Iraqis – and appointing Saad instead whenever in need of satisfying the British. This practice did not come out of nowhere: the politics – and thus the security – of Iraq through the mid- and second half of the 1920s was in the hands of about 30 people, all of whom were products of the Ottoman education system. These were split into two camps. Dominated by Yasin al-Hashimi, the 'Opposition' enjoyed widespread popular support and consisted of people that joined Faysal only after the end of the First World War: other than military officers it included figures with civilian backgrounds, like the lawyer Rashid Ali al-Khaylani. The other group consisted of former Ottoman Army officers that sided with Faysal after being captured by the British during the Great War, and had already served with him in the Arab Kingdom of Syria: colloquially known as the 'King's Party', it was dominated by Askari and his Kurdish relative, Bakr Sidqi al-Askari, but also included Nuri as-Saad, Nuri al-Jaafar, Ali Jawdat al-Ayyubi, and Jameel al-Madfaai. With the exception of Saad, members of the Kings's Party were all fiercely anti-British, and determined to resist the Mandate – but, pragmatic enough to accept foreign domination if this was serving their own interests.[12]

THE SECOND ANGLO-IRAQI TREATY

Of course, Hashimi not only refused to sign the treaty, but resigned in November 1923. Contrary to what much of the Iraqi public expected from him, he refused to take up arms and lead a popular uprising: instead, he went on to organise a major opposition party in the 100-member parliament elected in 1924. Certainly enough, the latter – finally – ratified the treaty, but this caused such damage to the government of General Askari that they were forced to resign. The near-continuous rotation of governments went on until 1927, when the ultimate showdown between the King's Party and the Opposition began: in that year, immense quantities of crude oil were discovered outside Kirkuk in Mosul province. Whether this was the reason for the British to conclude that the original Anglo-Iraqi Treaty needed a renewal is at least arguable (for details, see the box at the end of this chapter), but it is certain that they decided to strengthen their control over Iraq – even if pretending they would grant additional freedoms. The result was London's offer to grant 'complete' independence and admittance to the League of Nations to Iraq, together with an end of payments for the mandate administration, and regulation of mutual relations through the Foreign Office instead of the Colonial Office in London – in exchange for an exclusive oil-concession to the British-owned Iraqi Petroleum Company (IPC). This gave birth to the idea for the Second Anglo-Iraqi Treaty.

Related negotiations lasted nearly three years: Faysal then appointed Saad to form a new government (with Askari as Defence Minister), and he dutifully signed the new treaty in June 1930: consequently, the Imperial garrison was drawn down to a single brigade. The RAF was to retain two bases, both protected by the Iraq Levies: Hinaidi and Shaibah.

IRAQI PLANNING

For the Iraqi Army, the Second Anglo-Iraqi Treaty – and the subsequent quasi-independence – resulted in sweeping changes. Tight British supervision of all of its activities ended and, at least in theory, the government in Baghdad was free to expand the armed forces without approval from London. On 23 December 1929, Brigadier-General Taha al-Hashimi was promoted in rank to that of a General and appointed as the first Chief of General Staff (CGS). Askari and Hashimi then recalled an idea from 30 March 1925, when Baghdad requested that London deliver 36 aircraft, together with equipment, weapons, and training of personnel necessary to establish an air force consisting of two squadrons. Much to Iraqi disappointment, on 14 April 1925 the British High Commissioner turned down that request. Bitterly disappointed, the Iraqis kept on pushing: Saad and Askari retained the decision to fund a rudimentary air force, but nothing happened for the next two years.[13]

Shortly after the British opened the negotiations for the Second Anglo-Iraqi Treaty, on 19 May 1927, General Askari (who played a crucial role in introducing general conscription as a tool of national cohesion, around the same time) presented his new plan for establishment of an air force. Confident due to the knowledge that dozens of his officers had experience with military aviation during the Great War, and to make sure his idea would meet approval from London, he recommended a joint British-Iraqi service, including four native pilots and 24 technicians.[14] Keen to have the new treaty signed, the British reluctantly agreed: on 1 August 1928, the first six students – all young 1st Lieutenants of the Iraqi Army – joined the RAF College in Cranwell, starting a course that was to last for two years, while 16 students (selected from a group of 200 volunteers)

A de Havilland DH.9A of the RAF seen underway over central Iraq in the early 1930s. (Albert Grandolini Collection)

entered a four-month course to become technicians at RAF bases in Iraq. Three additional Iraqi students were sent to Cranwell in 1928, and at least two in 1929. Nevertheless, in order to retain their control of the related efforts, on 9 March 1929 the British appointed their (Iraqi-paid) 'Air Inspector' to the Iraqi CGS.[15]

The first five Iraqi pilots (one from the original group was washed out) – including Natiq Muhammad Khalil at-Tayi, Sami Abd al-Fattah, and Hussain Janabi – returned to Iraq in 1930, and were assigned to the RAF units deployed in the country: Tayi was appointed the first administrator of the nascent flying service, and received a corresponding office at RAF Hinaidi. Muhammed Ali Jawad, Hafiz Aziz, Mousa Ali, and Akram Talib Mustaq graduated from Cranwell by 1931 and were also assigned to RAF units in Iraq.[16]

ROYAL IRAQI AIR FORCE

Having thus secured the necessary personnel, the Iraqi Ministry of Defence took care to obtain aircraft. In 1930, Baghdad was granted permission to place an order for five de Havilland DH.60 Gipsy Moths (a version of the original DH.60 Cirrus Moth powered by the 100hp strong de Havilland Gipsy engine, named 'Metal Moth' by the Iraqis), and two DH.80A Puss Moths with enclosed cabins. While one of the latter was to serve as King Faysal's personal aircraft, and all were meant to serve as trainers, at least four of the DH.60s were equipped with shackles for four 10kg (20lb) bombs each. On 8 April 1931, Muhammad Ali Jawad (the most experienced of the early Iraqi pilots), Natiq Muhammad at-Tayi, Mousa Ali, Akram Mushtaq, and Hafiz Aziz flew the five Gipsy Moths – escorted by one of the Puss Moths piloted by an RAF officer named Carter – from de Havilland's aerodrome at Hatfield to Iraq. Following an arduous journey via France, Italy, Yugoslavia, Bulgaria, Turkey (where the pilots spent three days as official guests of the government), and the French Mandate of Syria, they arrived to a joyful reception from King Faysal, all the government ministers and dozens of other officials and dignitaries at al-Washash aerodrome in northern Baghdad, on 22 April 1931. Ever since, this day is commemorated as the day that the Royal Iraqi Air Force was established. Together with their ground crews, these pilots formed the RAF Hinaidi-based No. 1 Squadron. Nominally commanded by 1st Lieutenant Muhammad Ali Javad but supervised by a squadron leader deputed from the RAF,

A row of the first five DH.60 Metal Moths of the RIrAF: their arrival at Washash aerodrome on 8 April 1931 is celebrated as the Air Force Day in Iraq. Notable are the large national insignia atop their upper wings. (Tom Cooper Collection)

1st Lieutenant Akram Mushtaq in the Metal Moth with serial number 1, which he flew to Baghdad in April 1931. (via Ali Tobchi)

the unit was quickly worked up through bombing practice and aerial gunnery. Indeed, it flew its first operational sorties (dropping leaflets) against Kurdish insurgents in the north as early as 21 October 1931. On 27 January 1932, No. 1 Squadron was reinforced through the acquisition of four DH.60Ts: while one made a forced landing during delivery flight from Egypt, and had to be written off, the three others were delivered to Iraq by the fourth group of pilots qualified at RAF Cranwell.[17]

As the air force grew, so also did its significance. Appointed on 22 April 1931, the first official commander of the RIrAF, Major Mohammed Ali Jawad, was replaced by Lieutenant-Colonel Ibrahim Hamdi ar-Rawi, on 22 April 1932 – on the same day, the RIrAF flew its first combat operations against Sheikh Barzani's insurgents that attempted to take Kifri and Qanaqin. Indeed, the Iraqi aircraft played a crucial role in the battle for Aui-Barika, where Barzani's force was defeated and scattered, forcing survivors to flee into Persia once again. Northern Iraq remained a crisis zone, however: in February 1932, the British attempted to settle surviving Assyrians in the vicinity of Barzan, provoking another revolt, this time by Sheikh Ahmed Barzani. The RAF and the RIrAF then supported an Iraqi Army unit that quickly occupied the insurgent stronghold, and then succeeded in driving Barzani over the frontier into Turkey, in July 1932.[18]

Combined with intensive training, combat operations over the harsh terrain of northern Iraq resulted in significant attrition: while one DH.60 crashed into the Tigris River near RAF Hinaidi on 18 February 1932, killing its pilot Abdul Wahid Hilmi, another collided with Mount Shirin near Barzan during a reconnaissance sortie, on 19 April 1932: Natiq Muhammad Khalil at-Tayi and his observer, Sayed Mohammed Abbas, thus became the first combat fatalities of the air force. Although their actions were overshadowed by the RAF, the Iraqi pilots proved at least as effective: indeed, their experiences encouraged Baghdad into further expansion of the air force. Correspondingly, three DH.80 Puss Moths were acquired to replace losses: these arrived on 20 April 1932, all already equipped with racks for four 10kg bombs each, along with radios and reconnaissance cameras. With this, No. 1 Squadron was finally complete with its originally planned complement of 12 aircraft.[19]

INDEPENDENCE

On 3 October 1932, the Hashemite Kingdom of Iraq was officially granted independence under King Faysal I, and the Mandate of Mesopotamia ended. Of course, this was a mere quasi-independence: in addition to securing complete control over Iraq's oil and its military bases in Iraq, Great Britain also secured continuous supervision of King Faysal and his government, the security of Imperial communications, and a guarantee that Iraq would never accept any foreign military advisors other than the British. Moreover, Iraq was required to assist the United Kingdom

A row of DH.80A Puss Moths seen prior to their delivery to Iraq in 1932. Barely visible is the national insignia applied on the underside of the wing, near the wing-tip. At the time, this insignia was worn in six positions. Serials were subsequently applied in black on the rear fuselage. (BAE Heritage)

NATIONAL INSIGNIA OF THE RIRAF

Seeking to distinguish themselves from their British 'advisors' and also from their Ottoman origins, officers of the RIrAF went to some lengths to design an original national insignia for their aircraft. Correspondingly, instead of the fin-flash limited in size and containing three stripes, as on RAF aircraft, they decided to paint the whole ruder of their aircraft in the traditional pan-Arab colours of black, white, red and green (where green stands for the Islamic prophet Mohammad, red for courage in battle, white for generosity, and black for the era of Caliphates and the past glory). Instead of the usual RAF-style roundel, they opted for a triangle applied in the same colours: the centre field in green was outlined in black and represented a stylised Iraq. On the green field, a red line was applied in the form of a stylised Arabic letter 'Jim', which stood for Jaysh ('Army') and for the flow of the Euphrates and Tigris Rivers. Inside this insignia was a small white diamond.

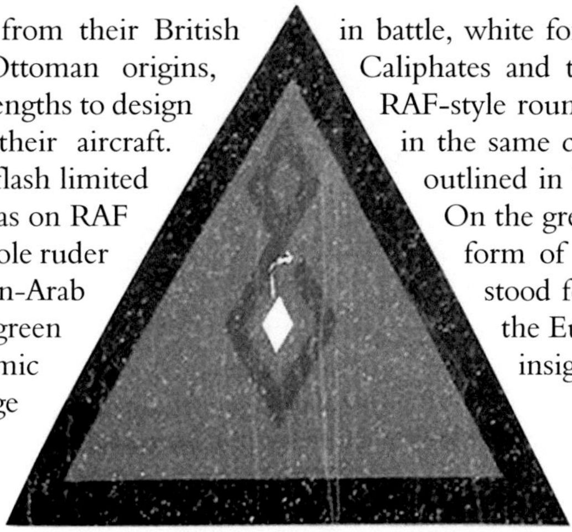

The classic 'triangle' – the well-known national insignia applied to all Iraqi military aircraft from 1931 until 2003 – as applied on the intake of a MiG-25RB reconnaissance-bomber captured by US Marine Corps troops in 2003. The green field, outlined in black, represents a stylised Iraq. The red 'line' is the stylised Arabic letter 'Jim', which stands for *Jaysh* ('Army') (See the colour section for further examples in situ). (Tom Cooper Collection)

in wartime and allow British troops to pass as they liked. Although their numbers were greatly decreased, the British advisors remained in the country and influential in all government affairs: it is almost unnecessary to say that the country continued suffering from permanent political instability and never-ending armed uprisings as a result.

Sticking to his usual practice, Faysal dismissed Saad shortly after independence, and requested Khaylani to form a government, before starting a long trip abroad in May 1933, leaving members of the 'Opposition' to attempt restoring order in a country shaken by mass demonstrations and a new series of violent uprisings. Whether on the advice of Askari or Hashimi, on 22 June 1933 Khaylani declared the Royal Iraqi Air Force – commanded since April 1932 by Lieutenant-Colonel Ibrahim Hamdi ar-Rawi – an autonomous branch of the armed forces. Corresponding to its new status, in November 1933 the RIrAF was taken over by Brigadier-General Ismail Ibrahim Namaq (a cavalry officer of the former Ottoman Army).[20]

In summer 1933, an uprising of the diminutive Assyrian minority erupted in north-western Iraq. The Iraqi government reacted fiercely, deploying units led by the 'rising star' of the Army – and the only Iraqi officer favoured by the British – Brigadier-General Bakr Sidqi al-Askari, to virtually smash the rebellion: the operation culminated in the Simla massacre in August when 315 Assyrians were murdered.[21] The RIrAF seems not to have taken part: for much of 1933 it was preoccupied with introducing into service eight

A nice profile view of the DH.84 serial number 22: notable is the gunner, demonstrating the deployment of a machine-gun from his elevated position atop the fuselage. (Tom Cooper Collection)

A DH.60 Puss Moth, serial number 12, with a row of DH.84A Dragons as seen during the parade celebrating the reorganisation of the RIrAF's combat fleet in 1934. (Ahmad Sadik Collection)

de Havilland DH.84A Dragon twin-engined biplanes, delivered in another direct overflight from Great Britain on 27 March.[22] Including a position for a machinegunner, shackles for up to a dozen 10kg bombs, and equipped for desert operation, this type entered service with No. 2 Squadron, officially established on 1 June 1933.[23]

King Faysal also missed the Sidqi-led massacre of the Assyrians: he was still abroad. Indeed, on 8 September 1933, he died of a heart attack while in Switzerland for his usual medical checks. His successor was his only son, Prince Ghazi Bin Faysal, crowned as king on the same day. Although a graduate of the Royal Iraqi Military College (where he was tutored by Taha al-Hashmi), and thus a staunch pan-Arab nationalist, propagator of the annexation of Kuwait to Iraq, and fiercely anti-British (and a passionate pilot), Ghazi's reign was considered to be weak by the Iraqis and seen as heavily dependent on Sidqi's support.[24] Considering that neither was to live for very much longer it is rather ironic that Ghazi's and Sidqi's alliance was to shape the future of the country for nearly a decade.

UNREST-INDUCED GROWTH

The RIrAF remained preoccupied with itself for most of early 1934. When it became obvious that major insurgencies were looming not only between the Shia in the centre, but also amongst the Kurds and Yazidis in the north and north-west, Namaq and his assistant – and the commanding officer (CO) of No. 1 Squadron – Akram Musthaq, reorganised the air force. Three additional DH.83 Tiger Moths were acquired and then, together with all the remaining earlier marks of that type, concentrated within the Training Flight.[25] Remaining pilots and aircraft, and all the new DH.84As were concentrated within No. 2 Squadron. This unit was intensively involved in operations against the Kurds during the successful campaign of the summer of 1934, but suffered the RIrAF's worst loss to date, when a Dragon flown by Ahmad an-Nasiri crashed shortly after taking off from RAF Hinaidi, killing the pilot and four other officers, on 11 September 1934.[26]

Moreover, seeking to obtain a serious combat capability, the RIrAF was granted permission to place an order for the first batch out of an eventual 34 Hawker Nisr scout bombers from Great Britain. Powered by Rolls Royce Pegasus Mk IIM2 engines, these were the first military aircraft designed as such to be purchased by Iraq. Initially, all were grouped within No. 3 Squadron, officially established on 1 October 1934 under the command of Mushtaq, who was also awarded a medal of courage for his operations against the Kurds.[27]

Muhammed Ali Jawad (centre) presenting the flag of No. 3 Squadron to King Ghazi in presence of Jaafar Askari, the then Minister of Defence (white suit). Notably, the Nisr in the background (wearing either the serial number 42 or 52) received the nick-name 'Basra' in Arabic, below observer/gunner's cockpit. (Ali Tobchi Collection)

Eventually, Iraq acquired a total of 34 Nisrs between 1934-1936: after serving with No. 3 Squadron for a few years, by 1941 the surviving 25 examples were re-distributed between that unit and the reformed No. 1 Squadron. (Ahmad Sadik Collection)

A row of Nisrs as seen in a parade celebrating the establishment of No. 3 Squadron, on 1 October 1934. They were powered by Bristol Pagasus Mk IIM2 radial engines and equipped with Osprey-type tail units. (Ahmad Sadik Collection)

RESOURCE CURSE: IRAQ'S OIL

Many narratives about Anglo-Iraqi relations in the 1920s, 1930s and early 1940s superimpose the issue of oil – and there seems to be next to no dispute that the primary purpose of the Second Anglo-Iraqi Treaty was to safeguard British control over the extensive underground oilfields discovered in the Kirkuk area in 1927. Indeed, most related histories create the impression that – combined with the oilfields of Persia – the Iraqi oilfields produced immense amounts of oil during the 1930s. Most of the oil imported by Britain at the time actually came from the USA, and the rest from Persia. On the contrary, due to their conflicting interests, the owners of the IPC – including the Anglo-Persian Oil Vompany (from Great Britain), Royal Dutch/Shell (a British-Dutch company), Compagnie Francaise des Pétroles (a French consortium), and the Near East Development Corporation (from the USA) – delayed development of the Iraqi oil sector and exported very little before the late 1940s. Certainly enough, and foremost thanks to French pressure, the IPC renegotiated its concession with Baghdad in 1931, obtaining a 75-year permission for oil exploitation almost anywhere east of the Tigris River, in exchange for minimal royalties, and the construction of two pipelines to the Mediterranean Sea. The British and the Iraqis preferred a terminal at Haifa, in the British Mandate of Palestine, but the French wanted the pipeline to transit their mandate in Syria to a coastal terminal at Tripoli. Correspondingly, the IPC constructed a pipeline in y-form. In 1934, the first part from Kirkuk to Haditha was completed: this K-pipeline was supported by multiple pumping stations (designated K-1 to K-5), which supported the flow of oil. Each station was constantly manned and included a small fort, a major power generator and facility with pumping machinery, a small airfield, and housing for civilian and security personnel. A year later, the other two branches were also ready: the T-pipeline through the French Mandate of Syria to Tripoli, served by stations designated T-1 to T-6, and the H-pipeline through the British Mandate of Transjordan to the British Mandate of Palestine, served by stations designated H-1 to H-6. Even then, no significant amounts of Iraqi crude were exported before 1939: a year later, production reached four million tonnes, but the T-pipeline was closed by the British shortly after the fall of France, in June 1940, and the production then severely reduced during the Second World War. The conclusion is therefore that the importance of Iraqi oil for Great Britain – whether as of 1927, 1930 or 1941 – was actually negligible. However, the issue of its *denial to other powers* was certainly a 'different pair of shoes'.[30]

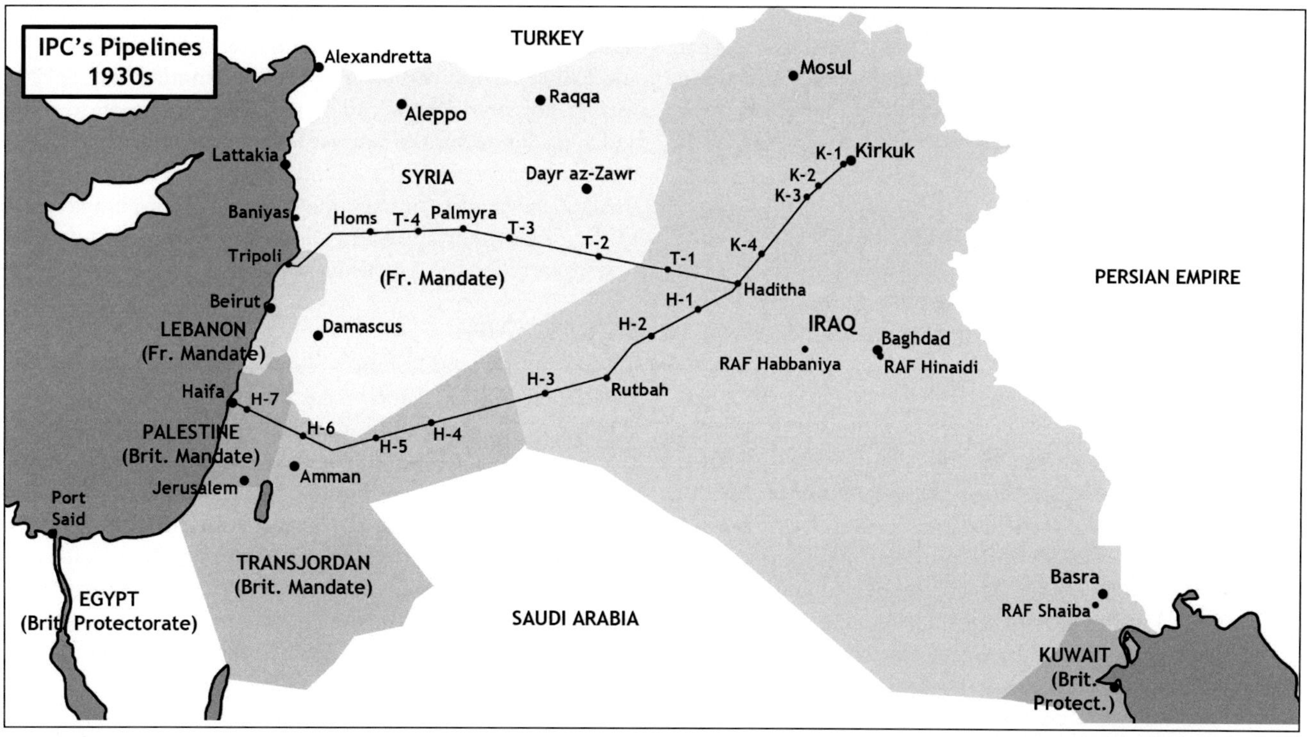

A map of the IPC's pipelines, including the K-pipeline, connecting Kirkuk with Haditha; the T-pipeline connecting Haditha with Tripoli, and the H-pipeline, connecting Haditha with Haifa. These pipelines were to play a prominent role in much of the subsequent history of Iraq. (Map by Tom Cooper)

FIRST EUPHRATES UPRISING

The rapid growth of the Sunni-dominated Iraqi armed forces was monitored with growing suspicion by the Shia majority. In late 1933, their only two ministers resigned in protest over the government spending money planned for civilian projects in order to acquire additional arms and establish additional military units instead. As the resulting unrest swept through the mid-Euphrates region during late 1934 and early 1935, the Shia leaders staged a major power demonstration in Baghdad, confronting the king with the People's Charter, which demanded major improvements to civilian life and the economy. Attempting to prevent a rebellion, in March 1935 King Ghazi dismissed the government of General Ali Jawdat al-Ayyubi, and appointed Jameel al-Madfaai. However, when Taha al-Hashimi refused Madfaai's order to deploy the armed forces against the Shia insurgents in Rumaytha, Ghazi was left without a choice but to appoint Yasin al-Hashimi as prime minister. Having good connections to the Shia, Hashimi took care to gather all the tribal and rural sheiks for a huge banquet in Baghdad, and then artfully used Ottoman statecraft – including reminders, cautioning, generous promises and subtle threats – to convince most of them to lay down their arms. The tribes that refused to take his offer were then subjected to a merciless campaign in which Sidqi made use of the full might of the Iraqi armed forces to effectively neutralise the armed opposition of what became known as the 'First Euphrates Uprising' in a matter of few weeks.[28]

As now usual for the RIrAF, the newly established No. 3 Squadron thus went into action before it was ready. Commanded by Magdy ad-Din, Nisrs of No. 3 Squadron became involved in combat against insurgents that, accustomed to air policing, resisted fiercely. On 15 March 1936, the Nisr piloted by Raouf Shabib – with Tawfiq Yahya as observer – was shot down by machinegun fire, and the crew killed. Only a day later, a Nisr piloted by Yeremiyah Nasir, with Abd Allah Hussein as observer was also shot down and its crew killed. Nevertheless, the RIrAF played an important role in the suppression of the insurgency in Diwaniyah, and then 'helped convince' the tribes in Rumaytha to negotiate – always by the means of (often extensive) air policing. Ultimately, the armed revolt was defeated by the end of May 1935.[29]

In October of the same year, Nisrs of No. 3 Squadron saw even more action in support of the Sidqi-led campaign against the Yazidi Revolt on Jebel Sinjar: the Yazidis formed the third largest non-Muslim minority within the kingdom, and had declared their independence. General Namaq deployed his combat aircraft in a series of devastating air strikes, after which the Sidqi-led army mopped up.

Yasin al-Hashimi, former Major-General of the Ottoman Army and the CGS of the Army of the Arab Kingdom of Syria, refused to take up arms and lead a general uprising against the British dominance on at least two occasions. Instead, he played a crucial role as an opposition politician and, while serving as Prime Minister in 1935-1936, completely reformed the administration of the nascent Iraq. (Ahmad Sadik Collection)

BISMARCK OF THE ARABS

Meanwhile, Hashimi launched an ambitious program of reforms based on his own visions of a modern, centralised, authoritarian and militaristic state, and aimed to assert full control over people, economy, territory, borders, and natural resources. Passing over 100 laws within less than 18 months, he introduced a new penal code, new tax laws, laws favouring local production of various products and new industrial ventures, laws that established new postal-, agricultural- and mortgage banks, and significantly improved civilian and military education. Moreover, he launched numerous irrigation projects and abolished the aristocratic titles, dismissed whatever officials had resisted him, expanded the parliament to include more of his allies, and alternately tightened and loosened press censorship. Finally, he launched a large expansion of the armed forces: the Army was authorised to establish division-sized formations, while military training for boys was introduced into the state middle and secondary curriculum, and a state youth military organisation came into being, where teenagers were subjected to strict military discipline, taught to use firearms, read maps, camp, read, and understand military manuals. For all practical purposes, Hashimi thus laid the foundations for the Iraqi state as known ever since.[31]

However, he also allowed the contracts for more than a third of the British advisors in Iraq – including the highest-ranking civilian (Sir Kinahan Cornwallis) and military positions (General John Charles Bruce) – to expire without replacement, while significantly cutting salaries for those that remained. An outburst of complaints by offended and jobless British officials left him unimpressed – even more so as a series of scandals sank the reputation of the royal family and King Ghazi in particular. Indeed, Hashimi's position was then further bolstered by his widely publicised intention to unify Iraq and Syria, his outspoken support for the Palestinian cause (including clandestine provision of arms and money to the to the insurgents in the British Mandate of Palestine), and his never-ending opposition to the Anglo-Iraqi Treaty. To add salt to the wound, the Baghdad newspapers then began praising him as the 'Bismarck of the Arabs'.[32]

SIDQI'S COUP

Of course, Yasin al-Hashimi's reforms were not something that the British were to tolerate for very long. Early on 29 October 1936, exploiting the opportunity that offered itself as Taha al-Hashimi was underway in Turkey, their favourite Lieutenant-General Bakr Sidqi launched the first military coup in the modern Arab history: as multiple units of the Army marched on Baghdad, 11 aircraft of the RIrAF dropped leaflets over the capital, in which Yasin al-Hashimi's dismissal and replacement by anti-reformist Hikmat Sulayman (younger brother of Mahmoud Shevket Pasha) was announced. Whether the British were involved in the coup, or 'just' supportive of it, remains unclear, but what is certain is that emboldened by the British ambassador, King Ghazi was happy to meet these and similar demands, and receive Yasin al-Hashimi's resignation. To make sure, during the afternoon the British smuggled their supporter Nuri as-Saad out of the country to Egypt, while Hashimi and Rashid Ali al-Khaylani fled to Lebanon. In turn, Sidqi then had Askari executed outside Baghdad, and finally marched with his units into the capital to stage a large military parade in a clear demonstration of *his* power.[33]

In the new government, Hikmat Suleiman concentrated on addressing social issues around the country, while Sidqi was appointed the CGS and focused on further expansion of the armed forces. Ironically, while both admired Atatürk for his reforms in

Turkey, they retained all of the reforms introduced by Hashimi, with one exception: before long there was no doubt about the fact that henceforth it was Sidqi who had the final say in nearly all affairs related to governance. Thus, it was actually the British-supported former Ottoman Army officer who established himself as a *de-facto* dictator of Iraq, and then one that began doing openly what Hashimi either did clandestinely, or never dared doing: openly challenging British interests. Sidqi intensified the flow of arms, ammunition and money for the anti-British and anti-Zionist insurgency in Palestine and intensified the expansion of the Army. Amongst others, in late 1936, he completed the process of establishing the 1st Division in Baghdad (this was commanded by Major-General Abd al-Latif Nouri), and then that of the Kirkuk-based 2nd Division (commanded by Sidqi). As could have been expected, both were organised following the patterns of the Ottoman Army, and included three brigades, each of three regiments, each of which consisted of three battalions. Moreover, while the army and the air force were then successful in putting down a local uprising in the Samawa region of southern Iraq – during which the RIrAF suffered its next loss, when losing a Nisr flown by pilot Anwar Mustafa on 13 June 1937 – and in contravention of the Anglo-Iraqi Treaty of 1930, Sidqi began searching for alternative sources of arms and equipment. Having 127 fully qualified pilots on hand, the RIrAF was eager to grow through acquiring modern combat aircraft.[34]

A row of Gladiators seen during the parade staged when the unit operating them, No. 4 Squadron, RIrAF, was established on 30 November 1937. (Ahmad Sadik Collection)

This became obvious on 3 June 1937, when a delegation led by Nouri – and including the commander of the RIrAF, Jawad; the CO of No. 2 Squadron, Hafiz Aziz; and technical officer Jawad Hussain – travelled to Rome in Italy. Welcomed by the highest Italian dignitaries, the Iraqis were shown the latest Italian-made aircraft and armoured vehicles, and on 7 July 1937 Jawad was given an opportunity to pilot one of the then brand-new Savoia-Marchetti bombers. The result was a series of Iraqi orders stipulating deliveries of 21 combat aircraft (in addition to light armoured vehicles of Fiat-Ansaldo design), which were to start in 1938.[35]

Not to be outdone, London promptly reacted with its own offer and – right after completing his visit to Italy – Nouri thus continued on to Great Britain, where he visited several aircraft factories and RAF bases. The result was a contract for 15 Gloster Gladiator Mk I biplane fighters. The first nine of these were delivered to Basra by the merchant SS *Clydewater*, by mid-November 1937, and assembled and test-flown by RAF personnel, they were handed over to No. 4 Squadron on 13 December 1937, two weeks after this unit was officially established. The other six were handed over to the RIrAF by 30 March 1938. Twelve were powered by the Bristol Mercury VI engines, while the last three had the more powerful Mercury IX. However, the unit suffered two mishaps in which two Gladiators were written off by 1941, and the RAF thus supplied another example as a replacement on 12 October 1940.[36]

One of very few photographs of Bakr Sidqi, perhaps the most controversial of all the former Ottoman Army officers to serve with the Iraqi Army, but also one that shaped the entire armed forces of the late 1930s. (Ahmad Sadik Collection)

Moreover, Baqr Sidqi prompted the British to withdraw to their last two bases in Iraq, as stipulated by the Second Anglo-Iraqi Treaty. Thus, in March 1937 the RAF vacated the sprawling complex of Hinaidi: the RIrAF renamed it Rashid Airfield (*Moascar al-Rashid*; after a Caliph under which Baghdad greatly prospered), and deployed most of its aircraft there. The next was RAF Kirkuk, which the Iraqis renamed to al-Hurriyah AB (Freedom), while on 2 June 1937 RAF Mosul was handed over to the RIrAF. In a great celebration, the Union Jack was lowered and replaced by the Iraqi flag, and the base became home to the personnel and Nisrs meanwhile re-assigned to No. 1 Squadron. Proving that the history of Iraq is full of irony, the garden of what the Iraqis named Firnas AB (after a legendary Middle Ages Andalusian Arab who attempted to fly using feathered wings) became a fateful place for Bakr Sidqi: he was assassinated there by a Kurdish soldier of the Iraqi Army while making a stop during an official trip to Turkey, together with the commander of No. 2 Squadron, on 12 August 1937.[37]

Purchased from Italy in 1938, the six Savoia Marchetti SM.79As were the nominal tip of the spear of the RIrAF. This photograph shows them pre-delivery, at the airfield of the Sesto Calende factory. (Ahmad Sadik Collection)

FIFTH, SIXTH AND SEVENTH SQUADRONS

It remains unclear whether Sidqi's assassination was a part of a bigger plot by Kurdish nationalists, perhaps the revenge of a few disappointed officers that he had failed to appoint to expected posts, or a spontaneous action of a disaffected soldier. What is certain is that his image with the Iraqi public was ruined soon after the coup, not only due to

Iraq acquired a total of 15 Breda Ba.65A-80s in 1937, all of which can be seen in this pre-delivery photograph. Two (serials 106 and 107) were equipped as trainers, while the remaining 13 belonged to the Ba.65A two-seat attack bomber variant, with a hydraulically powered turret for the rear gunner. Each was armed with one light machinegun and one heavy machinegun in each wing, and could carry up to 2,000lbs (1,000kg) of bombs. Operated by No. 5 Squadron, they were to see plenty of action in May 1941 and a few surviving examples served until at least 1947. (Ahmad Sadik Collection)

A pre-delivery photograph of one of 15 Northrop 8A-4D dive-bombers acquired by Iraq in 1939. Clearly visible is the insignia of No. 7 Squadron (see colour section for details) that operated this type. (Ahmad Sadik Collection)

RIrAF SERIAL NUMBERS

Serial numbers of the RIrAF aircraft followed a very simple pattern: they were assigned in the sequence of delivery. Thus, the first of five DH.60Ms to reach Iraq received a big black '1', the first DH.60T '6', the first DH.84M was '15', and so on. By 1941, the RIrAF is known to have issued a total of 150 consecutive serials, as listed in Table 1.

TABLE 1: SERIALS OF RIrAF AIRCRAFT, 1931-1941

SERIAL NUMBER	AIRCRAFT TYPE	NOTES
1-5	DH.60M	Five delivered in April 1931; two written off in 1932
6-9	DH.60T	Four delivered in January 1932
10-11	DH.80A	Two delivered in 1932
12	DH.60M	
13	DH.60T	Taken away by RAF as HK.507, 1942
14	DH.60M	
15-25	DH.80M	Eight plus one delivered in 1933–1934, two written off in 1934
26-27	DH.84M	Taken away by RAF as HK.908 and HK.909. 1942
28-39	Nisr	12 delivered in 1934
40-46	DH.82A & DH.83	Six delivered in 1933-1934
47-68	Nisr	21 delivered in 1934-1937
69-78	DH.82A	10 delivered in 1934
79-94	Gladiator I	Nine delivered in 1937, seven in 1938 (Nos. 80, 85, 86, 90 and 91 written off by 1940)
95-98	Nisr	Three delivered in 1938
99-104	SM.79B	Six delivered in August 1938
105-119	Ba.65A/65bis	15 delivered in September 1938
120-124	Vincent	Six delivered in 1940, five entered service
125-130	Nisr	Five delivered in 1940
131-145	8A-4D	15 delivered in September 1940
146-150	Gladiator I	Six ordered in October 1940, never delivered

DH.84 Dragons manufactured for Iraq – visible are serials (from front towards the rear): 22, 17, 20, 21, 19, and 18 – seen prior to delivery. The Iraqis originally ordered eight DH.84As (serials 15-23), but serial 15 was written off while still in the UK. A replacement was quickly acquired, but then serial 16 crashed during operations in Iraq, killing five officers, on 11 September 1934. (Tom Cooper Collection)

the execution of Askari, but especially because of his dictatorial behaviour and numerous irresponsible acts. What is also certain is that without Sidqi, Hikmat Sulayman lacked the support necessary to continue governing: he resigned and Ghazi had him replaced by Jameel al-Madfaai in August 1938.[38]

All of this had relatively little impact upon the conversion training of selected RIrAF pilots and ground personnel in Italy. On 10 August 1938, the Iraqis flew their six brand-new SM.79B bombers from Milano via Rome and Naples to Catania, at Sicily. A day later, they crossed the Mediterranean Sea to Tripoli in the then Italian Tripolitania (modern-day Libya), before continuing for Iraq, where all six arrived safely on 16 August 1938. Initially, all the SM.79s were operated by No. 5 Squadron, commanded by Hafiz Aziz and based at Rashid AB: this unit included all the Iraqi crews qualified to fly the Bredas and Savoia-Marachettis. However, once the Breda BA.65As arrived by ship at Basra, on 25 September 1938 the unit was split: the Ba.65s were retained by No. 5 Squadron, while the SM.79s entered service with a new unit, No. 6 Squadron, officially established at Rashid AB on 31 May 1939.[39]

During the same year, the last major Iraqi arms acquisition of this period took place, when another delegation of the RIrAF paid a visit to the newly-established Northrop Corporation in Hawthorne, in California. The result was an order for 15 Northrop 8A-4Ds, which were delivered by ship to Basra on 15 September 1940, and entered service with the newly established No. 7 Squadron based at Rashid AB.[40]

3

ANGLO-IRAQ WAR OF 1941

The never-ending political and security crisis in Iraq of the 1920s and the 1930s culminated in the Anglo-Iraqi War of 1941. The origins and background of this short, yet bitter conflict with far-reaching consequences are usually explained as being due to the importance of Iraq for Great Britain as a major oil source (and the denial of the same to Germany), the collaboration of the Iraqi military and political leadership with the Nazi Germany, and a threat to Egypt, to the French Mandate of Syria, and to Turkey – in the event of Iraq getting rid of British dominance. Ironically, while the cooperation of the Grand Mufti of Jerusalem, Muhammad Amin al-Hussein with Nazi Germany – and, consequently, also that of Iraqi Prime Minister Rashid Ali al-Khaylani – has been widely researched and published upon in the West, the fact that the *Iraqi* politics of that period was foremost influenced by 'normal' pan-Arabism, *Iraqi* interests, and the Palestine struggle (which had reached its peak in an uprising lasting from 1936 and 1939 and crushed by the British in blood), are almost completely left out. Similarly, the intentions of the Iraqi government, and the intentions and capabilities of its armed forces and the RIrAF are only superficially covered, not mentioned, or misinterpreted.[1]

GOLDEN SQUARE

Madfaai's conciliatory politics towards the members of Sulayman's government angered a group of influential colonels of the Iraqi armed forces. Led by Salah ad-Din as-Sabbagh, and originally known as the 'Circle of Seven', and later the 'Four Colonels' or the 'Golden Square', they included Fahmi Said, Kamil Shabib, and Mahmoud Salman. While fiercely anti-British, they were reinforced by Nuri as-Saad (fresh back from exile in Cairo) while exercising severe pressure upon King Ghazi. Under threat of another coup, on 24 December 1938 he dismissed Madfaai, and replaced him with Saad. Henceforth, the Golden Square de-facto ruled Iraq.[2]

In turn, on 4 April 1939, Ghazi was killed in a car accident. Greatly relieved – and while ignoring rumours that the king was murdered on order from Saad for planning to unify Iraq with Kuwait – the British rushed to replace him with Abd al-Ilah of Hejaz, elder brother of King Faysal, who was to serve as a regent. Another foreigner imposed upon the Iraqis, lacking vision, charisma and determination, and unpopular with the public, Abd al-Ilah was hopelessly overdependent on British support and instruction. Moreover, he took over only months before the Second World War erupted with the German invasion of Poland on 1 September 1939. Two days later, Great Britain declared war on Germany, and London requested Baghdad to sever its ties to Berlin, to intern all Germans, and provide assistance as required. Saad complied quickly, and on 5 September German ambassador Dr Fritz Grobba – highly-popular in Iraq for his anti-British agitation – left Iraq with his staff, while other German nationals were deported to India. Moreover, a week later the Iraqi government declared a state of emergency, introduced curfews, rationing, and requisitioning, virtually putting the country on a war footing.[3]

Saad's support for Britain caused unrest within nationalist circles: the latter found it made little sense to follow despised British orders and turn against the Germans at the time many were hoping for a better future for the Arabs *if* Great Britain and France were to lose the war. Nevertheless, caution prevailed and the situation remained calm until January 1940, when Saad exploited the assassination of one of his ministers to purge

Pilots of No. 4 Squadron, RIrAF in front of one of their Gladiators in early 1941. (Ahmad Sadik Collection)

This undated photograph shows the details of the 'unit insignia' applied to the rear of RIrAF Gladiator Mk I serial number 80 in the late 1930s: in the case of No. 4 Squadron, this consisted of five black circles. Reportedly, around the same time Nisrs of No. 1 Squadron received a similar insignia in red; Dragons of No. 2 Squadron in blue, and Nisrs of No. 3 Squadron in green. (Ahmad Sadik Collection)

his political opponents. This effort backfired: facing an outburst of criticism, he was forced to resign on 18 February 1940. In an attempt to avoid a dictate of the Golden Square, Abd al-Ilah then requested Rashid Ali al-Khaylani to form a coalition government including most senior politicians. Although the new cabinet included Saad as the foreign minister and Taha al-Hashimi as Minister of Defence, and implicitly stressed its acceptance of the 1930 Treaty, Khaylani's appointment was harshly criticised by London, where Churchill complained that Baghdad had failed to declare war on Germany and Italy. Khaylani reacted with several public expressions of his support for Great Britain and her allies, but refused to bow: on the contrary, he granted asylum to most of the leaders of the Arab uprising in the British Mandate of Palestine, and refused to restrict the political activity of the Grand Mufti of Jerusalem.[4]

After the fall of France in June 1940, the British Embassy in Baghdad announced the intention to deploy additional British troops outside Basra, Baghdad and Mosul, and construct a transfer route from Basra to Haifa.[5] The British request took the Golden Square and most of the anti-British camp in Baghdad by surprise: uncertain about the future of the French Mandate of Syria, they concluded that Great Britain was weak and the Axis Powers might win the war. Knowing that Britain was still a power to be reckoned with, Khaylani's government reacted with an attempt to extract concessions from London – not only for Iraq, but especially for Palestine. Noticing that the British had already cooperated with the Zionists during the Arab uprising of 1936-1939, and then agreed to arm them while withdrawing the mass of their troops from that territory (in turn significantly worsening the situation of the Palestinians), Khaylani offered to declare the war on Germany and Italy, in exchange for a complete British withdrawal from Iraq and from Palestine, and deliveries of advanced armament. The answer of the British government – entirely ignorant of Iraqi interests and intolerant of any kind of dissent, but keen to misunderstand the Iraqi position as influenced by Nazi-Germany – reached Baghdad on 29 August 1940: London rejected all proposals and postponed a solution for Iraq (and Palestine) to the 'post-war period'.[6]

APRIL 1941 COUP

To say that Churchill's refusal to work with the Iraqis on equal terms had shattered the position of the last few influential British allies in Baghdad – like Saad and Madfaai – would be an understatement: not only did the Golden Square withdraw its support for Saad, but many officers began openly disobeying orders from anybody considered pro-British, including the Regent Abd al-Ilah. In January 1941, Abd al-Ilah ordered the government to resign, but Khaylani refused and enlisted help from Sabbagh, who threatened a military coup. By sheer accident the following crisis took place at the same time as a similar crisis in Yugoslavia, which prompted Nazi Germany to invade that country, and then Greece – another major British ally, while the German Afrika Korps disembarked in Italian Tripolitania and launched its first offensive against the British troops in the Cyrenaica. Precisely at that point in time, Abd al-Ilah attempted to break-up the Golden Square by asking Taha al-Hashimi to form a new government. Resenting Hashimi as 'pro-British', the Golden Square reacted with a coup: during the night of 1 to 2 April 1941, together with the Acting CGS, Major-General Amin Zaki, the 1st Division was mobilised to enter Baghdad. While securing the Ministry of Defence, the plotters had failed to arrest the Regent: he escaped to the US Embassy and was then evacuated via RAF Habbaniya to Jerusalem. Supported by the Golden Square, on 4 April, Khaylani arranged a new government, which was confirmed by all 94 of the members of parliament present (out of a total of 135) during the session of 12 April 1941. To make sure, he publicly announced that his new government did not intend to bring Iraq into the war, but to follow its own, sovereign policy.[7]

However, convinced that Iraq had already reached an agreement with the Axis powers and was only waiting for their arrival, and insistent on preference for an armed intervention to further negotiations, London's reaction was provocative, quick, and ruthless. While it was the Golden Square that staged the putsch, London described the change of government in Baghdad as the 'Rashid Ali coup' and refused to recognise Khaylani's government. Instead, and on the advice of its Ambassador in Baghdad, Cornwallis, on insistence of the British Commander-in-Chief India, Sir Claude Auchinleck, and against advice from the British Commander-in-Chief Middle East, Sir Archibald Wavell, the decision was taken to launch an armed intervention in Iraq. On 8 April 1941, Churchill ordered the British Army of India to deploy troops to Basra. Auchinleck replied positively and re-routed the 20th Indian Infantry Brigade and a field regiment of the 10th Indian Division from a journey to Malaya to Iraq instead. As required by the 1930 Treaty, the British announced the arrival of their troops to Baghdad on 16 April: a day later, 384 officers and other ranks of 1 Battalion King's Own Royal Regiment (KORR) were flown to Shaibah and then to Habbaniya aboard 12 obsolete Vickers Valentia transports.[8] On 19

A row of RAF armoured cars assigned to the squadron that protected RAF Habbaniya, seen in the 1930s. (Albert Grandolini Collection)

April, the 20th Indian Infantry Brigade disembarked in Basra and quickly brought the dock area under control.[9]

While dock-workers went on strike (forcing the British to unload all of their equipment and vehicles on their own and, later on, bring in Indian laborers), Khaylani did not order a mobilisation of the Iraqi armed forces: instead, he reminded the British about restrictions set up by the Treaty, and demanded that their troops quickly transit to Palestine in small groups, and no additional troops to be deployed. Already well beyond the point of negotiating, London and New Delhi decided to deploy the entire 10th Indian Division to Iraq. Blatantly misinterpreting the treaty, Cornwallis answered only on 28 April 1941, explaining that the Iraqi government had no right to impose any restrictions on British military deployments in Iraq, and that Great Britain has the right to establish a new military base outside Basra. A day later, the second convoy arrived in Basra to disembark the rest of the 20th Brigade, while Cornwallis ordered an evacuation of about 350 British civilians from Baghdad and other cities to RAF Habbaniya (another 150 found refuge in the US Embassy), where the local garrison of 1,200 Iraq Levies (organised into four companies), and one company RAF armoured cars (with 18 vehicles) was put on alert.

TABLE 2: ROYAL IRAQI ARMED FORCES, MAJOR COMMANDS, APRIL-MAY 1941

COMMAND	HEADQUARTERS	NOTES
Chief-of-Staff	Baghdad	Colonel Amin Zaki
1st Division	Ba'aquba	Colonel Kammil Shabib (Golden Square)
2nd Division	Kirkuk	brigades in Mosul, Erbil, and Kirkuk
3rd Division	Baghdad	Colonel Salah ad-Din as-Sabbagh (Golden Square)
4th Division	Diwaniya	Colonel Mahmoud Salman (Golden Square); brigades in Diwaniya, Amara and Samawa
5th Division		Brigades in Nasiriyah and Basra
Mechanised Brigade	Musayyib	Colonel Mahmoud Fahmi Said (Golden Square)
RIrAF	Rashid AB	Colonel Mahmoud Salman al-Januby

TABLE 3: RIrAF ORDER OF BATTLE, MAY 1941[12]

SQUADRON	BASE	AIRCRAFT TYPE	COMMANDER
COMMANDER RIRAF: COLONEL MAHMOUD SALMAN AL-JANUBY			
No. 1	Firnas	25 Nisrs (nine operational)	
No. 2	Rashid	Seven DH.80A Dragons, five Vincents	
No. 3	Mosul	Nine Nisrs	
No. 4	Hurriyah	10 Gladiators (seven operational)	
No. 5	Rashid	13 Ba.65As (all operational)	Major Ismael Fatah
No. 6	Rashid	Four SM.79s (all operational)	Major Ibrahim Jawad
No. 7	Rashid	15 8A-4Ds (all operational)	Major Abdul Hamid Amar
Aviation School	Rashid	22 DH.60s (different marks), two Ba.65s	

IRAQI AIR FORCE OF MAY 1941

The Iraqi Army of 1941 boasted four fully deployed divisions: established in 1938, the 3rd Division was headquartered in Baghdad; in 1940, the 4th Division came into being in Diwaniyah. The 5th Division was in the process of establishment in southern Iraq, while there was also the Mechanised Brigade equipped with 16 Italian-made Fiat Ansaldo CV.33 tankettes and 14 British-made Crossley armoured cars. Overall, the army included a total of 44,000 officers and other ranks, organised into 45 battalions and 24 artillery batteries, deployed to protect major urban and economic centres, and was thus well away from the RAF bases in Habbaniya and Shaiba. After proving its mettle in earlier counterinsurgency operations, during 1938-1940, it had its skills honed in conventional warfare through extensive and intensive field exercises. Although following not entirely realistic scenarios, these took place at regular intervals, and significantly strengthened the capabilities of units most

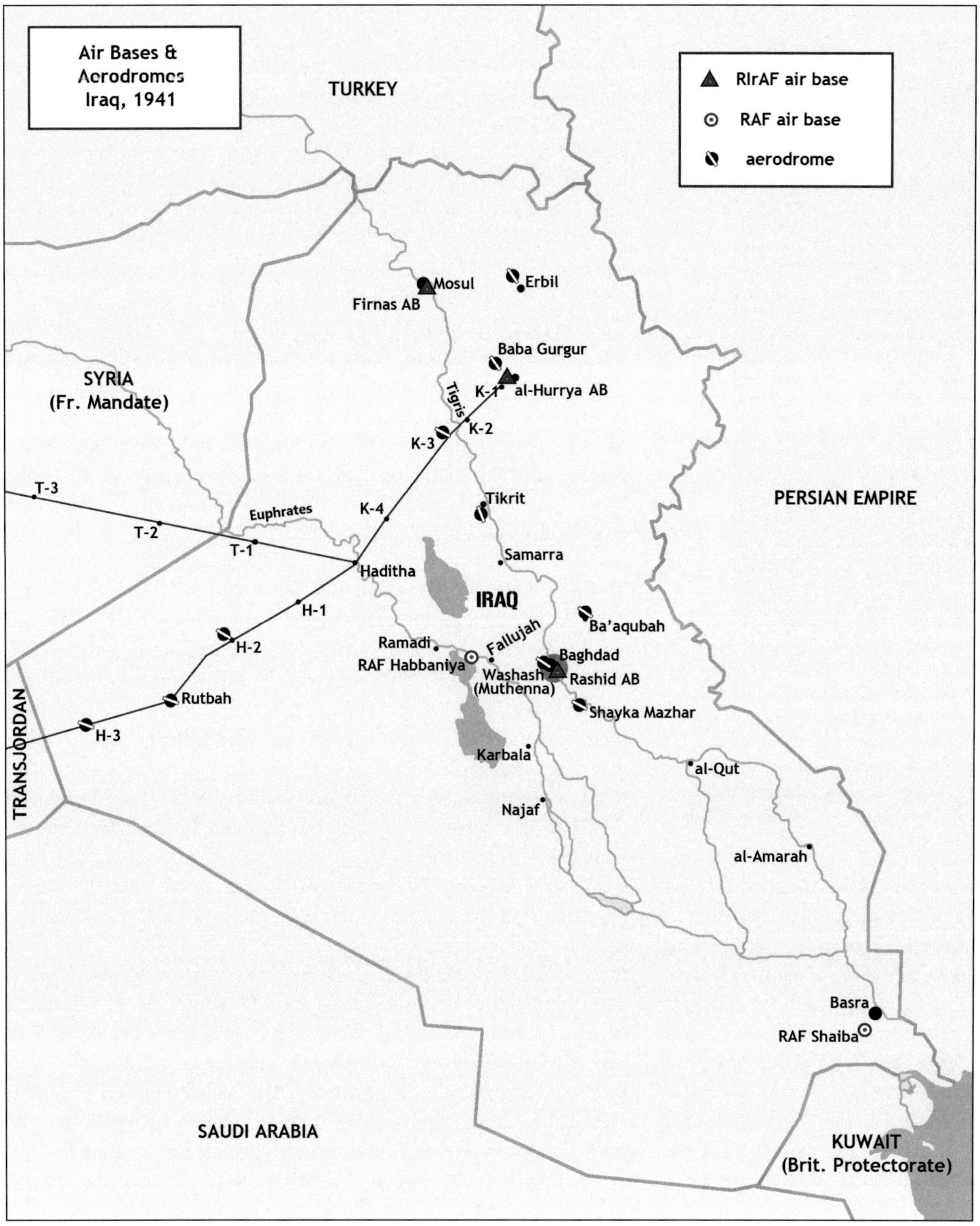

Deployment of the RIrAF as of April 1941. Notably, the Army had no major units near the two major British bases, Habbaniya and Shaibah. (Map by Tom Cooper)

A row of Nisrs of No. 3 Squadron seen in 1940 or 1941. By this time, they wore much larger serials than originally applied. (Ahmad Sadik Collection)

of which had been blooded in earlier fighting against various uprisings.[10]

As of April 1941, the RIrAF was commanded by Colonel Mahmoud Salman al-Januby, who was subordinated to the Army-controlled CGS. The air force included a total of 127 pilots and 116 aircraft, equipped and organised as listed in Table 3, but: it was already feeling the negative consequences of the outbreak of the Second World War. The British had impounded a ship carrying spares and armament for the Northrops of No. 7 Squadron in Singapore in 1940, while the acquisition of spares for Bredas and Savoias became impossible. The British did donate six Vickers Vincent light bombers (former mounts of No. 84 Squadron, RAF), but these were obsolete aircraft in poor condition, and only five were ever operated by the RIrAF. The situation reached the point where for the first four months of 1941, Iraqi pilots flew only two hours a month on average, while their ground crews were busy improvising frequently used spare parts.[11]

SAID'S PROVOCATION

Despite fruitless negotiations with Cornwallis, Khaylani still did not plan any kind of military action against the British. It was Sabbagh who made the next move. At 15:00hrs on 29 April 1941, two brigades of the 1st Division and one of the 3rd Division, reinforced with armoured cars from the Mechanised Brigade and commanded by Colonel Muhammad Fahmi Said (commander of the Mechanised Brigade), moved out of Baghdad along the road westwards with the task of securing and fortifying the towns of Fallujah and Ramadi. However, after leaving one battalion in Fallujah and directing one of the brigades to secure Ramadi, 14 miles (22km) west of Habbaniya, on

Born in Baghdad in 1896, Colonel Mahmoud Salman al-Januby was the last former Ottoman officer to serve as the Commander RIrAF (from 11 June 1938 until 30 May 1941). He graduated from the Military School in Istanbul in 1916, and fought as a lieutenant in the First World War. After joining the Iraqi armed forces and serving with the Royal Guard for a while, he graduated from the Military School in Baghdad in 1924 as a cavalry officer. After appointment as the commander of the RIrAF, he graduated as a pilot, a year later, but was to pay the ultimate price for siding with the Golden Square in 1941 and was shot by a firing squad on 5 May 1942. (Ahmad Sadik Collection)

his own initiative and without any planning, Said then led the rest of his force – including the 1st Infantry Brigade and one battalion of the Mechanised Brigade with 12 armoured cars and a machine gun company mounted on Vickers Bren carriers, one artillery regiment with 12 3.7in howitzers, and another with 12 18-pounder guns and 14 4.5in howitzers, and a mixed battery of anti-aircraft and anti-tank guns – to RAF Habbaniya. He did not launch an attack (and had no related orders at all), but ordered his troops to take defensive positions atop the 150-foot high (45m) plateau less than 1,000 yards (914m) south of the base. Although carrying live ammunition, the officers and other ranks were told that they were to take part in an exercise and, contrary to some reports, no order was ever issued to open fire at British aircraft taking off from the base.[13]

To say that this move was considered a provocation, and indeed alerted the British, would be an understatement and on the evening of 30 April, Cornwallis informed the commander of RAF Iraq, Air Vice Marshal Harry G Smart, that London was in the picture about the Iraqi deployment and was urging Baghdad to withdraw, but received no response. Furthermore, he declared the Iraqi actions as 'acts of war' and urged Smart to attack. Smart's units were already on a war footing and the commander of No. 4 Service Flying Training School (SFTS), Group Captain W. A. B. Savile distributed his 39 instructor pilots – many of whom were Greek and with only a rudimentary command of the English language – and their aircraft into four squadrons and one flight: three equipped with a total of 32 Audaxes, each armed with a pair of 250lb bombs (a few non-operational aircraft had their top wings removed in an attempt to deceive the Iraqis into thinking that the RAF had deployed its modern Hawker Hurricane fighters in Iraq), one with 29 Airspeed Oxford trainers (jury rigged with racks for 20lb bombs); eight Fairey Gordon biplane bombers (each armed with a pair of 200lb bombs), three Valentias and one Bristol Blenheim bomber. The separate single flight operated nine Gladiator fighters. That evening, the British Embassy in Baghdad was invaded by Iraqi troops and had all of its radio equipment confiscated. Out of touch with Cornwallis, Smart was then encouraged by Churchill's direct order to 'strike hard'. Expecting the Iraqis to 'withdraw within three hours', he ordered his pilots to attack at dawn.[14]

TURKEY SHOOT AT HABBANIYA

At 04:30hrs of 2 May 1941, 30 aircraft took off from RAF Habbaniya and showered the Iraqi troops dug-in on the plateau with bombs, before diving to strafe. Although shocked by the attack, heavily hit and showing no inclination to launch a ground attack, the Iraqis held their positions firmly and shot back. Indeed, Smart's expectation that they would fold and run proved seriously overoptimistic: after two hours of air strikes, they began shelling the air base. Moreover, the RIrAF was relatively quick to react by launching multiple attacks against RAF Habbaniya. The first of these took place at 10:00hrs, when six Gladiators destroyed two Audaxes and one Oxford on the ground in the course of multiple strafing runs. Next came the Savoias, one of which was intercepted by a lone RAF Gladiator, that caused little damage. Finally, a formation of Breda BA.65s bombed the British base, disturbed only by a lonesome RAF Gladiator, which reportedly damaged one of the Iraqi aircraft. At 18:00hrs, a pair of RIrAF Gladiators and 8A-4Ds intercepted a formation of 10 Vickers Wellington bombers from RAF Shaibah approaching RAF Habbaniya: although attacking them for nearly 20 minutes, the Iraqi pilots were repeatedly driven away by the heavy defensive fire of the British bombers and caused no damage. Ironically, nine of

Taken during its delivery flight in 1938, this photograph of one of six Savoia-Marchetti SM.79As of No. 6 Squadron (serial number 104) is illustrative of their appearance in May 1941. The type saw quite intensive action right from the start of the fighting, first in attacks on RAF Habbaniya and later while flying armed reconnaissance. (Pit Weinert Collection)

British bombers were declared unserviceable after returning to RAF Shaiba. Moreover, Iraqi Army troops deployed in blocking positions north of Basra shot down two Vincent bombers that launched from Shaiba to attack them. Overall, under the given circumstances Smart had no other solution but to order his pilots to continue their attacks: thus, by the sunset of 2 May, the troops of the 1st Infantry Brigade and the elements of the Mechanised Brigade on the plateau south of RAF Habbaniya were exposed to 193 recorded sorties of the SFTS alone. While the mass of British (and other) accounts of the Anglo-Iraqi War of 1941 stress the Iraqi armed forces' inability to offer sustained resistance to the British, low morale, desertions and confusion, the Iraqis actually fought back with everything to hand. They not only shot down 22 aircraft of the SFTS during the day, but also shot up one of the Wellingtons from RAF Shaiba, forcing it to land at RAF Habbaniya – where it was promptly set on fire by Iraqi artillery.[15]

Flying a Gladiator Mk I of No. 4 squadron, like this example, 1st Lieutenant Abdul Salam Yahya al-Katib scored the historic first-ever aerial victory for the Iraqi air force. (Tom Cooper Collection)

COUNTER-AIR STRIKES

In reaction to the British attack on its troops the Iraqi government declared martial law and decided to re-establish diplomatic relations with Germany, a termination of service of all British civilian and military advisors in Iraq, and authorised the prime minister to purchase arms, ammunition and services from whatever source he deemed propriate. Correspondingly, Khaylani – even if actually having next to no say in regards of all these affairs – ordered Major Majaddin an-Naqib of the RIrAF to Aleppo to establish contact and act as a liaison officer with the German and Italian military missions that were expected to travel to Iraq. Sabbagh was in command, however: around the noon of 2 May, he issued a direct order for Colonel Said to launch an attack on RAF Habbaniya. With his units in some disorder due to the air strikes, the latter then postponed the assault to the morning of 3 May, and then into the afternoon. As time was to show, he thus not only lost the initiative, but also the decisive battle of the war.[16]

Indeed, on the morning of 3 May, Smart ordered not only the continuation of attacks on Said's force, but also air strikes on Iraqi air bases. Three Wellingtons from RAF Shaiba bombed Rashid AB at early dawn, only to be intercepted by several Nisrs: while one of the RAF bombers was slightly damaged, their gunners claimed one of the Iraqis as shot down and another as damaged. In return, the RIrAF's SM.79s bombed Habbaniya, and one received some damage from a lonesome RAF Gladiator, while another British fighter hit one of the RIrAF's Northrops, forcing it to land on a piece of flat ground north-east of Lake Habbaniya where, reportedly, one Iraqi Savoia and a Nisr had also landed. Finally, the lack of an Iraqi ground attack enabled the British to reinforce the SFTS – which flew 119 sorties that day – with four Blenheims, while evacuating civilians and casualties aboard six Douglas DC-2s.[17]

AIR COMBATS OVER BAGHDAD

The air strikes on the Iraqi troops on the plateau south of RAF Habbaniya continued on 4 May, without the RIrAF attempting to interrupt them. The reason was that the Iraqis were busy redeploying their aircraft from Rashid AB to the airports of Washash and Baquba. This decision proved correct when at dawn eight Wellingtons – followed by two Blenheims – attacked Rashid AB. The British claimed to have destroyed one 'biplane' on the ground. In turn, their formation was then intercepted by multiple Iraqi fighters: one of a pair of Northrops was claimed as shot down by defensive fire, and another damaged. A pair of Iraqi Gladiators then approached, one of which caused slight damage to a Wellington. Finally, the second Iraqi fighter pounced on a bomber that had already been hit by anti-aircraft fire over Rashid AB and had fallen behind the rest of the formation. Using his .303in (7.7mm) Vickers machine gun, Abdul Salam Yahya al-Katib caused so much damage that the crew was forced to make an emergency landing outside Baghdad, where they were promptly taken prisoner. Katib thus scored the historic, first ever aerial victory for the Iraqi Air Force (and, indeed, for any Arab air force).[18]

The RAF continued striking, and two Blenheim NF. IVFs were particularly successful that afternoon. They first attacked a SM.79, a Ba.65, and a Nisr at Rashid AB, and claimed the latter as destroyed, and then went on to claim a Nisr and a Gladiator as destroyed at Washash airport. Finally realising that the bulk of the RIrAF was not at Rashid AB, the RAF then deployed a lonesome Blenheim to fly reconnaissance over Firnas and Hurriyah ABs in the north. The crew of this bomber reportedly strafed two Nisrs at the Iraqi air base outside Mosul, but in turn returned to RAF Shaiba with some damage from ground fire. Still busy with scattering its aircraft, the RIrAF suffered a particularly painful loss when a SM.79 piloted by Major Abdul Hamid Amar was shot down by friendly ground defences over Diwaniyah airfield that afternoon.[19]

Meanwhile, at Habbaniya, the Iraqi anti-aircraft fire remained intense: it, and the fact that the British and Greek pilots began diving very low to hit Said's artillery as precisely as possible, reduced the STFS to just 20 operational aircraft. Nevertheless, these still flew 53 combat sorties against Said's force. The British continued launching air strikes on 5 May 1941, and the crew of a lone Blenheim damaged two SM.79s and a Gladiator at Rashid AB. During the same evening, the artillery of Said's force ceased shelling RAF Habbaniya – because it had run out of ammunition, and no replenishment arrived from Baghdad. By the time, the STFS was down to only four flyable Oxfords and about a dozen pilots. Virtually all 20 remaining aircraft were badly damaged and undergoing repairs. The condition of the RIrAF was no better: the air force was down to about two dozen operational aircraft, most of which were now redeployed to Ba'aqouba. However, this facility lacked the ground equipment, tools and armament necessary to return them to service.[20]

TABLE 4: RIrAF, CONFIRMED LOSSES OF ANGLO-IRAQ WAR, MAY 1941[26]		
DATE	AIRCRAFT	NOTES
4 May 1941	SM.79, No. 6 Squadron	Major Abdul Hamid Amar, Lieutenants Mustafa Hassan Zalzabi & Saadi Mohammed Ali; shot down by friendly air defences over Diwaniyah
6 May 1941	Gladiator, No. 4 squadron	Lieutenant Saleh Mahdi al-Wazan; circumstances unknown (possibly flew the 'Nisr' claimed downed by a Blenheim night fighter into the Euphrates River)
8 May 1941	Gladiator, No. 4 Squadron	Lieutenant Lufty Ahmed al-Jameel, claimed shot down by an RAF Gladiator; Iraqis report shot down by their own air defences over Rashid AB
18 May 1941	Gladiator, No. 4 Squadron	Lieutenant Naji Mahdi al-Jaboury; crashed on take-off from Khan Bani Sa'ad

Although their primary task was ground attack, Iraqi 8A-4D pilots eagerly attacked RAF aircraft at every opportunity, and thus became involved in several air combats. This photograph shows serial number 132, warming-up the engine prior to its next mission. (Ahmad Sadik Collection)

EXHAUSTION

On the morning of 6 May 1941, six Wellingtons bombed Rashid AB again, leaving a hangar on fire and reporting hits on – reports differ – either an Iraqi Gladiator, or a 'twin-engined aircraft'. A lonesome Northrop 8A-4D then bombed RAF Habbaniya and was harried by a RAF Gladiator on the way back. Meanwhile, Sabbagh rushed another brigade from Baghdad to reinforce Said, while Khaylani urgently appealed to Germany and Italy for military assistance. However, it was too late: having lost nearly all of his artillery, Said had no option but to order a withdrawal from RAF Habbaniya.[21]

The Iraqi air force continued its action, nevertheless. At 10:45hrs of 7 May 1941, two Nisrs attacked RAF Habbaniya: a Blenheim NF.Mk IVF night fighter then caught the Iraqis on the way back and pursued one until it crashed into the Euphrates. Later in the day, an Iraqi Army column approaching Fallujah met the stream of units withdrawing towards Fallujah. In complete disregard for military procedures, both Iraqi units stopped on the highway only five miles (8km) east of RAF Habbaniya, and personnel jumped down from their vehicles to confer, leaving all of their armoured cars and trucks parked in plain view. Scrambling every available aircraft once again, the SFTS flew 139 additional recorded sorties within two hours and completely demolished the majority of the two convoys. The RIrAF did try to disrupt this action by launching three air strikes on RAF Habbanyia: the first two killed seven and wounded eight, and destroyed two Oxfords, a Gladiator, and an Audax on the ground. Only the third Iraqi wave – consisting of two Northrops – was intercepted by RAF Gladiators over Falluja and driven away.[22]

On 8 May 1941, the British could find no trace of the Iraqi troops near Habbaniya. At 16:35hrs, in reaction to intelligence that the Iraqis had concentrated 21 of their aircraft at Baquba airfield, Audaxes and Oxfords of the STFS raided that location accompanied by two Blenheim NF.Mk IVFs and Gladiators to claim the destruction of six aircraft on the ground. In the air, the escorting RAF Gladiators encountered a lonesome Iraqi Gladiator, hit it and last saw it in a steep dive. The Iraqis admitted the loss of pilot Lufty Ahmed al-Jameel, but stressed that he was shot down by friendly air defences while attempting to land at Rashid AB.[23]

The action was concluded on 9 May 1941, by which time RAF Habbaniya had been effectively secured, and the Iraqi ground troops forced back to Fallujah. Blenheim NF.Mk IVFs from Habbaniya raided Firnas AB in Mosul, where three or four Iraqi aircraft were claimed as destroyed, and Rashid AB, where a single SM.79 was reported as destroyed, while the STFS flew anther 54 sorties.[24]

Overall, there was no doubt that in five days of fighting for RAF Habbaniya, the 1st and 3rd Divisions, and the Mechanised Brigade of the Iraqi Army suffered crippling losses: when the British forces moved out to mop up the battlefield, they collected a total of 408 prisoners, one Italian tankette, 10 armoured cars and Bren carriers, six 3.7in howitzers, one 18-pdr gun, 79 trucks, three 20mm anti-aircraft guns and a sizeable collection of firearms. The number of Iraqi officers and other ranks killed by the British air strikes remains unknown but is usually estimated at 500 to 1,000 on the plateau, and up to another 1,000 in the Fallujah area. The number of sorties flown by the RIrAF remains unknown, but the Iraqis seem to have lost about 40 aircraft in the air and on the ground, together with about half a dozen pilots. While the STFS logged at least 650 sorties, it suffered 13 men killed and 21 badly wounded, and four suffered battle fatigue: the latter included Air Vice Marshall Smart, who had to be evacuated due to a nervous breakdown.[25]

SONDERKOMMANDO JUNCK

During the next phase of the Anglo-Iraq War of 1941, the focus of the air war moved away from a confrontation between the RAF and the RIrAF to one between the British and the Germans that were about to arrive on the scene. On 3 May 1941, German Foreign Minister Joachim von Ribbentrop persuaded Adolf Hitler to return exiled ambassador Grobba to Iraq, together with a contingent of the air force (Luftwaffe). Correspondingly, three days later Colonel Werner Junck

Two four-ships of Bf.110s of Sonderkommando Junck seen refuelling during their transfer to Iraq. The aircraft retained their original camouflage pattern, but their four-digit codes were overpainted with light grey, and they received Iraqi national insignia. (Pit Weinert Collection)

received the order to organise the 120-man strong unit designated Special Force Junck (Sonderkommando Junck) as an element of the German forces combed together for deployment to Iraq. With the Luftwaffe in the process of launching its airborne attack on the island of Crete, there were relatively few aircraft on hand for this enterprise. Sonderkommando Junck was originally to be equipped with only three Heinkel He.111D-2s from a reconnaissance unit, and three Messerschmitt Bf.110 drawn from the 2nd Squadron of the Destroyer Wing 26 (2. Staffel/Zerstörergeschwader 2./Z.G.26). However, on 7 May, Junck managed to convince his superiors to reinforce his unit through the addition of nine Bf.110E-1s twin-engine heavy fighters of the 4./Z.G.76, nine He.111P-4s twin-engine bombers of the 4th Squadron/Bomber Wing 4 (Kampfgeschwader 4: 4./K.G.4), and a battery of 20mm anti-aircraft guns. Moreover, he was assigned a contingent of transports, including 10 Junkers Ju.52/3m from Special Combat Group 106 (Kampfgruppe zur besonderen Verwendung 106: K.Gr.z.b.V.106), and three Junkers Ju.90A-0s drawn from Lufthansa: these were all to return to Greece as soon as possible in order to support the Crete operation.[27]

While retaining their original camouflage patterns, the first few aircraft deployed to Iraq wore French national insignia during their transfer flight: this was replaced by the Iraqi national insignia after arrival in Kirkuk. The Messerschmitts of 4./Z.G.76 had received Iraqi national insignia before their transfer. At least nominally, their crews were integrated into the RIrAF at one rank higher than their German rank. Consisting of such a miscellany of aircraft, the vanguard of Sonderkommando Junck (carrying German officials and liaison officers) began transferring to Iraq on 6 May 1941, along a route from France, via Italy, Greece, and – in agreement with Vichy French authorities – the French Mandate of Syria (with refuelling stops in Beirut and Palmyra).[28] One of the first three He.111s crashed into a hill while underway from Belgrade to Salonica on 10 May, killing all nine crew and passengers: it was replaced by two Ju.52/3ms, of which one carried long-range radios, and another equipment to test the fuel available in Iraq. The rest of Sonderkommando Junck transferred from Germany, via Yugoslavia, Greece and Palmyra (despite agreements with the Vichy French authorities, they were not welcome in Damascus) to Mosul on 13, 14 and 15 May.[29]

On arrival at Firnas AB, Sonderkommando Junck was 118-men-strong, and had five He.111s (4 operational), and 12 Bf.110s (7 operational). Only a few of the transports supposed to support it ever actually reached Iraq: these included a pair of Ju.90s (which also wore Iraqi national markings), that brought a consignment of anti-armour weapons for the Iraqis, while the third delivered 72 SC.50 bombs for the Heinkels and Messerschmitts. None of the aircraft was equipped for operations in the Middle East, and the Sonderkommando was critically short of ground equipment, which was to cause massive problems during its subsequent activities. Indeed, one of the Messerschmitts was lost in a crash during the first alert-launch on 15 May. Nevertheless, the German commander acted without hesitation and sent several Bf.110s on reconnaissance along the border between Iraq and the French Mandate of Syria, while one He.111 was sent to bring Luftwaffe liaison officer Major Axel von Blomberg to Khaylani in Baghdad. However, while approaching Rashid AB at low altitude and speed, the bomber was fired upon by Iraqi Army troops, and von Blomberg was killed. Junck flew to Baghdad on the following day to meet Khaylani, General Amin Zaki, Colonel Nur ed-Din Mahmud, and Dr. Grobba. They agreed for the Iraqi Army to defend Fallujah and then attack and capture RAF Habbaniya, supported by the German air power.[30]

HABFORCE

At the same time, Wavell, on direct order from Churchill, cobbled together about 6,000 troops from the 1st Cavalry Division in Palestine and on 11 May, sent these on a march from Haifa via Transjordan to reinforce the garrison of Habbaniya. On 13 May, the leading elements of the seven mile (11.2km) long British column – codenamed Habforce – entered Iraq and approached the fort of Rutbah, which commanded the roads leading from Baghdad to Haifa, and those to Damascus and Beirut. Subjected to heavy bombing and shelling for the previous three days, and after shooting down an RAF Blenheim on 11 May, the Iraqi garrison gave up and withdrew, leaving the doors open for the British advance on Ramadi. After conducting maintenance, the leading element of Habforce, codenamed Kingcol, moved out of Rutbah on 15 May, when it was detected by an Iraqi SM.79 bomber that strafed it and dropped a single bomb, without effect. After bypassing Ramadi, on 16 May, this column was attacked by three Bf.110s, which shot up several vehicles, killing one man and wounding four others. Moreover, three of Junck's He.111s bombed RAF Habbaniya from high altitude: one of them was intercepted and shot down by a RAF Gladiator, but the latter in turn fell to the gunfire from the Heinkels. The German crew survived its crash landing, but the British pilot was killed. This raid was closely followed by six Bf.110s at low altitude, taking the British by surprise, shooting down one Audax and killing several men on the ground.[31]

Reinforced by four Gladiators, six Blenheims and two Hurricanes flown in from Egypt, RAF Habbaniya hit back the next morning. Two Gladiators caught a pair of Bf.110s taking off from Rashid AB and shot both down. Meanwhile, other RAF aircraft raided Firnas AB, knocking out two German aircraft and damaging four, while losing one Hurricane. With his Sonderkommando down to only four He.111s and eight Bf.110s, Junck was forced to withdraw all of his assets back to Mosul.[32]

After resting and replenishing at RAF Habbaniya, on the morning of 18 May, the fastest section of Habforce – about 2,000 troops and 500 vehicles in total – sortied out to attack the Iraqi troops at Fallujah. Underway there, it was attacked by four Messerschmitts, but the latter received such heavy fire in return that three had to be written off after returning to Firnas AB. Moreover, supported by 134 sorties of the SFTS, Habforce then assaulted Fallujah from the west, while a detachment of the King's Own Regiment was airlifted by Bristol Bombay and Vickers Valentia transports to a position east of the town. Fallujah fell on 19 May 1941, and 300 Iraqi troops were taken prisoner.

COUNTERATTACK OF THE 6TH BRIGADE

On 20 May, Bf.110s and He.111s of the Luftwaffe made repeated attacks on RAF Habbaniya and Habforce. Six Messerschmitts strafed the air base, destroying a Blenheim, a DC-2, two Valentias and damaging two other Blenheims in the process. Later, four Bf.110s encountered a RAF formation over Fallujah and claimed a Blenheim and a Gladiator as shot down. In return, the British then raided Rashid AB, where a Messerschmitt was destroyed on the ground. Moreover, a Bf.110 that had probably been damaged during one of the actions on this date was later discovered on the plain outside Fallujah, from where it was towed by the British to RAF Habbaniya.[33]

On 21 May 1941, the Luftwaffe launched its airborne invasion of Crete. While this meant that the Germans were hopelessly out of position to reinforce Iraq – and, indeed, Berlin failed to respond to any of Junck's pleas for additional aircraft – Sabbagh felt emboldened enough to order the 6th Brigade of the 3rd Division, reinforced by tankettes of the Mechanised Brigade, into a counterattack on Falluja. Rumbling down the road from Baghdad, the Iraqi unit launched a combined-arms attack in the early hours of 22 May: its mortar fire forced the outlying units of the 1st King's Own Regiment to withdraw into the town, pursued by Iraqi tanks. This assault was stopped only after two Iraqi vehicles were knocked out inside Falluja, but not before the Iraqi infantry managed to secure a part of the town. Another attempt against the south-eastern side of the town was repulsed during a nine-hour battle – in time for the hard-pressed and depleted British to by reinforced by Habforce.

At this critical juncture – the counterattack on Fallujah almost succeeded and was likely to bring the British advance to an end while greatly emboldening the Iraqis – the effects of the early death of Major Blomberg became obvious: Sonderkommando Junck was late in launching attacks on the British and when it did so, it lost two Bf.110s and one He.111 while achieving nothing. Dispirited by the effects of 56 air strikes of the STFS (the RAF lost an Audax flown by a Greek pilot near Falluja, shot down by ground fire), the Iraqis withdrew towards Baghdad late in the afternoon, leaving behind about 100 prisoners and six tankettes. The British suffered about 50 casualties.[34]

THE END

Belatedly, the Luftwaffe did return to strafe the British columns advancing from Habbaniya and Fallujah on 23 May, but achieved little: in the air, the Germans claimed to have shot down two RAF Gladiators, while losing one Bf.110. In turn, Hurricanes from RAF Habbaniya shot down two He.111s, while a Gladiators from RAF Habbaniya was shot down by Iraqi ground fire. That said, while the British were pouring ever more reinforcements into Iraq, the Germans failed to do so: with its last two Messerschmitts in need of repairs and only one He.111 left in operational condition, and short

A very rare photograph of one of Squadriglia Speciale Iraq's CR.42s, seen during its two-day stay in the country. Clearly visible is the Iraqi national insignia on the undersurface of the lower wing (together with bomb shackles). (via Hakan Gustavsson)

Although taken before the May 1941 Anglo-Iraqi War, this photograph showing Ba.65 serial number 107 after a belly landing is symbolic of the sad fate that befell most of the RIrAF during that conflict. In addition to the serial and national markings, the application of the construction number (c/n) on the rear fuselage is of note. (Ahmad Sadik Collection)

on support equipment, spares and fuel, Sonderkommando Junck was out of the battle.

After mopping up the battlefield, the British resumed their advance in the direction of Baghdad on 24 May by deploying a column directly down the road from Falluja, while another traversed the desert towards the north, to cut off the road connecting the capital with Mosul. While the ground troops were working their way forwards, the air war went on with the RAF bombing Rashid AB early on 26 May. Junck reacted by sending his last operational He.111 to bomb RAF Habbaniya, but this achieved little: indeed, shortly after returning from that mission, the last operational German bomber in Iraq was destroyed in an air strike on Firnas AB. On the following morning, following a consultation with other German officials in the country, Junck decided to withdraw from Iraq. Ironically, precisely at this point in time – on 27 May 1941 – it was the Italians who arrived on the scene. Their support for Iraq included 12 Fiat CR.42 biplane fighters from No. 155 Squadron (155a Squadriglia) of the Italian Air Force (Regia Aeronautica). Reorganised as the Special Squadron Iraq (Squadriglia Speciale Iraq) they staged through Greece, the island of Rhodes, and then Syria, to arrive at Firnas AB already wearing full Iraqi markings. Although losing one aircraft *en route*, they were immediately pressed into attacks against the British units streaming from Fallujah to Baghdad. This, however, was too little, too late: on 28 May, the German Counsel to Baghdad informed Khaylani that the Luftwaffe was about to pull out of the country. Working feverishly, Junck's ground crews patched up the surviving two He.111s and these were then flown out via Aleppo to Rhodes on 29 May. The ground personnel and crews lacking operational aircraft followed in six Ju.52s. The Italians covered this evacuation, and during the day CF.42s encountered three Audaxes of the SFTS, and forced one of them down. A subsequent British air strike on Firnas AB caused little damage, because the Italians then also decided to leave Iraq, leaving behind the burned out hulks of two unflyable CR.42s.[35]

On 30 May, Habforce – meanwhile down to 1,200 troops, six artillery pieces, and a few armoured cars because of the need to guard the positions secured earlier – reached the outskirts of the Iraqi capital. The unit was diminutive, and it found itself subjected to several strafing attacks from the last few RIrAF Gladiators. However, it was facing a completely demoralised enemy: with RAF aircraft bombing and strafing their positions at will, there was not much fight left in the approximately 9,000 Iraqi soldiers still present in the Baghdad area. Therefore, Khaylani and most of his government fled to Persia (and from there to Turkey, then Italy, and finally to Germany), leaving behind the Mayor of Baghdad to request a truce.[36]

4

PAINFUL RECONSTRUCTION

A cease-fire ending the Anglo-Iraq War of 1941 was signed on 31 May 1941. Regent Abd All-Ilah returned to the capital a day later to be promptly reinstated, and he then appointed Madfaai as prime minister. Nominally at least, peace thus returned to Iraq on the same day that the island of Crete fell to Nazi Germany. In reality, there was no peace at all. Trying hard to disguise their quantitative weakness, the British forces remained outside the major cities of Iraq while these were torn apart by rioting and looting, much of which was focussed on the local Jewish quarters. Over 200 people were murdered in Baghdad alone and relative stability resumed only once the Iraqi Army curbed the violence. In the process, three colonels of the Golden Square – Said, Salman and Shabib – were arrested and hanged, while Sabbagh managed to escape to Turkey. By June 1941 the British Army of India completed the occupation of the country – once again under the premise of 'securing access to the country's strategic oil resources' (only to see its elements deployed in Iraq be re-assigned to the British Middle East Command). The Iraqi armed forces were then severely purged of all officers showing any kind of anti-British sentiments. Even then, concerned about the prospect of Nazi Germany defeating the Soviet Union and breaking through into the Middle East via the Caucasus, by 1942 the British reinforced their garrison in the country to 22 brigades – many of which subsequently redeployed to North Africa – and kept the Iraqi armed forces under extremely tight control.

WRECKED AIR FORCE

With the British military intervention in Iraq of 1941 abruptly ending the cycle of military coups in Baghdad, and establishing Nuri as-Saad as the dominant political figure, the recovery of the Iraqi armed forces – and that of the RIrAF in particular – was to prove particularly painful and very slow. In October 1941, Jamil

One from several batches of Gladiators sold to the RIrAF between 1943 and 1944, seen before delivery. Notable are multiple pieces of replacement fuselage skin around the fuel tank and the cockpit. (Albert Grandolini Collection)

Although of very poor quality, this is one of less than a handful of photographs showing an Iraqi Gladiator from the period 1943-1944 after their delivery. Clearly visible is the serial number 180, applied below the cockpit, and the traditional unit insignia in form of five black circles on the rear fuselage. (Ahmad Sadik Collection)

Madfaai resigned, and Abd al-Ilah appointed Nuri as-Saad as prime minister once again. From that period onwards, Saad's policy was heavily personalised in nature and characterised by continuous manipulation and immediate, short-term considerations. Deeply distrusting the armed forces, he constantly co-opted and cajoled potential adversaries and, if necessary, destroyed opponents through the ruthless use of force. The result was the development of a highly inegalitarian society, in which the major beneficiaries of public expenditure were a few Sunni families at the core of the system, and their client networks, while the great majority of the Iraqi population and the armed forces were completely ignored. Nowhere was this as obvious as in the case of the RIrAF, which had been devastated during the Anglo-Iraqi War of 1941.

The most crucial problem for Brigadier General Sami Fattah al-Musli, appointed as the commander of the RIrAF on 1 June 1941, was the fact that all the aircraft of the Flying School were destroyed. Just 10 out of 30 students of its 8th Course were still around, and all the instructor pilots were either killed during the war, or had fled to Syria, Turkey or Persia: for the next six years,

The other major type in service with the RIrAF of the late 1940s was the Avro Anson: 33 of these multi-role aircraft were acquired between 1944 and 1947, and they formed the backbone of the air force during the Palestine War of 1948. (Ahmad Sadik Collection)

One of three Northrops that survived the May 1941 Anglo-Iraqi War seen while about to fly *under* one of the Euphrates bridges in Baghdad in March 1944. (via Ali Tobchi)

the reconstituted air force was not able to train even one new pilot. The condition of the combat fleet was no better. Most of the officers of No. 1 Squadron had fled to Syria, while No. 2 Squadron had all of its aircraft destroyed: both units de-facto disintegrated. No. 5 Squadron was left with only five intact Ba.65s, and No. 6 Squadron with only one SM.79 – which was destroyed during its first post-war flight: therefore, both were disbanded. The only squadron left was No. 7: its technicians managed to salvage and repair three Northrop 8A-4Ds, and the unit then integrated the remaining six Gladiators from No. 4 Squadron. As if this was not enough, during the night of 26 to 27 March 1942, Rashid AB was suddenly flooded and whatever was left of the Nisrs of No. 3 Squadron destroyed. The unit thus had to be disbanded and its personnel assigned to other tasks. Finally, the British occupation authorities limited the number of flying hours to five per pilot per month.[1]

Madfaai's and then Saad's governments attempted to buy new aircraft but the British were reluctant and in March 1942, they took away three of the surviving Iraqi Gladiators. It was only on 10 September 1942 that the RAF provided five replacements, which were used to rebuild No. 4 Squadron, but these arrived without spare parts. The type had been out of production for years and the official explanation from London was that there were none left. In response to continuous Iraqi pleas, the British provided six grounded Gladiators as a source of spares in July 1943. In September the same year, the RAF then sold five operational examples to the RIrAF at a symbolic price (GBP £500 each), followed by another six in December (at a price of GBP £200 each): five of these were overhauled in Egypt before delivery and No. 4 Squadron flew just these. They were urgently needed because two operational Gladiators had collided on landing at Kirkuk on 9 January 1943, while Captain Abdul Rahman ash-Sheikh Abdul Wahhab crashed one of the remaining Northrops at Rashid AB in early 1944.[2]

Finally recognising the sad state of the RIrAF, London granted permission for the acquisition of five Avro A.652 Anson twin-engined multi-role aircraft. Upon their delivery, in early 1944, the RIrAF used this handful of machines to rebuild No. 1 Squadron, whose ground crews promptly had them equipped with bomb shackles. Finally, in May 1944, eight Gladiators in very poor state were transferred to Iraq from the RAF's stocks in Egypt: these were all used up as a source of spares. Thus, the RIrAF began its new life with about a dozen Gladiators, five Ansons, and three – then two – Northrops. The only positive development was of minimal value: in 1944, the British permitted the Iraqi pilots to fly up to six hours a month.[3]

RENEWED TUMULT

This gradual rebuilding of the RIrAF took place just in time for the force to face a new crisis: in June 1944, Saad resigned amid a growing dispute with Regent Abd al-Ilah, who appointed Hamdi al-Pachachi instead. This decision was opposed by the Kurds led by Mulla Mustafa Barzani, who launched a new rebellion because Pachachi had failed to respect earlier agreements with Saad. Once again, the Iraqi Army, supported by RIrAF Gladiators, Ansons and Northrops – which applied the old strategy of 'air policing' – quickly smashed the uprising, forcing Barzani and most of his followers to flee to Persia in October of the same year. However, unrest remained, and during follow-up operations, an Anson of the RIrAF hit a mountain outside Barzan on 22 September 1945, killing the crew consisting of pilot Abdul Majid Abdul ar-Razzaq al-Janubi, Anwar Aziz and Abdul Qader Ahmed Shukry. Another Anson was lost outside Ramadi, on 18 November 1946, when pilot Fathi Tawfik lost orientation in bad weather: the aircraft crashed, killing the pilot and his navigator, Khorshid Ali.[4]

While gaining Pachachi considerable prestige, the quick success against Barzani angered Abd al-Ilah who was meanwhile seeking to establish himself in a dominant position. The long dispute between the two culminated in February 1946, when Pachachi resigned and was replaced by Tawfiq as-Suwaidi. During his brief tenure in office, Suwaidi ended martial law and permitted the work of political parties, freed all those detained since 1941, lifted press censorship and introduced a new electoral law. However, Iraq's political scene was soon rife with old rivalries and anti-British sentiments: to these came the growing social unrest within a rapidly expanding population, and a financial crisis caused by a poor harvest. In 1946 and 1947, Iraq was hit by several big strikes, the most significant of which was the one of oil workers in the Kirkuk area. Moreover, major problems were looming on the international scene, foremost related to the question of Palestine. During his tenure, Saad attempted to find a solution in the form of a federation of the Arab states, including the British Mandate of Palestine. However, this was opposed not only by London but also by nearly all of the other Arab leaders – especially in Egypt and Saudi Arabia, and Abd al-Ilah's relative ruling in Transjordan – and thus the only result of this initiative was the creation of the Arab League in 1944-1945. Moreover, while ending their military occupation of Iraq in 1946, the British continued ignoring the Arabs (including their most-trusted allies, like Saad) and in April 1947 referred the issue of

Palestine to the United Nations instead: once again, foreigners were to decide the future of the Middle East.[5]

BAGHDAD FURY

Concerned by widespread unrest at home, and the growing tensions in Palestine, Baghdad recalled the effectiveness of 'air policing', and thus rushed to reinforce the RIrAF. Initially, London reacted by granting permission for deliveries of additional Ansons, and the number of these in Iraq eventually grew to more than 30. After protracted negotiations, in December 1946 an agreement was reached under which the Iraqis would return surviving Ansons in exchange for an order for 30 Hawker Sea Fury FB.Mk 11 (designated Fury F.Mk 1 but colloquially known as 'Baghdad Fury') and five (later reduced to 2) Fury Trainer T.Mk 52 conversion trainers. Baghdad agreed and the first batch of eight Furies reached Iraq in November 1947, accompanied by one two-seater.[6] These nine aircraft were allotted to the Rashid-based No. 7 Squadron, commanded by Lieutenant-Colonel Muhammed Rauf Hassan. Meanwhile, in July 1947, Baghdad followed with an order for three de Havilland Dove and three Bristol Freighter 170/C.Mk 31 twin-engined transports. The Doves were delivered in January 1948, together with the second batch of Furies: the former entered service with the re-established No. 3 Squadron, while the latter were taken over by the Firnas-based No. 1 Squadron, commanded by Lieutenant-Colonel Nadim Sadiq al-Ubaidi. Conversion from the Tiger Moths and Nisrs of the 1920s and the 1930s to high-performance Furies proved anything other than easy, and one of the new aircraft was lost in a crash at Rashid AB on 7 June 1948, killing the pilot, Hamid Mohammed ad-Dubuni. After this accident, all the pilots of No. 1 Squadron were subjected to stringent medical examinations, which revealed that most were unfit for flying duties. Correspondingly, they were given two months to meet fitness requirements.[7] Unsurprisingly, in his half-yearly report to the British Air Ministry, prepared in late spring of 1948, the British Air Inspector in Iraq, Wing Commander Fisher, commented: "The Furys' and Doves' performance has impressed the officers and men enormously. They do realise, however, that these types of aircraft are a big jump from anything they have flown or maintained before."[8]

Meanwhile, the Flying School was also re-established: equipped with a few Tiger Moths and Nisrs left from 1941, it launched its ninth course in September 1947. Obviously pleased with the work of the school, Fisher observed: "The Flying Training School is working well and to programme, with 27 pupils (including three Syrians), after an unfortunate start when an instructor and pupil committed suicide…."[9]

Overall, as of spring 1948, the RIrAF boasted a strength of 101 officers (of whom 95 were aircrew), and 1,066 other ranks,

The first three Fury F.Mk 1s prepared for Iraq (serial numbers 233, 232 and 231), and the first Fury Trainer T.Mk 52 (serial number 261), seen prior to their transfer flight in November 1947. (Albert Grandolini Collection)

The 'Baghdad Fury' serial number 245 as seen on delivery to Iraq. Notable are not only details of the camouflage pattern, national markings, and the serial number, but also two underwing drop tanks used for ferrying purposes. (Albert Grandolini Collection)

The first of – the little-known – Freighter C.Mk 31s manufactured for Iraq wore the serial number 330, as visible in this photograph. Although ordered in 1947, Iraq received its first three examples only four years later, when they entered service with the re-established No. 3 Squadron: the unit was to fly them for almost 30 years. (Albert Grandolini Collection)

The serial number 331 identifyies this Bristol Freighter C.Mk 31 as the second from the first batch of three transports ordered by the RIrAF in 1947. They entered service with the re-established No. 3 Squadron. (Albert Grandolini Collection)

organised into four operational squadrons (Nos. 1, 3, 4, 7) and the Flying School.

PALESTINE CRISIS

On 29 November 1947, the General Assembly of the United Nations adopted a resolution for a Partition Plan for Palestine, recommending the creation of two independent states – one Arab and one Jewish – and the creation of an international enclave in Jerusalem. While initially refusing to comply with the idea, concluding it was unable to maintain control, London announced its intention to withdraw from Palestine by 15 May 1948. Arabs protested, Jews celebrated, while British authorities ceased opposing the successive waves of escalating violence: riots, atrocities, attacks, bombings, ambushes, reprisals and counter-reprisals, and the Grand Mufti of Jerusalem's call for Jihad in Palestine converted the situation into a civil war, spreading panic among the local population. However, while about 70,000 Arabs fled between December 1947 and January 1948, and the operations by Zionist militants then successively increased that number to 100,000 by March, and to 250,000-300,000 by mid-May 1948, the Jewish Agency ordered the settlers to hold their positions at any cost. Working feverishly on securing the influx of additional troops, arms and supplies from abroad, the Zionists knew that the popular opinion abroad, and time, were on their side. Combined with the revelation of secret negotiations for a new Anglo-Iraqi Treaty, which was to secure British influence and interests for another 25 years, signed at Portsmouth on 15 January 1948, the plight of the Arabs in Palestine caused an outburst of public protest and mass demonstrations all over Iraq. The situation stabilised only once Prime Minister Muhammad as-Sadr proclaimed martial law and ordered the armed forces to deploy to the Palestine War.

As so often, the order for this deployment caught the RIrAF wrong-footed, with both of its two major fighter units still in the process of conversion to the Furies. Therefore, a detachment of 12 Ansons drawn from Nos. 1 and 7 Squadrons, and two Gladiators of No. 4 Squadron commanded by Hassan was deployed to Mafraq airfield in Transjordan on 12 May 1948. While potent, this unit was insufficiently supported with spares and armament: none were available because the British had withheld them for years. However, worst of all was the fact that the Arab governments had no overall strategic plan, and even less idea about the kind of threat they were facing. Certainly enough, their Chiefs of Staff did meet on 1 May 1948, and they agreed – in general terms – what each of the involved armies was supposed to do. However, every government also had its own individual designs: in addition to disagreements and different interpretations (and, subsequently, mutual accusations of treachery), this resulted in every force fighting on its own, without any kind of coordination. Moreover, many of the involved forces were not yet ready, and even less so had they *all* invaded Palestine – and thus the future Israel – on 15 May 1948 (the date on which the independence of Israel was proclaimed and which is thus considered the 'official' first day of the war in the West, although, and as described above, the conflict had been ongoing for months).

PALESTINE WAR

Early during the Palestine War (or 'War of Impendence' in Israel), it was the Royal Egyptian Air Force (REAF) that bore the brunt of air warfare. Operating following the RAF's *Land/Air Warfare Pamphlet No. 1 Air Support Command*, the REAF concentrated on supporting ground troops and on searching for airfields used by the nascent Israel Defence Force/Air Force (IDF/AF). Other Arab air forces operated only sporadically, and rarely coordinated with their ground forces. Theoretically, the task of the RIrAF contingent deployed at Mafraq was to support their own troops and those of the Arab Legion, the armed forces of Transjordan. However, due to the lack of arms and supplies, the Ansons are known to have flown only two combat sorties during the first phase of the Palestine War: on 18 May 1948, a pair led by Tallid at-Tikriti bombed the Israeli airfield of Ein Shemer, with unknown results. Even after this mission, the Iraqi ground crews had to work for days to improvise new bombs and manufacture spares necessary to make their aircraft operational again. Moreover, when the RIrAF attempted to reinforce its contingent in Transjordan by deploying additional Gladiators, one

Major (later Major-General) Hardan Abd el-Rhefal at-Tikriti, seen with a group of pilots from No. 7 Squadron in front of one of their Furies (serial number 316), together with a collection of unguided rockets and bombs – the mass of which were delivered by the British to Iraq only well after the Palestine War. (Tom Cooper Collection)

One of the RIrAF's Ansons as seen around 1948. Notable is the nose, apparently painted in green or blue and containing a reconnaissance camera, and the application of the serial number (in black). (Ahmad Sadik Collection)

of these suffered malfunction and was forced to land in the desert, on 7 June 1948. The aircraft was found only 15 days later, but its pilot, Captain Abdul Sattar Abdullah, was never found.[10]

The fighting stopped, temporarily, through an UN-mediated armistice of 11 June. The following four weeks proved vital for the Israelis because once the fighting erupted again, the IDF/AF had been greatly strengthened by a constant influx of ever more capable aircraft, additional arms and equipment, and more than 200 foreign pilots and ground personnel (all of them rich with combat experience from the Second World War). On the contrary, short on armament and supplies, the Iraqi air power continued to decline. When the RIrAF sent additional Ansons to Mafraq in early July 1948, two of these crashed: one at H-3, and another inside Transjordan. The unit launched its next sortie over Palestine only on 6 July 1948, when Major Rashid Ali Awad flew combat reconnaissance of the port of Haifa in response to intelligence that several ships were unloading contraband there. He found no targets and thus dropped his bombs on Ramat David on the way back.

Haifa and Ramat David remained the principle targets for the Iraqi unit once the Israelis renewed the fighting with an offensive against the Syrian forces holding Mishmar Ha'Yarden in the north, and the Iraqi and Transjordanian forces in the Jerusalem Corridor in the Ramleh/Lydda area on 8 July 1948. On 15 July, two Ansons led by Tikriti bombed the port of Haifa with unknown results, while two led by Awad bombed Megiddo airfield. A day later, two Ansons hit Meggido once again. Much more action was to follow because the IDF/AF then introduced to service three Boeing B-17 heavy bombers, which flew a series of indiscriminate attacks on the Arab capitals. Damascus was bombed in the early hours of 18 July 1948: ordered to find and destroy the B-17s, but lacking any kind of meaningful intelligence and depending on little more than rumours, Hassan first deployed Tikriti with two Ansons to target Ein Shemer airfield in the morning, before sending another pair, piloted by Major Anwar and one of the youngest pilots in the unit, Lieutenant Arif Abd ar-Razzaq, to bomb the former RAF Ramat David, in the Jezreel Valley, in the afternoon. Anwar led another attack at Ramat David a few hours later and, overall, the Iraqis claimed the destruction of three B-17s on the ground using a total of eight incendiary bombs. However, one Anson involved in the latter strike was hit by anti-aircraft fire and made an emergency landing near Afula, where its crew of two was captured by the Israelis. That, however, was about all the RIrAF detachment at Mafraq could do at the time: by the time another UN-negotiated armistice took effect, later the same day, it was out of ammunition and spares once again.[11]

For easier visual identification, the RIrAF's Fury F.Mk 1s deployed to Syria during the Palestine War of 1948 all received two wide white strips around their wingtips; some also received one white strip around the rear fuselage. This photograph, taken during the parade celebrating the hand-over of RAF Shaiba to the RIrAF in 1955, shows exactly the same markings on two examples, indicating that either the Egyptians returned four aircraft donated to them in October 1948, or that another batch of Baghdad Furies was subsequently deployed to Transjordan or Syria. Visible are serial numbers applied 'RAF-style' in black on the bottom of the wing, including 326 (front), 302 (left), 319 (right), and 325 (background). (Albert Grandolini Collection)

Not related to the Palestine War, this photograph shows the fin of RIrAF Fury F.Mk 1 from No. 7 Squadron, RIrAF (only the first two digits of the serial, 23? are readable), with its pilot, Hassan Rajab Arim. Arim's Fury was badly damaged in a collision with another Fury during a training sortie over RAF Shaiba on an unknown date in 1948. Although losing both the ruder and most of the horizontal stabilator, Arim managed a safe landing. (Ali Tobchi Collection)

WITHDRAWAL

The appearance of the B-17 prompted the governments of Syria and Transjordan to demand that the Iraqis replace their remaining Ansons with Furies. However, concerned about a possible Israeli air strike on Baghdad, the Iraqi Minister of Defence Sadiq al-Bassam – who was denied much say about the conduct of the war in Palestine – insisted on retaining his best interceptors for protection of the capital. Correspondingly, in late July 1948, all Ansons were withdrawn (two were donated to Syria, and the Iraqis then helped convert a group of Syrian C-47 pilots to this type), and in their place six Furies from No. 7 Squadron transferred via airfield H-3 in western Iraq to Almazza AB in Damascus. Tired after the long flight, one of the pilots involved crashed on landing, and his aircraft was written off. Another Fury was written off after a hard landing sometime in September 1948, when its pilot was injured. The remaining four were to see only a bare minimum of action during the Palestine War: because of the armistice, and because the British supplied only 6,000 rounds of ammunition for 20mm Hispano V cannons, and no bombs, they only flew armed reconnaissance. Thus, and although meanwhile nearly all of the pilots of Nos. 1 and 7 Squadrons had completed their conversion course to the type, they never received the opportunity to prove their mettle in combat against the IDF/AF. Their only known combat sorties over Palestine were flown by Tikriti and Razzaq from Almazza AB on an unknown date, probably sometime in October 1948: they first sought for ships off the port of Haifa, but when finding none, strafed Ramat David AB, claiming one B-17 as destroyed. Eventually, the governments in Baghdad and Cairo then agreed to hand over the four surviving aircraft to the REAF: they were transferred to Almaza AB in Egypt later the same month. The RIrAF did retain its detachment of Ansons at Mafraq AB in Transjordan for a few months longer but these saw no action. On the contrary, the poor condition of the remaining Ansons became obvious on 2 October 1948, when the aircraft piloted by Lieutenant Qasim Mohammed Qasim crashed on take-off because its left wing fell off. The pilot and his crew – including Sergeants Mulah Salom and Abid Jawad – were killed.

5
JET AGE

The outcome of the Palestine War was received with bitterness and anger by the entire Arab world, and so also the Iraqi public. As the power that created the Mandate of Palestine, suppressed repeated revolts of the local population, and then handed it over to the Zionists, Great Britain was blamed for the disaster by nearly everybody in Baghdad. Britain was also Iraq's primary arms supplier or, rather, the party that had refused to supply what was considered necessary. Unsurprisingly, anti-British hostility began to dominate public life. Ironically, the British now reacted by delivering almost everything the Iraqis demanded – and could afford. The 1950s thus saw a period of unprecedented growth of the RIrAF, which introduced to service nearly a dozen new types of aircraft, including its first jet-powered fighters and first helicopters.

KOREAN BOOM

Reacting to critique, complaints and protests, on 6 January 1949 Regent Abd al-Ilah dismissed the government and re-appointed Nuri as-Saad as prime minister for what was now the tenth time. Saad dealt with the situation in his usual way: ruthlessly and short-sightedly. Accusing 'communists' and 'Jews' of causing all the Iraq's problems, he ordered a wave of arrests and court martials, and then unleashed his Minister of Defence Bassam to initiate systematic harassment of the Iraqi Jewish community. Ironically enough, while such policies made the situation appear 'under control' on the surface, they were to transform the negligible and unpopular Iraqi Communist Party (ICP) into one of the best-organised and most popular political parties in the country, while intimidating the majority of around 120,000 Iraqi Jews into leaving the country by 1952 – much to Iraq's loss. Concerned, the British concluded that a major change was necessary and thus ordered Saad to concentrate on economic development instead. Rather by accident than design, the so-called 'Korean Boom' (prompted by US economic activities related to the Korean War of 1950-1953) then boosted the export of agricultural products, while the conclusion of a new agreement with the IPC considerably increased the income from oil exports.[1] Instead of sharing with the population and spending for development, Saad then authorised a comprehensive re-equipment of the armed forces. This is how not only an additional 20 Fury F.Mk 1s were acquired in 1951 – bringing the total orders to 55 single-seaters and two two-seaters operated by three squadrons (Nos. 1, 4, and 7) – but also the RIrAF took care to replace obsolete Tiger Months through the acquisition of de Havilland Canada DHC-1 Chipmunk T.Mk 51 basic trainers, Percival Provost T.Mk 53s and US-made North American T-6

Together with Chipmunks from Canada, in 1951 the RIrAF also placed an order for 15 Provost T.Mk 53s. Upon their delivery in 1954, they served as advanced trainers at the Air Force College up until 1970. This example (serial number 374) was photographed while in a turn, thus nicely showing its national markings and serial numbers applied underwing in RAF-style. (BAE Heritage)

Taken during a parade at Rashid airfield in 1955, this photograph shows a row of seven Chipmunk T.Mk 51s (the front aircraft wears the serial number 280). The RIrAF acquired a total of 15 such trainers from 1951, and they served with the Air Force College until replaced by Czechoslovak-made Zlins in 1970-1971. (Albert Grandolini Collection)

Three Westland WS.51 Dragonflies were the first helicopters obtained by the RIrAF: they arrived in 1951 and were operated by No. 3 Squadron. Their camouflage colours were similar to those of the Furies and included light earth and dark brown on top surfaces and sides, and PRU blue on the undersides. (Tom Cooper Collection)

Six de Havilland Doves (all reconditioned former FR.Mk 3s) were acquired by the RIrAF starting from January 1948. (David Nicolle Collection)

Another of the Dove FR.Mk 3s delivered to the RIrAF (serial number 267) seen wearing unusual marking in the form of a yellow-coloured camel applied on the red cheat line below the cockpit. (David Nicolle Collection)

Harvard advanced trainers. Finally, in the same year the RIrAF placed its first order for three Westland WS.51 Dragonfly helicopters (a licence-built version of the US-made Sikorsky S-51): these were operated by No. 3 Squadron, alongside Doves and Freighters.[2]

This proved to be one of very few of Saad's decisions with positive long-term effects: the new equipment enabled the Flying School of the RIrAF to be expanded into the Air Force College, which began providing a much-improved curriculum to a significantly larger number of students. Dozens of new pilots and hundreds of technicians were graduated during the following years, founding a solid basis for future growth of the air force.

INTIFADA OF 1952

Saad's failure to address the social discontent and improve the economy proved a short-sighted decision. From the point of view of ordinary Iraqis, it was clear that nothing had changed: the same regency governed in the same old manner, through the same narrow ring of privileged oligarchs, under the same pretence of constitutional politics. Certainly enough, the unpopular Saad was replaced by a succession of Abd al-Ilah's political allies, through 1952. However, influenced by developments in neighbouring Iran and the revolutionary events in Egypt, unrest began to spread in Iraq once again. In October 1952, a major student strike followed by riots, erupted and then spread into a general strike supported by all oppositional parties. When police opened fire at demonstrators and killed dozens, rioters brought most of Baghdad and the whole of Najaf under their control. Keen to retain power at any cost, Abd al-Ilah then appointed a government consisting of military officers and led by General Nuraddin Mahmoud – the former commander of the Iraqi Army during the Palestine War. Although knowing that most of his troops sympathised with the demonstrators, and most of his officers still resented a Regent that relied on the British, Mahmoud imposed martial law and prohibited demonstrations: when the demonstrators re-appeared, on 24 November, the Army opened fire killing dozens. Immediately afterwards, another wave of arrests followed in the course of which all of the top opposition politicians were imprisoned. As if this was not enough, the government then rigged elections of January 1953, providing Saad and his followers with an overwhelming victory.[3]

FAYSAL II TO THE THRONE

Theoretically, the events of 1952-1953 could have initiated a new era in Iraqi history. However, nothing changed even once Faysal II ascended the Iraqi throne, upon reaching his majority, on 2

During the early 1950s, the RIrAF also acquired several de Havilland Heron C.Mk 2Cs. Only one of these – serial number 393, visible here – is known to have ever received air force serials: the rest served with the Royal Flight. (John Fircker Collection via Simon Watson)

The aircraft assigned to the Royal Flight all wore the same livery, including the white top to the fuselage, a red cheatline, and the rest of the fuselage and wing either left in bare metal, or painted in light grey. As far as is known, they wore registrations in the range RF1 – RF6 on the fin. (Pit Weinert Collection)

A Vampire FB.Mk 52, serial number 340, seen on delivery to Iraq in May 1953, where it served with No. 5 Squadron. Within only two years, the type was replaced by more advanced Venoms. (John Fricker Collection, via Simon Watson)

May 1953. Young, Western-educated, having democratic ideas, and popular but out of touch with the Iraqi public, he appointed a reformist government that included Kurdish representatives, lifted martial law, ended press censorship and allowed party activity. However, the young reign remained dependent on Abd al-Ilah, the British, conservative oligarchy, and the armed forces – for advice, and to keep himself in power. Indeed, he and his government 'had to pay the price' for military support. Correspondingly, in 1953 Baghdad placed another series of orders for arms in London. Increased oil income enabled the RIrAF to fund the acquisition of 12 de Havilland Vampire FB.Mk 52s and 10 T.Mk 55s between May 1953 and November 1955. These entered service with the re-established No. 5 Squadron (declared operational on 13 August 1953), initially based at Rashid AB and commanded by Arif Abd ar-Razzaq, who – after his two tours in Palestine and then converting to Furies – served with the King's Flight and flew Doves and de Havilland Herons in 1951, before graduating from the Staff College, two years later.[4]

In 1954, after another conversion course in Great Britain, Razzaq was appointed the first commander of the re-

A wonderful study of a Venom F.Mk 50 serial number 362, seen pre-delivery to Iraq, where it initially served with No. 6 Squadron. After being replaced by Hunters, surviving Venoms were operated by No. 1 Squadron well into the 1960s. (John Fricker Collection via Simon Watson)

A quartet of RIrAF Vampire FB.Mk 52s passing low over RAF Habbaniya and showing details of their camouflage pattern and national insignia. Visible are serial numbers 389 (the first of the Iraqi FB.Mk 52s), 338 (rearmost aircraft), and 337 (front). (Ahmed Hussain Collection)

A trio of RIrAF Venom F.Mk 50s in left turn, showing details of their top-side camouflage pattern. Notable is the application of fin flashes on the outside and inside of each fin. (Pit Weinert Collection)

established No. 6 Squadron: this was equipped with more powerful de Havilland Venom F.Mk 50s (an export variant of the Venom FB.Mk 1). Deliveries of the first batch of 12 began in May of that year and were completed by January 1955; the second batch of eight followed between April 1955 and February 1956.[5]

BAGHDAD PACT

In the wake of recent developments in Egypt and Iran during the mid-1950s, an increasing number of Iraqi politicians concluded that British power was in decline (a feeling further increased by the approaching expiration of the Anglo-Iraqi Treaty of 1930), and there would be a need to seek an alliance with the USA instead. This played directly into the arms of the administration of US President Dwight D Eisenhower: having lost China to communism in 1949-1950, and after barely saving South Korea in 1950-1953, the administration became obsessed with 'preventing communist encroachment' through the means of 'collective defence'. On the basis of experience with the creation of the North Atlantic Treaty Organisation (NATO) in Europe, the establishment of a similar structure in the Middle and Near East was proposed. The purpose of this was to link-up the southernmost member of NATO – Turkey – with the westernmost member of the Southeast Asia Treaty Organisation (SEATO), Pakistan. Knowing that Baghdad was still considered to be the proverbial 'bastion of British colonial rule in the Middle East' in London, Faysal II and Abd al-Ilah re-appointed Saad as prime minister and authorised him with regards to the related negotiations. In February 1955, Iraq and Turkey signed a 'pact of mutual cooperation': when Great Britain reacted with the announcement that it would adhere to this treaty, not only Iran and Pakistan decided to join, but even Jordan and Lebanon considered this option. Rather surprised by the Iraqi move, while not joining the resulting Baghdad Pact, the USA participated as an 'observer' – and strongly influenced what was expected to become the next step in the development of the RIrAF. In turn, the new pact ended the Anglo-Iraqi Treaty of 1930 without replacement, and Baghdad thus avoided provoking a new wave of demonstrations at home.[6]

Stills from a film with symbolic character, taken during the hand-over of RAF Habbaniya to the RIrAF in May 1955: British Military Policemen removing the sign 'Royal Air Force Habbaniya'…

… and Iraqi Military Policemen installing the sign 'Habbaniya Airfield' in Arabic. (Albert Grandolini collection)

The biproducts of the related negotiations were three-fold. On one side, the USA donated at least six Stinson L-5 Sentinels and seven Cessna O-1A Bird Dog aircraft to Iraq: apparently planned to be used by an army aviation service, all were taken up by the RIrAF instead. On the other, Great Britain agreed to hand over RAF Shaiba, and to start sharing RAF Habbaniya with the RIrAF in May 1955. Renamed as Wahda AB, Shaiba became the new home of the Air Force College in the same month. Finally, the RIrAF established cooperation with the Lebanese air force and later on (on 16 May 1957), donated its surviving six T-6s to the Lebanese.[7]

Encouraged by the creation of the Baghdad Pact, Washington began signalling its preparedness to start providing military aid to Iraq. Initially at least, the commander of the RIrAF, Major-General Abdel-Kadam ash-Shiah Abadi (appointed in November 1954), proved reluctant: he preferred British-made aircraft and, in early 1956, presented a five-year development plan that envisaged a massive expansion of his service, including the training of no fewer than 200 additional pilots and the establishment of three new fighter squadrons and two bomber squadrons by 1960.[8] While arrangements were made to ensure that sufficient vacancies would be available for Iraqi students at training facilities in Great Britain, due to recruiting and financial difficulties, only about 120 students arrived between March and May 1958. To improve the situation (and retain their influence), the British reacted by deploying a team of 24 officers and 16 non-commissioned officers (NCOs) headed by Group Captain Wells of the RAF to Iraq: this not only helped improve the recruiting and basic training, but also reorganised the RIrAF's supply and maintenance system and links with supply depots in Britain. This activity also then supported the introduction to service of the first two radar stations equipped with Marconi Type 13 and Type 14 radars.[9]

After taking over RAF Habbaniya, the RIrAF staged a large parade, proudly putting all of its aircraft on display. Thus came into being this 'group photo', showing (from left to right) Herons, Doves, Vampires, and O-1As. (Ahmad Sadik Collection)

This row of Venom F.Mk 50s was also photographed on the same occasion. (Ahmad Sadik Collection)

A wonderful view of one of the first batch of Hunter F.Mk 6s destined for Iraq, seen during the transfer flight in December 1957, when it was wearing the transfer-code N on the top of the fin and a temporary registration XG236. (Air Pictorial via Albert Grandolini)

The same report concluded that estimated serviceability was at 60 per cent, but with poor spares backing, and that the RIrAF apparently had only 65 pilots, of whom 33 had trained on jets (10 had completed the Hunter OCU course and 15 were in the process of conversion at Chivenor). Another report indicated that 40 additional Iraqi pilots were expected to arrive in the UK in May 1958.[11]

Only a month later, in February 1958, a US Military Survey Team visited Iraq and – amongst other points – agreed not only to financially support the construction of a new air base with a 2,500 metre-long (8,202ft) runway near RAF Habbaniya, but also to donate at least six Cessna O-1A Birddog liaison aircraft (in addition to at least six Stinson L-5 Sentinels donated at an earlier date), and 36 F-86Fs free of charge. Delighted, Abadi promptly seized the opportunity and dispatched 15 of his pilots for conversion training in the USA. At least four, but probably six, O-1s reached Iraq by June 1958, followed by the first five Sabres, on 15 of the same month. The new jets were scheduled to enter service with No. 4 Squadron, a unit then still flying Furies and under the command of Lieutenant-Colonel Shams Idlin.[12]

Encouraged, Abadi then expressed his interest in acquiring 10 Hawker Hunter F.Mk 6 fighter-bombers. Guided by their traditional mistrust for the Iraqis, the British initially expressed their doubts that Baghdad could afford these jets, and offered older Hunter F.Mk 4s instead. This caused protracted negotiations finalised only once London could not but express its gratefulness for Saad's support during the Suez War against Egypt in 1956. In February 1957, Whitehall announced its readiness to sell a package of six Hunter F.Mk 6s and three-months of spares. By this time, the first group of 11 Iraqi pilots has already completed its conversion training on the type at RAF Chivenor: the second group – including six pilots and 25 technicians, followed by the end of the same year. Thus, the type entered service with the re-organised No. 6 Squadron, as soon as delivered, between April and December 1957.[10]

STILLBORN COOPERATION WITH THE USA

All of these acquisitions resulted in the RIrAF of early 1958 being organised as described in the semi-annual report of the RAF Attaché in Baghdad, as follows:

- Habbaniya: 15 Hunter F.Mk 6s, 20 Venoms (14 operational), eight Vampire FB.Mk 52s (6 operational), and six Vampire T.Mk 11s
- Wahda: 40 Sea Furies (15 operational)
- Rashid: six Stinson L-5 Sentinels (4 operational), 11 Austers (6 operational), one Piper PA-18A Cub, four Bristol Freighters (3 operational), two Herons (1 operational), five Doves (4 operational), and two Westland S.51 helicopters (1 operational).

14 TAMMUZ REVOLUTION

The massive build-up of the Iraqi armed forces during the 1950s had next to no impact upon the simmering disaffection, widespread anti-British sentiment, and deep hatred for the Hashemite rule and its endless list of failures in domestic and international matters amongst Iraqi military officers. A coup plot by the so-called 'Free Officers' – an underground movement active since at least 1927 – was revealed in early 1956, but the government found itself in no position to do any more than to disperse the plotters by re-appointing them to other positions. Ironically, Nuri as-Saad subsequently lulled himself into a false sense of security, created by his repressive tactics, lavish distribution of new equipment, and appointments to the armed forces, but also by his preoccupation with developments abroad. On 1 February 1958, Egypt and Syria announced the formation of the United Arab Republic (UAR). Widely regarded in the West as an 'expression of imperialist ambitions' by the Egyptian President Gamal Abdel Nasser, but initiated by the Syrian government, this short-lived experiment created much unease amongst the rulers in Amman and Baghdad (and in the West). On an Jordanian initiative, a union of Iraq and Jordan was negotiated between 11 and 14 February 1958, and ratified by the Iraqi parliament on 12 May. In the new state King Faysal II assumed the position of the head, with King Hussein of Jordan as his deputy, along with a federal government. Attempting

PILOT-POLITICIANS

During the mid-1950s an entire generation of Iraqi fighter-pilots emerged: they mostly joined the RIrAF in the late 1940s, graduated from its Air College in the early 1950s, and underwent multiple advanced training courses in Great Britain. They usually first flew Furies, then Vampires and Venoms, before the best amongst them were assigned to No. 6 Squadron in 1957. Commanded by Arif Abd ar-Razzaq, the first complement of this unit included Nimma Abdullah ad-Dulaymi, Mumtazz Abdel Ali as-Saydoon, Mufeed Said, Khalid Jerjis Sarah, Hamid Shaaban at-Tikriti, and Jamal al-Windawi. Most of them could be described as well-educated, skilled pilots, and capable administrators. Nominally, they were quiet and calm, yet strong-willed young men, determined to fulfil their duty, but also to exploit the opportunities offering themselves through the rapid expansion of the air force. During their early military service, they trained very hard and accumulated extensive knowledge about aerial warfare: subsequently, they developed managerial skills and excelled in staff work. Frequently involved in politics, they were repeatedly side-lined and appointed to secondary positions, sometimes arrested and jailed, sometimes even pensioned-off or forced into exile, only to be released and/or pardoned and then appointed to ever higher positions. The older of this 'class of pilot-politicians' flew, fought and commanded units during three wars with Israel (1948, 1967 and 1973), and during more than a dozen coups and uprisings in Iraq in the 1950s and 1960s. Unsurprisingly they were to play a crucial role not only for the future of the Iraqi Air Force, but indeed the entire country, for the next 30 years.

King Faysal II (centre, with glasses) shaking hands with Mumtazz Abdel Ali as-Saydoon during a visit to No. 6 Squadron, shortly after the unit was declared operational on Hunters in December 1957. Visible on the right of the photograph is Arif Abd ar-Razzaq, the first commanding officer of this unit. Just six months later, Saydoon and Razzaq would take part in the 14 Tammuz Revolution, during which King Faysal II was executed together with most of his family and the government. (via Ali Tobchi)

Iraq's involvement in the Baghdad Pact resulted in the acquisition of advanced British weapons and various US arms. Some of the equipment was proudly put on display in a parade staged during the visit by King Saud Ibn Saud in 1956. This photograph shows two Centurion main battle tanks of British origin. (Albert Grandolini Collection)

A reconstruction of the first of five DH.60M Gipsy Moths acquired by the RIrAF in 1931. Painted in silver dope overall, the aircraft received the full Iraqi insignia, including classic 'triangles' on the fuselage, and all four national colours on the fin. While not armed originally, Iraqi ground crews adapted four of them to carry bomb shackles for four 10kg (20lb) bombs. Notable is the oversized serial number '1': probably as a matter of pride and prestige, this was applied in a much larger size and greater thickness than the numbers on the other four DH.60Ms or the subsequent nine DH.60Ts and DH.83s acquired by the RIrAF by 1934. (Artwork by Tom Cooper)

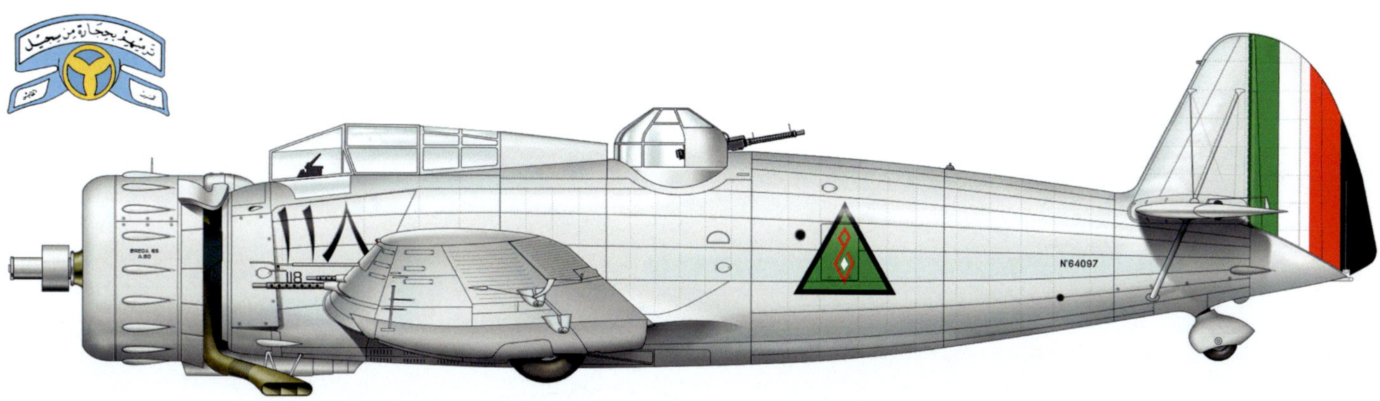

The 15 Breda BA.65A-80s that Iraq ordered from Italy in 1937 represented the first ground-attack of the RIrAF designed as such from the start. While serials 106 and 107 were equipped as trainers, the other 13 examples, including 118 shown here, belonged to the Ba.65A variant equipped with a hydraulically powered turret for the rear gunner. Other armament included one 7.62mm light machinegun and one 12.7mm heavy machinegun in each wing. Moreover, the type could carry up to 1,000kg (2,000lbs) of bombs. Inset is shown the insignia of No. 5 Squadron as in use during the late 1930s. The RIrAF's Bredas saw much action during the Anglo-Iraqi War of 1941, and a few survivors continued serving until 1947. (Artwork by Richard Caruana)

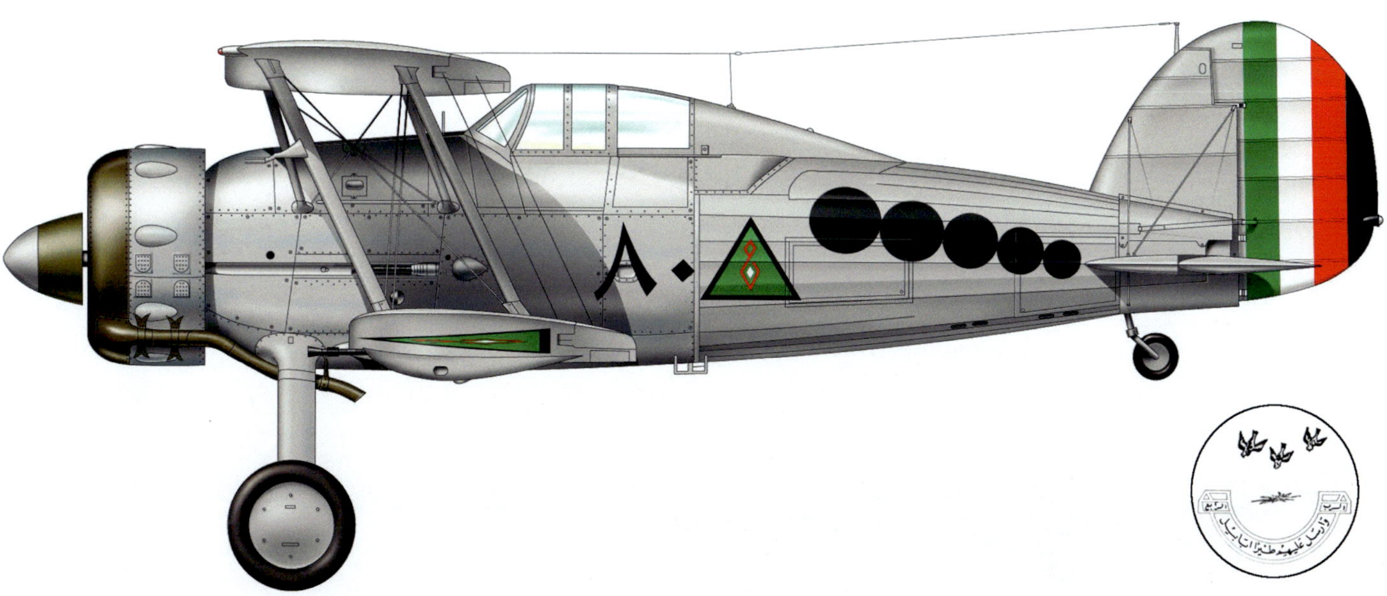

The type to see most action with the RIrAF in the late 1930s and through the 1940s was the Gloster Gladiator: 15 Mk Is and Mk IIs were acquired in 1937, of which six survived to June 1941. After taking away three of these, the British eventually supplied 19 additional Gladiators by 1944, and they thus formed the backbone of the RIrAF's fighter fleet until 1947-1948. As far as is known, all Iraqi Gladiators were painted in silver dope overall, and wore the usual set of insignia including large black serials and triangles applied under the cockpit, and the fin painted in national colours. Their primary armament consisted of four 7.7mm machine guns (two installed low in the centre fuselage, and two under the wing). This artwork shows the classic 'five balls' insignia applied on the rear fuselage and – in the lower right corner inset – the insignia of No. 4 Squadron as in use in the 1940s. (Artwork by Richard Caruana)

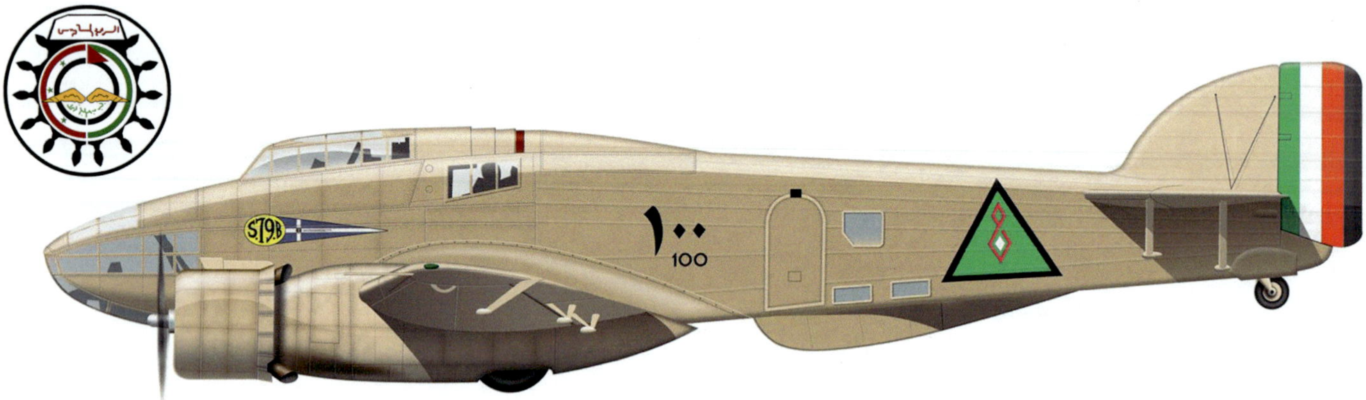

The acquisition of six Savoia Marchetti SM.79B bombers for No. 5 Squadron in 1937-1938, propelled the RIrAF into the world of modern military aviation of that period. While other versions of this bomber were powered by three engines, this one received a re-designed nose with the bomb-aimer's position, an elevated cockpit with a movable machine gun, and two Fiat A.80 RC.41 engines. The centre fuselage included a large bomb bay, in which either two 500kg, five 250kg, or 12 50 or 100kg bombs could be installed – all vertically. The SM.79Bs operated by the RIrAF all appear to have been painted in yellow sand overall: large type insignia, serial number and the triangle were applied on the fuselage sides and national colours on the ruder. Inset is shown the insignia of No. 5 Squadron as in use from 1938s until the 1980s. (Artwork by Goran Sudar)

The Douglas/Northrop 8A-4D (or A-17) was the most advanced ground attack type in service with the RIrAF during the Anglo-Iraq War of 1941. The type was a predecessor of the famous Douglas SBD Dauntless dive bomber from the Second World War, but apparently not yet equipped for dive-bombing (the most precise bombing tactics of the 1930s and the 1940s). Fifteen were acquired from the USA and used to equip No. 7 Squadron, but their subsequent operations were severely hampered by the British confiscating a shipload of spares and armament in 1940. As far as is known, all were left in bare metal overall, and wore the usual set of insignia. However, the exact position and size of the serial numbers (131-145) – applied after delivery – remains unclear. Inset is shown the crest of No. 7 Squadron, as applied on all of the Iraqi 'Northrops'. (Artwork by Luca Canossa)

Starting in 1944, Iraq acquired at least 30 Avro A.652 Anson twin-engined aircraft of different marks. Assigned to the reconstituted Nos. 1 and 7 Squadrons, these were used for a wide variety of purposes, from transport and reconnaissance to ground attack against several uprisings in Iraq of the 1940s, and against Israel in 1948. As far as is known, most were painted in silver dope overall, but the few available photographs also indicate the application of an unknown shade of light- or medium-grey overall. Several examples seem to have received nose-turrets with reconnaissance cameras, and these were painted either in green, as shown here, or in blue. (Artwork by Tom Cooper)

Between 1947 and 1951, the RIrAF acquired a total of 55 Hawker Sea Fury FB.Mk 11 fighter-bombers (re-designated Fury FB.Mk 1 for export but colloquially known as the 'Baghdad Fury') and two Fury T.Mk 52 two-seat conversion trainers. These were operated by Nos. 1, 4, and 7 squadrons, of which the former and the latter saw action during the Palestine War of 1948. Subsequently, four Furies were donated to Egypt, and another four to Morocco. While a debate about their camouflage colours is still raging, authentic colour photographs from the 1950s show them painted as illustrated here: in BS381C/362 mid stone and BS381C/350 dark earth on upper surfaces and sides, and BS381C/172 pale roundel blue on undersurfaces. Armament consisted of four 20mm Hispano cannons, up to two 454kg (1,000lb) bombs or 12 76mm unguided rockets. Inserts show two versions of the original insignia of No. 1 Squadron: the left one was applied in the form of a small black stencil, below the rear portion of the cockpit of the machines of this unit. (Artwork by Tom Cooper)

A total of 15 de Havilland Canada Chipmunk T.Mk 51s served as basic trainers at the Air Force College from 1951 until the early 1970s, and were thus used to graduate several generations of future Iraqi pilots. All were painted in silver dope overall, and originally wore yellow fuselage bands. Serials were applied RAF-style on the wings, and – over time – in several different positions on the rear fuselage (this example has the serial number 288). Insets show the crest of the Iraqi Air Force and the fin of the little-known North American T-6/Harvard IIB, 15 of which were acquired around the same time. These were left in bare metal overall, but next to nothing is known about the position and size of their insignia – except for that of the fin flash. Six Iraqi Harvard IIBs were donated to Lebanon in 1956. (Artwork by Tom Cooper)

One of the rarest types ever operated by the Iraqi air force was the Bristol Freighter 170/C.Mk 31, at least four of which were ordered in 1947 but delivered between 1953 and 1957. All were left in highly-polished bare metal overall, but had most of their engine nacelles painted in black, and wore the typical set of individual and national markings on the rear fuselage and fin. The example illustrated here is shown with the fin flash in use from July 1958 until the second coup of 1973. Having a large cargo door in the nose, the Freighter was capable of loading even small vehicles and was thus highly appreciated by the Iraqis: unsurprisingly, it remained in service until replaced by much more advanced types in the early 1970s. The inset shows the insignia of the only unit to operate this type: No. 3 Squadron. (Artwork by Luca Canossa)

Twelve de Havilland Vampire FB.Mk 52 fighter-bombers and no fewer than 10 Vampire T.Mk 55s acquired between 1953 and 1955 became the first jet fighters of the Iraqi air force. All were camouflaged in a standard pattern consisting of BS381C/362 mid stone and BS381C/350 dark earth on upper surfaces and sides, and BS381C/697 Sky S on undersurfaces and sides, and wore their serials applied in black, RAF-style, on booms, and wing-undersides. Following their overhauls and upgrade in Great Britain, the T.Mk 55s received ejection seats as shown in this example that was eventually donated to Somalia in the mid-1960s. The inset shows details of the camouflage pattern on upper surfaces, and the RAF-style application of serials. (Artwork by Tom Cooper)

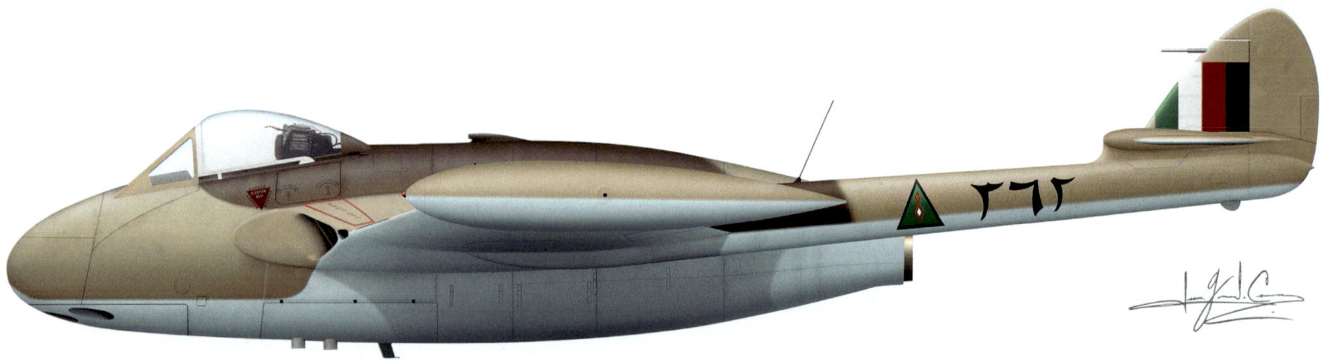

The RIrAF acquired 20 de Havilland Venom F.Mk 50s and these were initially operated by its No. 6 Squadron. All wore the same camouflage pattern as the Vampires, consisting of BS381C/362 mid stone and BS381C/350 dark earth on upper surfaces and sides, and BS381C/697 light admiralty blue on undersides. It remains unclear if they ever received their serials in RAF-style on wing-undersurfaces, though the usual set of national markings and serials was applied on the booms and the fins. In addition to four 20mm Hispano Mk. V cannons installed low in the forward fuselage, the type could be armed with up to two 454kg (1,000lb) bombs, or eight unguided 76mm or 88mm rockets. The type ended its service career in Iraq while flown by No. 1 Squadron in the COIN role, in around 1967-1968. (Artwork by Luca Canossa)

The Hawker Hunter was certainly the most important and most influential combat aircraft in service with the Iraqi air force of the mid-20th century. A total of 15 Hunter F.Mk 6, 12 T.Mk 66/69s, 12 F.Mk 59A, and 13 F.Mk 59As were acquired between 1957 and 1967: they served well into the 1980s, and were crucial for the emergence of several generations of highly-influential officers. All Iraqi Hunters wore the same, standardised camouflage pattern consisting of BS381C/638 dark sea grey and BS381C/641 dark green on upper surfaces and sides, and high-speed silver on undersurfaces. The usual set of national markings and serials was applied on the rear fuselage, and the serial repeated – usually in small white digits – on the cover of the front undercarriage. As well as the four 30mm ADEN guns installed internally, standard armament consisted of 76mm, 88mm or 127mm unguided rockets: up to four 'banks' of three rockets could be installed under each wing. The inset shows the insignia of No. 6 Squadron – the first Hunter-unit in Iraq – and different national markings worn on Hunters over time, including the original fin-flash of the RIrAF on the F.Mk 6 serial number 400, and the one worn from 1958 until 1963 on the fin of the F.Mk 6 serial number 402. (Artwork by Tom Cooper)

Perhaps the most famous Iraqi Hunter ever was the F.Mk 59A serial number 580. Delivered to Iraq in 1964, its standard camouflage colours were soon partially overpainted in bright red – a visual identification measure introduced by the United Arab Command during the same year. The jet served with No. 6 and then the newly-established No. 29 Squadron during the mid-1960s. The insignia of the latter unit is shown inset in the left upper corner: it consisted of the Iraqi and Palestinian flags, surrounding a golden hawk with a silhouette of a Hunter and the number 29. After the June 1967 Arab-Israeli War, this aircraft was decorated with two kill markings for Israeli jets claimed shot down by the Pakistani pilot Saif-ul-Azam, shown in other insets. (Artwork by Tom Cooper)

In addition to the Hunters, the backbone of the IrAF's offensive capabilities in the 1960s was a total of 12 Il-28s, two Il-28U conversion trainers, and two Il-28BM target tugs: additional examples may have also been acquired from Egypt in the early 1960s. All were operated by the IrAF's second dedicated bomber unit: No. 8 Squadron – the insignia of which is shown in the upper left corner – which saw constant and intensive utilisation in all campaigns against Kurdish insurgents in the north of the country during the 1960s and 1970s. Like the Hunters, Iraqi Il-28s wore different fin flashes over time: indeed, it seems they retained the 'preliminary' version of the ex-RIraF flash with a yellow disc even through the 1958-1963 period, after which this was crudely removed, and the new red-white-black tricolore with three green stars applied atop of it. For most of their operational carrier, Iraqi Il-28s were left in the colours as on delivery: painted in two layers of clear lacquer mixed with 5% and 10% aluminium powder, respectively. (Artwork by Tom Cooper)

Iraq is known to have received at least 17 MiG-17Fs (shown inset) and 17 radar-equipped MiG-1PFs between 1959 and 1962. Equally divided between Nos. 5 and 7 Squadrons, both were originally operated as interceptors, but the former unit was disbanded and the entire fleet concentrated within the latter unit, following the second coup of 1963 (the insignia of No. 7 Squadron as in use since 1963 is shown inset in the left upper corner). All were painted in two layers of clear lacquer mixed with 5% and 10% aluminium powder, respectively, applied directly over their bare metal surface. Notably, Iraqi MiG-17Fs also received rare add-on underwing pylons for the carriage of UB-16-57 pods for 57mm S-5K unguided rockets. These were extremely useful as the type saw much combat against the various uprisings of the 1960s. Notable on the top of the fuselage of each of the aircraft shown here is the IFF-antenna, added in 1962. (Artwork by Tom Cooper)

In 1960, the newly established No. 9 Squadron (insignia shown inset) became the first Iraqi unit to operate MiG-19S interceptors. Iraq originally ordered up to 50 such jets – including the radar-equipped MiG-19Ps – but, displeased by their poor technical condition and reliability, the IrAF accepted only some 16-19 into service. All were painted in an undertermined shade of grey overall and wore the usual three-digit serials (500 in this case) on the forward fuselage. The serial was frequently – but by far not always – repeated, in much smaller fonts, on drop tanks, which were left in bare metal overall. While many of No. 9 Squadron's MiG-19Ss were destroyed during the two coups of 1963, the type remained in service with No. 11 Squadron for at least a year longer, until all the surviving examples were donated to Egypt, where they served with No. 20 'Araba' Squadron until June 1967. (Artwork by Tom Cooper)

In 1961, the IrAF placed an order for 16 MiG-21F-13 supersonic interceptors. Deliveries to the newly established No. 11 Squadron, home-based at the brand-new Taqqaddum AB, began a year later. All early Iraqi MiG-21s were painted in the usual two layers of clear lacquer mixed with 5% and 10% aluminium powder, respectively, resulting in the colour colloquially known as 'silver grey'. Although Iraq received older RS-2U air-to-air missiles for its MiG-19Ps, these were never pressed into service: thus, the R-3S infra-red homing air-to-air missiles (ASCC/NATO-code 'AA-2 Atoll') became the first guided missiles operated by the IrAF, and indeed, in the entire Middle East. Inset is shown the insignia of No. 11 Squadron. (Artwork by Tom Cooper)

In April 1966, Iraq placed its next order for MiG-21s: as well as additional MiG-21F-13s, this included 23 MiG-21FLs; an improved variant lacking an internal gun, but including the RP-21 Sapfir airborne intercept radar with a range of about 20km (12.5 miles). Painted the same way as earlier MiG-21F-13s, the new variant first entered service with the newly-established No. 17 Squadron (insignia in the left inset): several of its aircraft had the cover of their avionics bay painted in black, as shown in the main artwork. No. 17 Squadron subsequently served as an operational conversion unit for this type. Starting in 1967, a batch of MiG-21PFMs was acquired, which arrived together with little-known Kh-66 radar-guided air-to-ground missiles – the first such weaponry in the Middle East; the primary user of this variant became the reconstituted No. 9 Squadron. (Artwork by Tom Cooper)

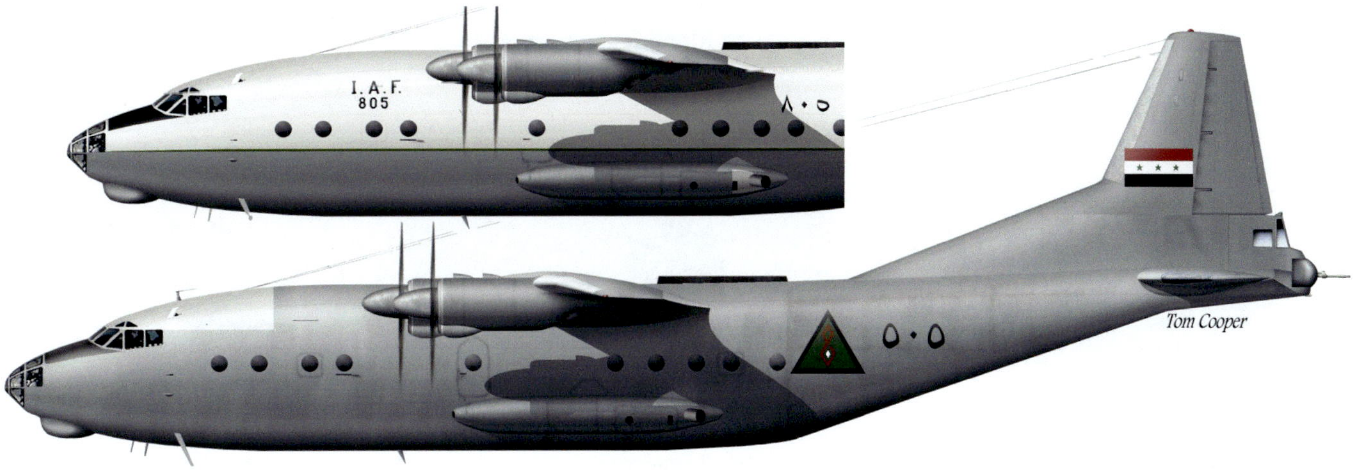

During the 1960s, Iraq acquired a total of 21 Antonov An-12BP transports. The first six served with its traditional transport unit, No. 3 Squadron, alongside An-2s and Freighters, and were painted as shown in the main artwork, in mid-grey overall and with white atop the cockpit. In 1965, the IrAF then split this unit to create No. 23 Squadron, destined to support the rapid intervention of ground forces in the case of another coup attempt. Based at the former Washash AB, now renamed Muthenna, No. 23 Squadron primarily operated An-12BPs that had only their undersides and wings painted in grey, while the rest of the fuselage was painted in white. From around the same time, most Iraqi An-12BPs began wearing two sets of serials. The serial number 505 was probably the example destroyed in the first Israeli air strike on H-3 airfield on 5 June 1967. (Artwork by Tom Cooper)

In 1967, the IrAF began reciving Sukhoi Su-7BMK fighter-bombers. Although comparable in size to the US-made McDonnell-Douglas F-4 Phantom, almost as fast, and capable of carrying up to 2,000kg of bombs, the type was very short-ranged. Nevertheless, it came as a welcome replacement for the old Furies and Venoms of No. 1 Squadron, which proudly developed its new unit insignia around the same time: seen inset, this showed a white-caped mountain, symbolic of northern Iraq, where this squadron was heavily involved in fighting against various insurgencies. Notably, Iraqi Su-7BMKs (illustrated is the example with serial number 755) retained not only their 'silver grey' overall livery, but also had no rear-view mirror atop of the cockpit-canopy. Prior to 1973, they also had only one hardpoint under each wing. (Artwork by Tom Cooper)

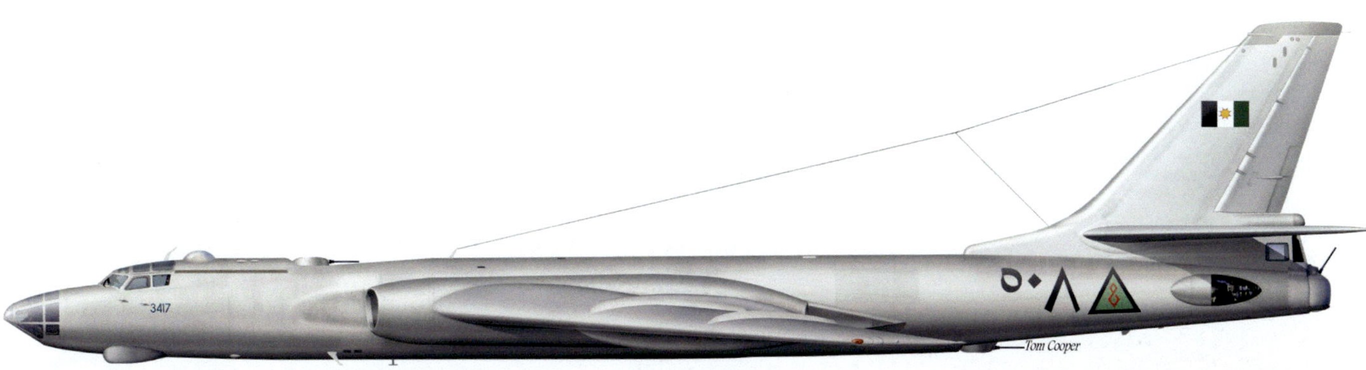

Iraq was the first Arab air force to introduce to service medium jet bombers, in the form of 10 Tupolev Tu-16s, starting in 1962. Operated by No. 10 Squadron, the big Tupolevs were left in 'silver-grey' overall and wore the usual set of serials and national insignia on the rear fuselage and the fin (this example is shown with the fin-flash from the period 1959-1963). Because all were second-hand aircraft formerly of the Soviet bomber aviation, they also had the 'last four' of their construction number: while that of the Iraqi Tu-16 serial number 508 illustrated here remains unknown, construction number 3417 from another example is shown for the purpose of illustrating the size, colour and position of that marking. Two Iraqi Tu-16 bombers successfully penetrated Israeli air defences on the morning of 6 June 1967, but they missed their target (Ramat David AB) and one was then shot down by Israeli interceptors and ground-based air defences. (Artwork by Tom Cooper)

Unit Insignia of RIrAF & IrAF Squadrons
1931-2003

No. 1 Squadron
1931-1941
1944-1967
1967-1995

No. 2 Squadron
1934-1941
1949-2003

No. 3 Squadron
1935-1941
1949-2003

No. 4 Squadron
1937-1941
1948-1967

No. 5 Squadron
1938-1941
1953-1963

No. 6 Squadron
1938-1941
1954-1974
1982-1995

No. 7 Squadron
1939-1941
1944-1975

No. 8 Squadron
1959-1992

No. 9 Squadron
1961-1963
1966-1995

No. 10 Squadron
1962-1992

No. 11 Squadron
1961-1995

No. 14 Squadron
1966-1995

No. 17 Squadron
1966-1995

No. 23 Squadron
1965- ?

No. 29 Squadron
1966-1995

TABLE 5: SERIAL NUMBERS OF RIrAF AIRCRAFT, 1941-1958		
SERIAL	**AIRCRAFT TYPE**	**NOTES**
151-180	Gladiator I/II	30 delivered 1943-1944, only 10 actually operated
181-230	Anson	33 delivered from March 1946
231-260	Fury F.Mk 1	30 delivered from November 1947
261-264	Fury T.Mk 52	'262' and '264' never delivered
265-270	Dove FR.Mk 3	Six delivered from January 1948
271-285	Chipmunk T.Mk 10	15 delivered from 1951
286-301	Harvard T.Mk IIB	16 delivered from 1951
302-326	Fury F.Mk 1	25 delivered from 1951
327-329	Fury T.Mk 52	Three ordered in 1951: order cancelled
330-331	Freighter C.Mk 31	Two delivered in 1953
332	Dragonfly	One delivered in 1953
333-335	Vampire T.Mk 55	Three delivered in May 1953
336-344	Vampire FB.Mk 52	Six delivered in May 1953, three delivered in Aug 1958
345	Dragonfly	One delivered in 1953
346-351	Chipmunk T.Mk 10	Six delivered in 1953
352-367	Venom FB.Mk 50	16 delivered from May 1954
368-369	Freighter C.Mk 31	Two delivered in 1955
370	Venom FB.Mk 50	One delivered in 1955
371-385	Provost T.Mk 53	15 delivered from 1954
386-388	Vampire T.Mk 55	Three delivered from 1954
389-391	Vampire FB.Mk 52	Three delivered from 1954
392	Dove FR.Mk 3	
393	Heron C.Mk 2C	delivered in July 1956
394-409	Hunter F.Mk 6	16 delivered 25 Jan – 19 Dec 1957
410-414	F-86F Sabre	Five delivered in June 1958; serials 52-5209, 52-5222, 52-5231 and 52-5235, and 53-1077
415-420	O-1 Birddog	Six delivered in June 1958

TABLE 6: RIrAF, ORDER OF BATTLE, JULY 1958[14]			
UNIT	**BASE**	**EQUIPMENT**	**REMARKS**
LAST COMMANDER RIrAF: BRIGADIER-GENERAL ABDUL KADHIM ABADDI **FIRST COMMANDER IRAF: COLONEL JALAL JAFFAR AL-AWQATI**			
Flying Units			
No. 1 Squadron	Firnas	Fury F.Mk 1	In process of conversion to Venom FB.Mk 50; last RIrAF CO Lt Col Abdallah Naji al-Jasin; first IrAF CO Maj Qasim Mohammad el-Azawi
No. 2 Squadron	Rashid	Anson, L-5, O-1A, Dragonfly	Light transport and liaison unit, operating first Iraqi helicopters.
No. 3 Squadron	Rashid	Dove FR.Mk 3, Heron C.Mk 2, Bristol Freighter C.Mk 31	Heavy transport and VIP-transport unit; until 14 Tammuz Revolution, (Herons were operated by the Royal Flight)
No. 4 Squadron		Fury FB.Mk 1	Expecting conversion to F-86F Sabre; CO Lt Col Hassan Rajap A'rem
No. 5 Squadron	Rashid	Venom FB.Mk 50	Last RIrAF CO Lt Col Mahmmoud Aziz; first IrAF CO Maj Nimma Abdullah ad-Dulaymi
No. 6 Squadron	Habbaniya	Hunter F.Mk 6	Last RIrAF CO Maj Arif Abd ar-Razzaq; first IRAF CO Maj Mufid Sayd
No. 7 Squadron	Hurriyah	Fury F.Mk 1	CO Lt Col Abd el-Saheb Mohammad
Air Force College	Wahda	Chipmunk T.Mk 51, Provost T.Mk 53	

US-made M24 Chaffee light tanks were photographed on the same occasion. British-built Churchill tanks can also be seen in the far background of this photograph. (Albert Grandolini Collection)

to make this union palatable to the Iraqis, Saad then undertook great efforts for Kuwait to join it – which was something London strictly opposed. However, by then it was already too late: in May 1958, civil war broke out in Lebanon and pan-Arab nationalists began causing problems within the Jordanian armed forces. Fearing for his own position, King Hussein requested help from Baghdad and Saad thus ordered the 19th and 20th Brigades of the Iraqi Army to re-deploy to Jordan. However, instead of marching west, early on 14 July 1958 both units – commanded by Brigadier-General Abd al-Karim Qasim (brother-in-law of the former RIrAF commander, Jawad) and Colonel Abd as-Salam Arif – entered Baghdad. They quickly seized all major public buildings, including the radio station, from where Arif announced a revolution, declared the downfall of the monarchy, and proclaimed a republic. Immediately after, the Royal Palace was subjected to short bombardment, after which entire royal family – including King Faysal II and Crown Prince Abd al-Illah – and most of the government, including the Prime Minister of Jordan was arrested. Whether by design or in an outburst of all the hatred that had accumulated since 1918, all were summarily executed. Nuri as-Saad avoided the tragedy for just 24 hours: escaping early on, he was caught, and shot in the street, on 15 July 1958. The 14 Tammuz Revolution ended the period during which Iraq was dominated by British-supported former officers of the Ottoman Army.[13]

Now largely forgotten is the fact that the RIrAF pioneered the acquisition and deployment of so-called 'unmanned aerial vehicles' in the Middle East, when it acquired a batch in the mid-1950s, one of which is visible here. Sadly, next to nothing is known about their operational service. (Albert Grandolini Collection)

6

NINE YEARS OF UNREST

Although based on a plan developed at least a month earlier, and usually credited to the 'Free Officers' movement, exactly as in Egypt of the 1940s and 1950s, this movement actually included people linked to very different political parties, with very different ethnic and religious backgrounds, and who thus followed very different ideologies. Unsurprisingly, the 14 Tammuz Revolution was almost an ad-hoc operation carried out and then consolidated by Qasim, Arif and relatively few aides, entirely on their own. Foremost, of modest and very diverse backgrounds (for example: Qasim's father was a Sunni Arab but his mother was a Shia Kurd), the new rulers of Iraq were quickly seduced by the power of their new positions, and their growing conviction that they represented all Iraqis and that they alone could define the common good. Ironically, they began exploiting the old system of patronage to centralise power in their hands – in turn managing to turn all of their potential allies against them. Qasim's rule not only caused an entire series of – sometimes massive – armed uprisings and outrages, but even his downfall resulted in a protracted political struggle: as one clique within the top ranks of the armed forces staged a coup against the other, Iraq slowly descended into a sort of 'organised chaos'. The country was to experience a rude awakening from the resulting apathy only as a result of the catastrophic defeat during the June 1967 Arab-Israeli War.[1]

Masterminds of the 14 Tammuz revolution: Colonel Abd as-Salim Arif (left) and Brigadier-General Abd al-Karim Qasim. (Albert Grandolini Collection)

QASIM AGAINST ALL

Early on 15 July 1958, Qasim established a Revolutionary Council as the new government of Iraq. This included members of all three main ethnic groups, but he appointed himself as the prime minister and minister of defence, while Arif became the minister of interior and deputy commander of the armed forces. The last commander of the RIrAF, Major-General Abadi, was forced into early retirement and then into exile, and replaced by Brigadier-General Jalal Jawad al-Awqati.[2] Immediately afterwards, a curfew was imposed to stop the public violence that spread through the streets of Baghdad, culminating in the destruction of the British Embassy and the murder of dozens. Initial reports from Iraq in those days fuelled the expectation that Iraq would quickly join the UAR. However, Qasim soon dampened all such expectations and gradually turned against the pan-Arab nationalists, explaining that whilst he was not against the union, he was also not keen to make a headlong rush into it. On the contrary, and to help stabilise his rule, Qasim courted several political parties: none proved as forthcoming as the ICP – which held very good influence with the masses, and staged multiple demonstrations in favour of the new ruler over the coming weeks and months.[3]

To satisfy the widespread pan-Arab nationalism (and Arif, who was pro union with the UAR), Qasim then invited President Nasser to deploy a squadron of Soviet-made Mikoyan i Gurevich MiG-17F fighters of the United Arab Republic Air Force (UARAF) to Iraq, to protect the country from possible counter-coups and interventions from the outside. The unit is known to have remained in Iraq for four months, and to have participated in some joint exercises with the IrAF. However, the Iraqi Air Force proved not only loyal but also perfectly capable of curbing internal unrest during the coup: when pro-Royalist elements of the 1st Division attempted to march on Baghdad, during the afternoon of 14 July, they were promptly strafed by Hunters of No. 6 Squadron, and forced to withdraw into their barracks.[4]

Over the following weeks and months, Qasim continued distancing himself from the Nationalists: he failed to hold promised elections, and then – and much to the relief of the Shia majority – ordered the arrest and trial of major nationalist leaders, including Arif. Logically, the influence of the ICP continued to grow, and

A row of MiG-17Fs of an unknown UARAF unit temporarily deployed to the newly-constructed Taqqaddum AB, in Iraq, in support of Qasim's government in mid-1958. (Photo by Osman Mahmoud, via Nour Bardai)

In addition to appointing a new commander, the first change for the IrAF prompted by the 14 Tammuz Revolution was the rapid acquisition of a large number of aircraft of Soviet origin. Instead of British-made Canberras, as originally planned by the RIrAF, in January 1959 the air force received its first two Il-28Us – a conversion-trainer variant of the classic Soviet-made medium bomber, recognisable by the unusual cockpit arrangement installed atop the front fuselage. (Ahmad Sadik Collection)

Hard on the heels of the first two Il-28Us, the IrAF received the first of an eventual total of 14 MiG-15UTI jet conversion trainers. This example (serial number 549), belonged to the batch delivered in 1962, and was photographed showing the fin flash introduced in 1963. (Ahmad Sadik Collection)

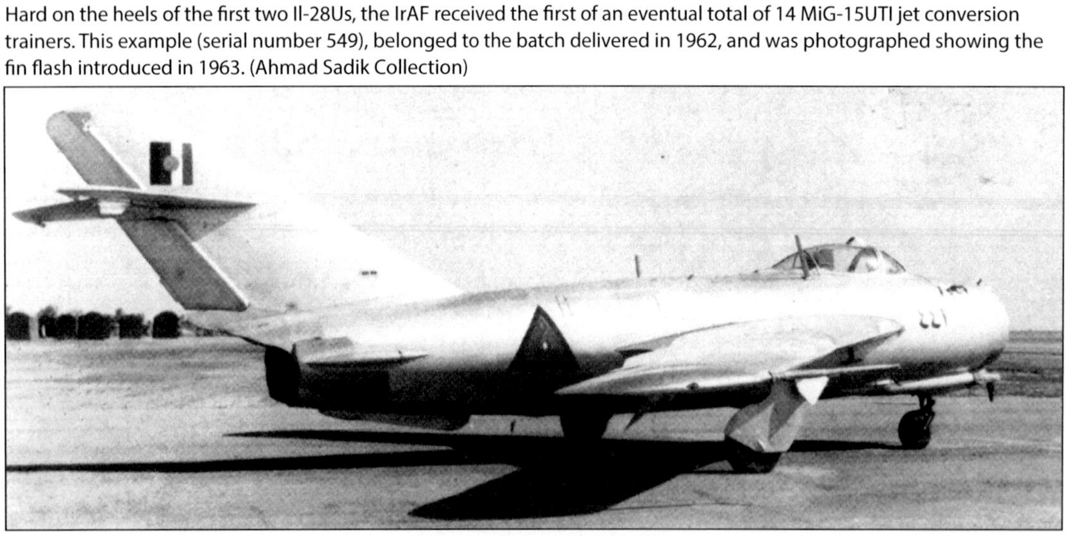

The third Soviet-made type to enter service with the IrAF in 1959 was the MiG-17F: serial number 441 was one of the first to reach Iraq, in January of that year, and this photograph shows it wearing the initial variant of the fin-flash in use between 1958 and 1963: this consisted of black, red, white, and green fields, as during the times of the Hashemite Kingdom, but with a yellow disc in the centre. (Ahmad Sadik Collection)

Awqati – an outspoken communist – encouraged Qasim to improve relations with the USSR. While allowing the third group of pilots to complete their conversion course for Hunters at RAF Chivenor, he shelved plans to re-equip the IrAF with US-made F-86s, and instead sought to order Soviet-made aircraft. Emboldened by the realisation of strong communist influence in Baghdad, Moscow proved exceptionally forthcoming: during autumn 1958, Iraq signed a series of contracts with the USSR and Czechoslovakia stipulating deliveries of – amongst others – MiG-15UTIs, MiG-17s, Ilyushin Il-28 bombers, Antonov An-2 and An-12 transports, and other Soviet-made arms. Proceeded by deliveries of MiG-15UTIs required to facilitate the swift conversion of Iraqi pilots and ground crews to the Soviet-made equipment, the first batches of Il-28s and MiG-17Fs arrived by ship in Basra in January 1959: the former were assigned to the newly-established No. 8 Squadron, initially commanded by Major Adnan Ameen Rashid, and the latter to No. 5 Squadron. Commanded by Major Dulaymi, and then Major Khaled Sarah, and officially declared operational on 13 February 1959, No. 5 was to see its first action only a month later.[5]

UPRISING IN MOSUL

In early March 1959, Free Officers led by Colonel Abdul Wahhab ash-Shawwaf assigned to the 5th Infantry Brigade in Mosul – a traditionalist and conservative city, the population of which still resented its separation from the former Ottoman Empire – staged a mutiny against what they saw as a 'sell-out to the communist infidels'. Originally, their plot was to be supported by the commanders of the 1st Division in Diwaniya and the 2nd in Kirkuk, but these never moved because the majority of their officers opposed pan-Arabism. On 7 March 1959, elements of the 5th

By early 1959, Hunter F.Mk 6s of No. 6 Squadron had received the next version of the fin flash, consisting of the black, white and green tricolore, with a yellow disc (symbolising the sun) on a white field – as visible on the fin of the examples with serial number 399 on the first photograph, and number 403 on the second. (Ahmad Sadik Collection)

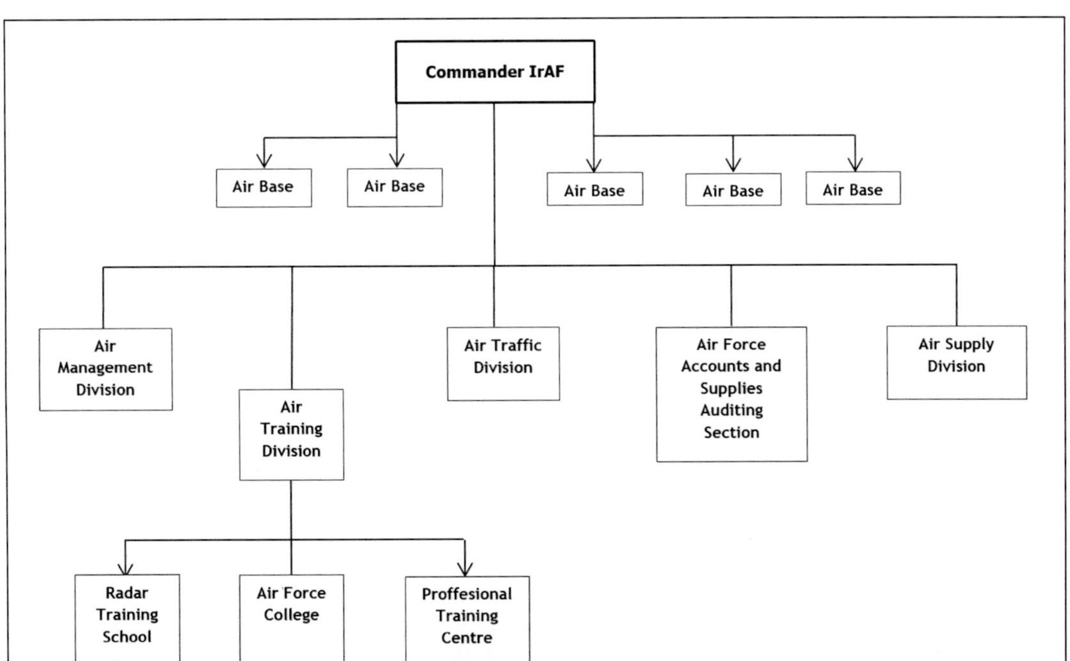

A diagram depicting the organisation of the IrAF as of 1960 – retained for most of the following decade. Notably, every base commander was responsible directly to the commander of the IrAF, while exercising administrative control over all the units stationed at 'his' base. However, the second most powerful position was that of the Director of the Air Traffic Division: equivalent to what was subsequently named the Deputy Operations, this position was responsible for organising and controlling all flying operations of the air force. (Diagram by Milos Sipos)

Brigade, supported by members of the Shammar tribe, attacked an ICP rally in Mosul. After shooting some and arresting dozens, Shawwaf's troops secured the city and the local radio station and he broadcasted the 'Manifesto', which declared Qasim to be a traitor of the Revolution and called for a mutiny of the Army. However, the revolt then received no support, while Qasim and Awqati reacted quickly. On the morning of 9 March 1959, Hunters of No. 6 Squadron and MiG-17Fs of No. 5 Squadron flew about 20 sorties deploying unguided rockets to demolish Radio Mosul, the headquarters of the 5th Brigade, and several other key positions. Seriously wounded in one of the air strikes, Shawwaf then lost the control over his unit and his coup collapsed. However, and tragically, the unrest then exploded into an orgy of murder and looting as the Arabs began fighting each other and the Kurds, and as peasants attacked their landlords. The frenzy only increased when it became known that the much-beloved peace activist, lawyer and poet Kamil al-Qazanchi had been murdered in prison. Still, the high point was delivered by the Kurds loyal to Qasim, who then literally sacked Mosul and reinforced by troops of the 5th Brigade (many of which were Kurds), they looted, murdered, robbed and wrecked most of the city over two days, until order was restored by other Iraqi Army units. By this time, about 2,000 people had lost their lives, and much of the city was completely ruined. Even the IrAF could not avoid suffering losses in this mess: on 9 or 10 March 1959, the Communists nearly overran Tal Aftar airfield in northern Iraq. There they caught a Fury of No. 1 Squadron refuelling: the pilot, Saeb Sabri as-Safy attempted to scramble, but was shot down and killed in a crash.[6]

Although the air force remained loyal to Qasim, the uprising in Mosul had significant repercussions for it: the leader in Baghdad subsequently purged nearly 800 nationalist officers. Arif Abd ar-Razzaq, who meanwhile served as the commander of Habbaniya AB (which the RAF completely vacated only on 31 May 1959), and Colonel Abdullah Naji (commander of Firnas AB), Captain Qasim Mohammed Amin al-Azawi, and Lieutenants Ahmed Mehdi Ashour and Fadil Nasir were amongst air force officers known to have been arrested and imprisoned. While several squadron commanders were removed from their positions, pilots suspected of either being pan-Arabist nationalists, or even royalists, but not obviously involved in any kind of plots against the government, were concentrated within Nos. 1 and 7 Squadrons, which continued flying Furies (No. 1 Squadron also flew Venoms well into the 1960s), and No. 6 Squadron, whose Hunters appeared as candidates for early retirement. The remaining operational units of this period were No. 2 Squadron (commanded by Major Wahid Ibraheem Adham Mohammed al-Bayati, and equipped with liaison aircraft and a total of 12 Mil Mi-4s), No. 3 Squadron (which operated all the transports), and No. 4 Squadron (which subsequently converted from Furies to helicopters). However, the most trusted pilots were concentrated within the MiG-17 equipped No. 5 Squadron. Indeed, having thus reorganised the IrAF following his preferences, Awqati then placed two additional orders in Moscow – one for radar-equipped MiG-17PFs, and one for MiG-19 supersonic interceptors – with a declared intention to form a sort of 'flying praetorian guard', a force that would be responsible for the defence of Qasim's rule.[7]

As a convinced communist, Colonel (later Brigadier-General) Jalal Jaffar al-Awqati was quick to place numerous orders for Soviet-made aircraft in late 1958. His most-significant acts of this kind followed in 1959-1961 when he secured deliveries of MiG-19s, MiG-21s, and Tu-16s. (Ahmad Sadik Collection)

Although of poor quality, this highly interesting photograph shows a line of MiG-17s from No. 5 Squadron, including two radar-equipped MiG-17PFs in the foreground (serials 457 and 455), followed by MiG-17Fs. Notable is the 'intermediate' version of the fin flash from the 1958-1963 period, including green, white and black fields with the yellow disc. (Pit Weinert Collection)

A trio of MiG-19S of No. 9 Squadron, IrAF, as seen high above Baghdad in 1960. Only the serial number 498, in the foreground, is readable. (Photo by Osman Mahmoud, via Nour Bardai)

PRAETORIAN GUARD

Many details of what exactly happened next remain obscure. What is known is that a group of IrAF pilots and ground technicians underwent conversion training to MiG-19s in the city of Gorky in the USSR (nowadays Nizni Novogord in the Russian Federation), while the Soviets proved not only quick in delivering at least 17 MiG-17PFs, but went as far as to deliver about 50 MiG-19s in no less than three variants. An approximate break-down of the latter order is as follows:

- 30 MiG-19S, equipped with three 30mm Nuddelmann-Richter NR-30 guns and capable of carrying two ORO-57K pods for 57mm S-5K unguided rockets;
- 10 MiG-19Ps, equipped with the RP-1 Izumrud radar and only two NR-30 guns; and
- 10 MiG-19PMs, equipped with the RP-1 Izumrud radar and four Kaliningrad K-5M (ASCC/NATO-codename 'AA-1 Alkali') beam-riding, guided air-to-air missiles (instead of 30mm guns).

Contrary to the majority of MiG-17Fs exported to other air forces, the examples sold to Iraq received outboard underwing pylons, which enabled them to carry UB-16-57 pods for 57mm S-5K unguided rockets – in addition to the usual drop tanks necessary for almost every sortie due to the type's very short range. Such pylons are visible in this front view of an Iraqi MiG-17F. (Ahmad Sadik Collection)

The mass of these aircraft – further increased by the first batch of MiG-15UTI two-seaters, acquired to facilitate quicker conversion of additional pilots in Iraq – reached Basra by ship in late 1959 and early 1960, and were then trucked to Wahda AB for assembly and test-flying by Soviet pilots and ground personnel. While the MiG-15UTIs entered service with the Air Force College, the MiG-17PFs were used to re-equip No. 7 Squadron. Eventually, the IrAF took up only 16 MiG-19Ss, and they entered service with No. 9 Squadron, based at Rashid AB and commanded by Major Khaled Sarah. The other aircraft of this type were not accepted and were never paid for by Baghdad: they remained stored inside a hangar at Wahda AB for several years longer. As so often before and after, MiG-19Ss of No. 9 Squadron were to see action even before that unit was officially declared operational on 11 June 1961.[8]

HOT HEADS IN THE COOL NORTH

By the time MiG-15UTIs, MiG-17PFs, MiG-19s and Tu-16s were officially declared as ready for combat operations, the political situation in Iraq had undergone a fundamental transformation. The tragedy that befell Mosul in March 1959 – followed by another, similar massacre in Kirkuk caused by major clashes between Arabs and Kurds, and which left over 120 killed on 14-17 July 1959 – proved both the climax of the ICP's onslaught on its opponents and the beginning of its recession. Confronted by bitter complaints from all over the country, Qasim was forced to denounce the communist attacks as 'barbaric'. Indeed, despite ICP-organised mass demonstrations run from May to August 1959, and after surviving an assassination attempt by the Ba'ath Party (which included a youngster named Saddam Hussein at-Tikriti, who subsequently found refuge in Egypt) on 7 October 1959, he not only began releasing pan-Arab nationalists and Free Officers from prison, but also distanced himself from the ICP. Nevertheless, knowing that any other kind of government would repress it severely, the party continued supporting him for the duration of his regime.[9]

Meanwhile, emboldened by relatively good relations to the leader in Baghdad and the ICP, Mustafa Barzani returned from the exile in the USSR. He quickly found himself at odds with several Kurdish parties, tribes and clans: initially, the reason was his cooperation with Qasim and his attempts to impose himself upon various tribes. For example, in May 1959, a combined force of the 2nd Division and Barzani's militias – supported by IrAF Hunters, Il-28s, MiG-17Fs, and Furies – ran such a ferocious campaign against the Pishdari tribe, that about 20,000 survivors felt forced to flee to Iran. However, concerned at Barzani becoming too powerful, by 1960 Qasim began supplying arms to his adversaries. Moreover, he failed to fulfil any of his promises for free elections or negotiations about autonomy and in early 1961 refused to even talk about a petition asking for public use of the Kurdish language. While back in the mountains from March 1961, Barzani first sought to pay off a few old scores with his rivals: with some 5,000 tribesmen, reinforced by Assyrians, torching villages and crops as he went, he pushed most of the Zibari tribe into Turkey.[10]

The spark that turned the situation upside down was provided by the Kurdish Arkou tribe in an entirely unrelated action. On 11 September 1961, one of its groups ambushed a column of the 2nd Division outside Bazyan, causing casualties. Although such ambushes had taken place at regular intervals ever since Iraq came into being, and although taking time to select the method of retaliation and the target, on 16 September 1961 Qasim ordered IrAF Il-28s and Hunters to bomb Barzan, Barzani's stronghold. Unsurprisingly considering the Kurdish tradition of blood revenge, this act instantly converted Mustafa Barzani into an outspoken enemy of Qasim: in a matter of two weeks, his forces attacked and overran nearly all army and police outposts, and also all of the Kurdish tribes loyal to Baghdad – from Zakho in the west to Sulaymaniyah in the east – bringing almost a third of Iraq under his control. After bribing several additional tribes to side with him, on 22 September 1961 Qasim ordered the 2nd Division into a counteroffensive. Supported by IrAF fighter-bombers – including Furies, Hunters, MiG-17s, Venoms and even a few Vampires – deployed at Firnas and Hurriyah ABs, the first phase of this operation was characterised by an extensive campaign of 'air policing' in which more than 500 villages were bombed, and up to 270 completely demolished. When the ground troops then pushed towards Zakho, the IrAF attacked insurgent positions: skilfully guided by airborne forward air controllers (FACs) that flew L-5s and O-1A Bird Dogs, it caused heavy losses to the insurgency, forcing it to disperse. Zakho was thus recovered against very little resistance only two days later, and on 10 October 1961 Qasim proudly announced that the 'Kurdish uprising' had been put down.[11]

NEW MIGS AND FIRST TUPOLEVS

Although successful in recovering Zakho and subduing the activity of the Kurdish insurgents for the next six months, Qasim's campaign against Barzani was highly unpopular within the armed forces, where dissent was already widespread due to serious economic difficulties. The financial situation of the government in Baghdad become no better when Qasim almost provoked a showdown with Great Britain over Kuwait in late summer of 1961.[12] However, the quick British military intervention impressed the leader in Baghdad sufficiently to order Awqati to place an order for yet

MiG-21F-13 serial number 523, as seen shortly after delivery to Iraq. This was the first from the the first batch of 16 jets of this type acquired by No. 11 Squadron IrAF. Notable is the muzzle of the single NR-30 cannon low on the fuselage below the cockpit. (Pit Weinert Collection)

A group of IrAF MiG-21 pilots with their ground personnel and aircraft (including MiG-21F-13s with the serial numbers 526, 527, and 522) at the newly-constructed Taqqaddum AB in the early 1960s. (Photo by Osman Mahmoud, via Nour Bardai)

additional aircraft from the USSR, including MiG-21s supersonic interceptors and Tupolev Tu-16 medium bombers. Once again, many details about these acquisitions remain unclear, because most of the original documentation has since been destroyed. What is certain is that the two groups of IrAF crewmen selected to convert to the new MiGs and Tupolevs travelled to the USSR in late 1961. Deliveries of Tu-16s seem to have lasted well into 1963, but the unit equipped with them – No. 10 Squadron – was officially established at an unknown date in 1962. The first Iraqi MiG-21 pilots – including Hamid Dhahee, Munir Habib Jamil Redfa, Georges Sada, Farhad Abdel Haleq as-Saydoon, Munthir al-Windawy, and Shaker Mahmoud Yusuf – completed their course at Lugovaya AB, and were back in Iraq by June 1962, followed by 16 MiG-21F-13s, each armed with one 30mm NR-30 gun and a pair of brand-new R-3S (ASCC/NATO-codename 'AA-2 Atoll') air-to-air missiles. They entered service with No. 11 Squadron. Both units were home-based at Taqqaddum AB (also known as Tammuz), and it was there that Soviet instructors helped convert the second group of Iraqi pilots to both types in late 1962 and early 1963.[13]

CLASH WITH TURKEY

In March 1962, Barzani regrouped his forces and then launched a new offensive: caught by surprise, the 2nd Division suffered heavy losses and withdrew to Zakho and Dahouk. Qasim reacted by ordering Awqati's IrAF into action: indeed, a steady stream of air strikes by Hunters, Il-28s, MiG-17s and Furies from Firnas and Hurriyah, caused losses to Barzani's insurgents and – because they lacked air defence weapons – seriously shook their morale. Moreover, this operation developed into a particularly devastating air policing campaign: just in June 1962, the Iraqi air force may have killed up to 3,000 people and made about 180,000 more homeless. While the insurgents dispersed and changed their tactics to those of disrupting military communications by blocking defiles, blowing up bridges and ambushing supply convoys instead, the civilians had no options but to flee over the frontier to Iran and Turkey. The IrAF pursued them to the point where it began flying air strikes against settlements inside Turkey. In one such attack on 9 August 1962, two Il-28s hit a Turkish military outpost in error, killing one border guard and injuring another. However, when another pair of Il-28s crossed the frontier on 16 August, they were intercepted by four Republic F-84G Thunderjet fighter-bombers of the Turkish Air Force, and one Il-28 was shot down by gunfire from the jet flown by 1st Lieutenant Muretin Gül of No. 181 Squadron. The Iraqi crew of three ejected safely. While Baghdad apologised, the Turkish Army subsequently cleared a 12-mile-wide strip of territory along the border, where no Kurdish civilians were supposed to move. In turn, the IrAF stopped its air strikes and no further incidents of this kind occurred.[14]

RAMADAN COUP: HUNTERS VS MIG-19S

The rear section of Iraqi Il-28 serial number 427 photographed at Taqqaddum AB in March 2006. Clearly visible are traces of the application of no less than three different fin flashes – all of these applied in 1959-1963. (Tom Cooper Collection)

Wreckage of two of No. 9 Squadron's MiG-19Ss as seen in the aftermath of Windawy's and Saydoon's air strikes during the Ramadan Coup. (Photo by Osman Mahmoud, via Nour Bardai)

Through late 1962 and early 1963, the fighting in northern Iraq settled down into a brutal routine: Barzani's insurgents controlled the countryside by night, while by day the IrAF ranged and bombed wide and far, and the Iraqi Army concentrated on maintaining control over major towns and the communications in between. To much of the Iraqi public, this situation appeared a failure and internal dissent continued to grow, but none of political movements could find a way to remove Qasim from power. One exception was the Ba'ath Party, whose leadership came to the realisation that, since the strongman in Baghdad kept himself in power with the help of the armed forces, there was no alternative but to remove him *with* the help of the armed forces. Finding out that the IrAF had been organised into units sorted by the political affiliation of their commanders, the Ba'athists sought contact with officers serving with Nos. 6 and 7 Squadrons, home-based at Habbaniya AB. Thus came into being a coup plot emphasising an early destruction of Nos. 5, 9, and 11 Squadrons at Rashid AB, all of which were 'staffed by Communists'. Whether by accident or design, on 4 February 1963, Qasim ordered the early retirement of some 48 officers with links to the Ba'ath Party, thus prompting the plotters – led by Colonel Abd as-Salam Arif and retired Major-General Tahir Yahia – into action.[15]

Early on 8 February 1963, mid-way through the holy month of Ramadan, troops of 20th Brigade's armoured battalion quickly seized the Radio Baghdad station in Abu Ghrayb. Simultaneously, two Hunters from No. 6 Squadron – flown by Munthir al-Windawy and Mumtaz as-Saydoon – repeatedly attacked the apron of No. 9 Squadron at Rashid AB, destroying between four and six MiG-19Ss on the ground. Minutes later, two MiG-17Fs from No. 7 Squadron destroyed three MiG-21F-13s. The only 'loyal' pilot that managed to take-off, Lieutenant Fahad Abd el-Haley as-Saydon from No. 5 Squadron, was then shot down by 40mm Bofors AAA defending the air base. With the 'flying praetorian guard' out of the way, thousands of the Ba'athist militia took to the streets of Baghdad: Awqati narrowly survived an assassination attempt, but he, Qasim and about 700 loyal troops were then besieged inside the building of the Ministry of Defence. After clashing with several groups of Communists (who still did not want to see their favourite deposed), the Ba'athists called for help from Habbaniya AB: fresh out of prison, hurriedly promoted in rank to Lieutenant-Colonel and assigned as the provisional commander of the air force, Arif Abd ar-Razzaq ordered all pilots ready to fight with him into action. Around noon, two MiG-17s from No. 7 Squadron – though both flown by pilots from No. 11 Squadron – showered the Ministry of Defence with 57mm unguided rockets. Up to 60 air strikes by additional MiGs and Hunters followed, completely demolishing the building. After a 10-hour battle, a badly shaken Qasim gave up. He was arrested together with Awqati: after a short trial, both were executed on 14 February 1963.[16]

PURGES

The government that took over in Baghdad on 8 February 1963 was composed of Ba'athist civilians and pan-Arab nationalist military officers: presided by Abd as-Salam Arif – who subsequently advanced himself to the rank of Field Marshal (the first ever in Iraq's history) – one of the first decisions was to terminate all military cooperation with Moscow and force over 3,000 Soviet instructors to leave the country. Political developments in Iraq during the following months can only be summarised as a confusing campaign of manoeuvring for power against the backdrop of multiple campaigns of murder

At least two 30mm hits to MiG-19S serial number 489 caused an internal fire, effectively ending its career on 8 February 1963. The MiG in the rear of the photograph received at least one hit to the fin and had its cockpit hood shattered by another. (Photo by Osman Mahmoud, via Nour Bardai)

A row of MiG-21F-13s and a hangar of No. 11 Squadron at Rashid AB, all converted into heaps of wreckage by the repeated attacks of two MiG-17Fs from No. 7 Squadron. (Photo by Osman Mahmoud, via Nour Bardai)

and terror. Particularly fiercely hit was the ICP and its sympathisers, which were mercilessly prosecuted by the 'National Guard', an armed militia of the Ba'ath Party, the command of which was assigned to Munthir al-Windawy – who achieved the status of national hero for his actions on 8 February. Unsurprisingly, the IrAF was hit hard by a series of purges. Amongst others, Lieutenant-Colonel Sarah, commander of No. 9 Squadron, was imprisoned and replaced by Major Wafiq Abdallah ar-Ramadani, while Lieutenant-Colonel el-Emir, commander of No. 11 Squadron, was replaced by Fahad Saydoon. The purges intensified once Brigadier-General

The building of the Ministry of Defence was completely demolished by about 60 air strikes flown by IrAF Hunters and MiG-17s on 8 February 1963. (Nour Bardai Collection)

On his return to Baghdad, Windawy received a hero's welcome: he was subsequently appointed the commander of the Ba'ath's National Guard, but retained his proficiency on Hunters of the IrAF. (Photo by Osman Mahmoud, via Nour Bardai)

A T-54 of the 20th Brigade seen on the streets of Baghdad during the Ramadan Coup against Qasim's government on 8 February 1963. (Albert Grandolini Collection)

The Hunter F.Mk 59 serial number 570, belonged to the second batch of this type, ordered by Iraq in 1963, and delivered between March 1964 and January 1965. This jet was to see plenty of action in several campaigns against Barzani's insurgents and two wars against Israel. (David Nicolle Collection)

One of three Hunter T.Mk 66 two-seat conversion trainers delivered to the IrAF in April 1964: this variant played a crucial role in training of at least two future generations of Iraqi Hunter pilots – many of whom in turn played a crucial role in the future of the air force and the country. (Pit Weinert Collection)

Hardan Abd el-Rhefal at-Tikriti (a declared right-wing Ba'athist) was appointed as the new commander of the IrAF on 1 May 1963. With the exception of five officers who had taken part in the Ramadan Coup, all the pilots of Nos. 9 and 11 Squadrons were arrested and further flying by both units frozen: many of the remaining personnel of both units fled to Jordan and Syria.[17]

Finally, because all the Soviets were expulsed from Iraq, and all the communists purged from the armed forces, the IrAF also abandoned the project of introducing into service four battalions of Soviet-made S-75 (ASCC/NATO-code 'SA-2 Guideline') surface-to-air missiles (SAMs) delivered in 1961. These were returned to Moscow in mid-1963 and the Iraqi personnel undergoing training on such weapons in the USSR were recalled. The IrAF thus missed the opportunity to become the first air force to introduce SAMs to the Middle East.[18]

SECOND HUNTER ORDER

On the international level, Arif sought to create a union with Egypt and Syria. However, Nasser conditioned such a creation upon the complete subordination of Iraq to his direction. When the related negotiations collapsed, and the Egyptian president launched a campaign of challenging the legitimacy of the Ba'ath government in Baghdad, Arif reacted by improving his ties to the West, particularly Great Britain and the USA. In addition to returning the four F-86Fs stored at Habbaniya AB since July 1958 to the USA, in April 1963 he assigned Major Fahad Abd el-Haley as-Saydoon to the post of Air Attaché in London. Together with Tikriti and Razzaq, Saydoon then proved critical for the IrAF's decision to renew the acquisition of Hawker Hunters. Related negotiations were opened as early as mid-May 1963. A few days later, on 21 May 1963, the British Air Attaché to Baghdad reported to London:

> Tikriti said he now wished to commit the Iraqi Air Force irrevocably to British sources of supply and training and in this he was supported by the Minister of Defence… Tikriti said that although the Soviets seemed to have accepted that they had lost the political battle in Iraq, they were still anxious to supply Iraq with arms. For example, they had recently offered two squadrons of MiG-21s at knockdown prices. Tikriti hoped that Britain would be prepared to assist by supplying him with what he needed to rebuild his air force; otherwise there would be really no alternative but to resume the ties with the USSR. [19]

Eager to obtain new orders and recover its standing in Iraq, the Hawker Siddeley company promptly dispatched its Hunter T.Mk 66 demonstrator of the two-seat conversion variant to Habbaniya AB, and signalled its preparedness to follow-up with more, while the RAF announced its readiness to provide the necessary armament from its own stocks 'within days' – and then to accept 50 Iraqi pilot and navigator trainees, 20 pilots, and 20 ground staff to its educational facilities starting in the summer of 1963.[20] Hardan

Tikriti then visited London in July 1963 and negotiated an order for 22 Hunter F.Mk 59s.[21]

RESUMPTION OF THE WAR IN THE NORTH

Meanwhile, the war against Mustafa Barzani's insurgency was stalemated: multiple delegations from Baghdad travelled north to visit him throughout 1963. However, concerned by Arif's attempt to create a union with the UAR, Barzani then declared that he would be satisfied with local autonomy within the Iraqi state, but would demand autonomy on a federal basis should the country join Egypt. Finally, encouraged by support that the Soviet leadership began to provide to him (both for his quasi-leftist ideological orientation, but also in revenge for the prosecution of the Iraqi communists), he began demanding an ever bigger share of the oil income. Concluding there was no option but to resume the war, Arif ordered the preparation of a major offensive. In May 1963, all the involved units were assigned to the command of Brigadier-General Fathi Sakalli, and the air bases of Habbaniya, Firnas and Hurriyah were put under a lock-down. On 7 June 1963, Baghdad issued an ultimatum to the Kurds, on the one hand demanding impossible conditions but on the other offering amnesty to those who would surrender. When this passed unanswered, on 10 June 1963, 12 brigades of the Iraqi Army, reinforced by a brigade of the Syrian Arab Army, and supported by artillery and armour, launched their attacks on three separate fronts. The IrAF deployed all of its might to, initially, target dozens of roadblocks and minor ambushes, before switching to close air support (CAS) with the help of FACs. The insurgents rapidly withdrew into the mountains, where an almost total lack of roads and even motorable tracks made any further movement by the conventional Iraqi Army extremely problematic: this in turn prompted the IrAF to switch back to the old and 'proven' strategy of air policing. By 30 June, Barzani claimed that 167 villages had been 'wiped out' and 643 civilians killed by air strikes. The insurgents claimed to have shot down three or four IrAF jets and one Syrian, but the air force is not known to have suffered any losses in this operation.[22] On the contrary, and despite immense problems caused by the terrain and sporadic resistance, by 10-12 August 1963, the Army secured not only Zakho and Barzan in the north, but also Ruwanduz Gorge in the centre, and the entire Sulaymaniyah Governorate in the east, forcing Barzani to switch to the tactics of deploying small commando units to mount attacks on oil installations in the Kirkuk and Mosul areas.[23]

18 NOVEMBER COUP

Despite its apparent success, this offensive failed to push the Kurdish insurgents out of Iraq: indeed, it petered out during September and October, by when the Iraqi armed forces had run out of steam. This outcome caused a major crisis within the Ba'ath party, where a deep rift emerged between the civilian and military leadership. The conflict between the two wings culminated on 1 November 1963, when civilians dismissed Munthir al-Windawy from his post as commander of the National Guard. He refused to budge and threatened to bomb the party headquarters with one of the IrAF's Tu-16 bombers. His resistance encouraged other Ba'athist military officers (including Tikriti) to order an arrest of the civilian leadership of the party and send them into exile. Then the Syrian Ba'athists led by Michel Aflaq over-spilled the barrel by appearing in Baghdad in an attempt to iron out differences: this was too much – especially for Arif. The latter took action in cooperation with his brother, Brigadier-General Abd ar-Rahman Arif (commander of the 5th Division) and Brigadier-General Abd al-Karim Farhan (commander of the 1st Division), Colonel Said Sulaybi (commander of the military police), Major-General Tahir Yaha (Chief of Staff), and Hardan Tikriti. At dawn of 18 November 1963, at least two MiG-17Fs launched from Rashid AB to bomb the headquarters of the National Guard. This time, Windawy reacted by commandeering a Hunter at Habbaniya AB, scrambling and rushing to the aid of his party: however, after repeatedly strafing the Presidential Palace in Baghdad, he ran out of ammunition and was then intercepted by a pair of MiG-17s led by Nimaa Abdullah Dulaymi. Windawy was shot down in a short air combat and forced to eject: after landing by parachute, he joined several other Ba'athist officers that helped him flee to Syria. Arif then issued a proclamation announcing that the National Guard was to surrender its arms and to be dissolved immediately. The Ba'athists refused and street fighting broke out in Basra, Baghdad and Mosul: roundly defeated and after losing between 300 and 500 killed, the Ba'athists began melting away. By 20 November, the first short rule of the Ba'ath Party over Iraq was over.[24]

Brigadier-General (later Major-General) Hardan Abd el-Rhefal at-Tikriti, former Fury-pilot and a declared Ba'athist, served two tours of duty as the commander of the IrAF: from 2 March until 5 December 1963 and from 17 July 1968 until being forced into exile in Kuwait in July 1970. (Ahmad Sadik Collection)

Subsequent disarmament of the National Guard and arrests of most of the party's leadership were followed by purges of the Ba'athists from the armed forces. In December 1965, for example, the entire No. 5 Squadron was disbanded: its aircraft, and all personnel not arrested or forced into early retirement, were re-assigned to No. 7 Squadron, which thus became the biggest unit of the IrAF, with a total of more than 30 MiG-17F/PF and MiG-15UTIs.[25]

EXPANSION

The coup of 18 November 1963 ended all hope for the establishment of Iraq as a functioning democracy. Arif's rule thus had no other source of legitimacy but that conferred by military force. However, with most of his aides being not only pan-Arab nationalists, but indeed followers of Nasserist doctrine (and either the members of the Tikriti clan, or born in Tikrit), the Iraqi president had few options but to renew his efforts to form a union with Egypt, in the form of the United Arab Republic. After the 1964 Arab League summit in Cairo, he introduced a provisional constitution that stressed Iraq's relations with other Arab states, nationalised all banks and insurances, and all large manufacturing companies, eased out the remaining Ba'athists (including Hardan at-Tikriti) from his government, and – at least in theory – subjected the Iraqi armed forces to the United Arab Command (UAC) headquartered in Cairo. Correspondingly, remaining MiG-19Ss of the disbanded No. 9 Squadron were donated to the UARAF, while a brigade from the Egyptian Army was deployed in Iraq nominally to run joint manoeuvres with the Iraqi Army – though actually to bolster protection of the government which knew that its own armed forces had been exhausted by the recent battles against the Kurds and the Ba'ath Party, as well as subsequent purges.[26]

In line with these developments, but also on the basis of experiences from the war against Barzani's uprising, in early 1964 Tikriti travelled to London to sign a contract for 12 additional Hunter F.Mk 59As, 12 Westland Wessex HU.Mk 52 helicopters, and 12 (later increased to 20) British Aerospace Corporation (BAC) Jet Provost T.Mk 52s. Deliveries of all these aircraft were to last into May 1967, and prompted another reorganisation of the IrAF. Aiming to produce as many jet-pilots as possible within the shortest period of time, the Air Force College intensified its curriculum: students were now flying Chipmunks and Provosts for elementary training, before converting to Jet Provosts (the first of which arrived in Iraq on 27 August 1964), and then receiving advanced training and weapons training on Vampire T.Mk 55s (before these were donated to Somalia in 1964), and MiG-15UTIs. Wessex helicopters entered service in the assault and transport role with the reorganised No. 4 Squadron: some of the remaining Mi-4s were handed over to No. 3 Squadron that used them as VIP-transports, while others were used for helicopter pilot training at the Air Force College. Hunter F.Mk 59s ordered the previous year were taken up by No. 6 Squadron, whose older F.Mk 6s were then sent to Great Britain for overhauls

A nice view of an Iraqi Wessex HU.Mk 52 (serial number 588). The type entered service with No. 4 Squadron, IrAF, in 1965 and continued soldiering-on until replaced by Mi-8s and Alouettes in the early 1970s. As far as is known, the top-side camouflage consisted of the same colours as applied on Hunters (i.e. dark grey and dark green on top surfaces and sides), but with undersurfaces painted in light grey. (Pit Weinert Collection)

The little-recognised, but highly important acquisition of early 1964 included 12, later 20, BAC Jet Provost T.Mk 52s. Initially operated as advanced trainers by the Air Force College, they were later to serve with the Flying Leaders School (FLS) – the IrAF's fighter weapons school assigned to the Air Force Academy. (Albert Grandolini Collection)

One of the original Hunter F.Mk 6s seen in 1964 – already wearing a new fin flash (and still mounting Mk. 14 launch rails for unguided rockets), shortly before being sent to Great Britain for overhaul and an upgrade to the FGA.Mk 9-like F.Mk 59 standard. (Pit Weinert Collection)

Renewed cooperation with Great Britain enabled the IrAF to have not only its Hunter F.Mk 6s overhauled and upgraded to the F.Mk 59 standard, but to introduce similar measures to various of its older training aircraft. A good example was this Vampire T.Mk 55. On its return to Britain, it was worn out to the level where the entire cockpit section was replaced by one from an ex-RAF T.Mk 11, including ejection seats. Ironically, only just returned to Iraq, in 1964 this Vampire was donated to Somalia. (Albert Grandolini Collection)

INDIAN CONNECTION

Preoccupied with a constant build-up and expansion, the acquisition of new aircraft and equipment, and also due to the heavy involvement in politics of many of its personnel, the IrAF found itself short on qualified flight instructors. Correspondingly, in 1962, Baghdad reached an agreement with New Delhi for the latter to deploy a group of six instructor pilots of the Indian Air Force to serve at the Air Force College, then still based at Rashid AB. Delayed by the outbreak of the Sino-Indian War of 1962, and reduced to three, the first Indian instructor pilots arrived in Baghdad in mid-1963. At the time, the Air College had one course for fighter pilots under training: this was split into two groups, of which one converted to MiG-15UTIs and then MiG-17Fs, and the other to Vampires and then to Hunters. The second course was for transport pilots. Six months later, the same group of Indian instructors then provided basic flight training to a group of Iraqi novices (on Provosts). This is how it came to be that nearly all of the dramas that seemingly occurred on a daily basis in the Iraq of the 1960s were witnessed – usually first hand – by a number of Indian officers.[29]

In 1964, the first group of Indian instructors helped move the Air College to Wahda AB, and in 1965 to transfer newly acquired Jet Provosts from Great Britain to Iraq. Months later, they were replaced by another three instructors. Over the following years, the number of Indian pilots serving with the Air Force College and then – from 1970 – with the Air Force Academy in Iraq continued growing, until stabilising at about 20 in the 1980s.

A four-ship of MiG-15UTIs underway along the Shatt al-Arab over Basra, in 1965, when the Air Force College moved to the former RAF Shaiba. (Air Marshal Paghvendran Collection, via Pushpindar Singh)

Captain Farouk al-Tail (foreground, left), standing in front of two Tu-16s and one of the crews of his No. 10 Squadron, during an inspection at Taqqaddum AB, in 1966. Notable are the 'last four'(3417) of the construction number below the cockpit of the bomber in the foreground, and the serial number 508 on the jet to the rear. (Pit Weinert Collection)

and an upgrade to a similar standard. For a while, Tikriti then became seriously interested in the acquisition of the latest British interceptor, the English Electric Lightning. Correspondingly, Razzaq was sent to Great Britain to inspect and test-fly the type. To his great disappointment it turned out that the early variant of the Lightning was a pure missile-armed interceptor that lacked not only guns, but also hardpoints for bombs and rockets. As such, it was ill-suited to the IrAF requirement for a Mach 2-capable fighter-bomber with secondary interception capability. Therefore, Tikriti opted for acquiring additional Hunters instead and, later in 1964, placed an order for 13 F.Mk. 59Bs and six T.Mk 66 and T.Mk 69 two-seat conversion trainers.[27] Finally, additional Hunters were used to establish the Habbaniya-based No. 29 Squadron (officially declared operational on 18 November 1965), commanded by Major Ismail Waqti, and then the Hunter OCU, reportedly commanded (or at least 'supervised') by a British officer only recalled as 'Captain Crow'.[28]

RAZZAQ'S FIRST COUP ATTEMPT

All of Arif's efforts to form a union with Egypt were in vain: in the course of further negotiations with Nasser and several visits to Cairo, he gradually realised that the differences between two countries were much too massive. On 12 June 1964, he publicly announced that he no longer advocated union with Egypt, and by early 1965, even felt forced to distance Nasserists from his cabinet. To protect himself from a possible backlash from within the armed forces – and acting not only as President of the Republic but also the as Commander-in-Chief of the Armed Forces, and having his brother Abd ar-Rahman Arif as the CGS – Arif then reorganised the 20th Infantry Brigade into the Republican Guards. Consisting of three infantry battalions and a tank regiment, and with Arif's friends and relatives in key positions, this was converted into a powerful strike force responsible for the protection of the President.[30]

Although no longer acting as the flying praetorian guard, the IrAF was keen to further expand its capabilities. Correspondingly, in February 1965, the Brigadier-General took care to send 15 of his pilots on a staff course at the Randolph Air Force Base (AFB), outside Lackland, in Texas, USA. Finally, because he was tasked with developing a capability to rapidly move intervention troops around the country, whenever necessary, he split all of the available

The former Anson, Fury, Vampire, Venom and Hunter pilot, Colonel – later Brigadier-General – Arif Abd ar-Razzaq served two tours of duty as the commander of the IrAF: from 8 February until 1 March 1963, and from 17 December 1963 until 6 September 1965. Only a few days later, on 15 September 1965, he launched his first coup attempt. (Ahmad Sadik Collection)

Antonov An-12s transports from No. 3 Squadron, and re-grouped them within the newly-established No. 23 Squadron, based at the former Washash AB (renamed Muthenna AB around this time). [31]

Both the Republican Guards and No. 23 Squadron, IrAF, played an important role in the months after their establishment. Attempting to moderate the growing disappointment of the Nasserist officers, on 6 September 1965 Arif appointed a new government, with Brigadier-General Razzaq – a staunch Nasserist – as Premier and Minister of Defence. However, Razzaq knew what was actually going on and thus began plotting a coup. His plan for action called for IrAF aircraft to attack the aircraft carrying President Arif to Casablanca in Morocco, for an Arab League Summit on 15 September 1965. Subsequently, the IrAF was to hit back against any

Army elements loyal to the government, while his allies were to secure the most important buildings around Baghdad. However, this plot was uncovered early, and Major-General Abd ar-Rahman Arif and the commander of the Republican Guards (and Arif's kinsman) Colonel Said Sulaybi quickly moved to shatter it. When all their attempts to gain control failed, Arif and his allies were all forced to flee to Egypt on 21 September 1965: in their wake, the government arrested over 3,000 members of the Ba'ath Party, driving others underground. Arif Abd ar-Razzaq's coup not only caused a major rift between Arif and Nasser but made moot even the prospects for a loose federation including Egypt, Iraq, and Syria. Nevertheless, it was not to remain his last such attempt.[32]

Munir Helmi Moheidin was the only Kurd to command the IrAF in the 1931-2003 period. Originally, he was selected from amongst more than 200 candidates to join the first group of 16 technicians trained by the British in 1929-1931, and worked himself up the chain of command. After graduating from the Military School in 1930, he served with the rank of lieutenant until undergoing a staff course in 1940. He served as the Deputy Commander RIrAF from May until November 1954, and then as Inspector Armed Forces before being appointed the Commander IrAF from 3 May 1954 until 2 October 1954, and again from 11 September 1965 until 21 September 1966. (Ahmad Sadik Collection)

THIRD OFFENSIVE AGAINST THE KURDS

In the meantime, the relative – even if temporary – weakness of the Iraqi armed forces, Barzani's expressions of support for Arif's anti-Ba'ath coup, and the winter, brought the fighting in northern Iraq to a halt in late 1963. Indeed, a cease-fire was negotiated in February 1964. As a symbol of its goodwill, the government then released over 1,200 Kurds from detention, and declared a general amnesty for all those who had supported Barzani's revolt since 1961. Keen to establish his own support base, the Kurdish leader then took care to expand his force to about 25,000, including about 70 officers and other ranks that defected from the Iraqi Army. However, knowing he was lacking popular support within his own ethnic group, Barzani then entered negotiations with Baghdad. The resulting talks led nowhere however: although Arif formally abrogated martial law (in force since the 14 Tammuz Revolution), and relinquished his 'special powers', the break actually only served for both sides to prepare for the next big battle.[33]

On 3 April 1965, nine brigades of the Iraqi Army launched an offensive all along the 400 kilometre (250 mile) arc from Zakho to Khanakin. As usual, this operation was extensively supported by the IrAF, which repeated the usual pattern of first smashing all the roadblocks before switching to air policing. Supplied with anti-tank rocket-propelled-grenades (RGPs) of Soviet origin, and even some captured artillery, Barzani's insurgents offered more serious resistance than ever before – even more so once the government lost one of its most valued Kurdish allies, the 30,000-strong Lowlan tribe, which switched to join the insurgents. In a single blow, the balance of power tilted in favour of Barzani, who now had more combatants than the Army could deploy against him. The result was a stalemate on the entire front: once again, the Iraqi Army failed to penetrate the labyrinth of mountains in the north.[34]

Disappointed, Arif took a surprising decision. Although confronted by near-simultaneous coup-attempts plotted by former monarchists and by the ICP, he travelled to Moscow to – amongst other things – sign a contract for 19 additional MiG-21 interceptors and up to 34 Sukhoi Su-7BMK fighter-bombers. As well as obtaining additional combat aircraft, this action was a successful attempt to isolate Barzani's insurgency on the international level: in similar fashion, Arif had already agreed for Iran and Turkey to close their borders,

A group of Barzani's insurgents – known as the *Peshmerga* ('Those who face Death') – with five unexploded FAB-250M-46 bombs left behind by the IrAF during the fighting of 1965. Weapons of this type were most frequently deployed by Il-28 bombers. (Albert Grandolini Collection)

and thus curb the movement of insurgents in and out of Iraq.[35] Although originally opposed by the contemporary commander of the IrAF, General Munir Abbas Hilmi, this acquisition was eventually much welcomed by the air force: not only did MiG-21s prove to be easy to maintain (at least unless they had to be sent to the USSR for overhauls), but the Soviets were quick to deliver. Following their shipment to Basra in December 1965, they were transferred to Rashid AB: combined with a group of 12 pilots that had completed their conversion courses in the USSR, on 8 January 1966 they entered service with the newly-established No. 17 Squadron, commanded by Major Durhit Ibrahim.[36]

FOURTH OFFENSIVE AGAINST THE KURDS

Mass demonstrations by the Shia in Baghdad of late 1965 clearly demonstrated that the majority of the Iraqi population was not only against a continued war with the Kurds, but also against Arif's nationalisation measures. Always a proponent of conciliatory policy towards the Shia, the President reacted by appointing a civilian government led by Prime Minister Abdul Rahman al-Bazzaz, the task of which was to find a way out of the crisis. At the same time, Arif ordered the Army to take the insurgents by surprise by launching another a local offensive in the middle of the winter. Deploying two brigades, on 8 January 1966 the Army took the Kurds by surprise and secured Panjwin. Certainly enough, the insurgents quickly regrouped and hit back in full force, while the IrAF was grounded due to bad weather: after suffering more than 200 killed, the Army was forced to withdraw from the town by 18 January. However, and although unsuccessful, this operation provided a terrific morale boost to the entire Iraqi armed forces, who began preparing for a major spring offensive. In turn, it shocked Barzani, who then also found himself facing a coup from within his own movement, plotted by Jalal Talabani, and also cut off from Soviet aid.[37]

Preparations for the next offensive were rudely interrupted on 13 April 1966 when an IrAF Mi-4 helicopter (delivered to Iraq only a few weeks earlier) piloted by Captain Khalid Mohammed Nuri, and carrying President Abd as-Salim Arif, crashed outside Qurna, killing everybody on board. Bazzaz took care for a smooth take-over by Abd ar-Rahman Arif, the late president's brother, even though he was away in Moscow on another arms-purchasing mission. Indeed, the new President promptly exploited the opportunity to widen the rift between the Soviets and the Kurds: in exchange for demonstratively denouncing the US policy in Vietnam, he was granted permission to buy 49 additional MiG-21 interceptors.[38]

Hardly back in Baghdad to take part in the funeral of his brother, the new Iraqi president Arif then also overruled Premier Bazzaz and ordered the spring offensive: aiming to hit about 3,500 insurgents pressed with their backs against the Persian border, and thus to cut the Kurdish-controlled territory in two, this was launched on 4 May 1966, and saw the deployment of nine brigades with 40,000 troops. Supported by more than 100 aircraft of the IrAF, the Iraqi troops forced their way over the Ruwanduz Gorge before concentrating for a major attack on Mount Handrin and Mount Zozik. At that point in time, they were hit by Barzani's counterattack: on 11 and 12 May, an entire brigade was trapped at Mount Handrin. The IrAF did its utmost to support the besieged unit, and seems to have lost one of its MiG-17s to the ground fire, but to no avail: the brigade was then overrun by the insurgents, losing up to 1,000 killed and all of its arms, equipment and supplies. Although the fighting – including fierce Iraqi air strikes, some of which hit Iranian territory – went on for nearly two weeks longer, this was effectively the end of the fourth Iraqi offensive against the Kurds. Arif and Bazzaz then entered negotiations with Talabani, resulting in a cease-fire that took effect on 21 May 1966, and the so-called Bazzaz Declaration, which fulfilled nearly all Kurdish demands, including recognition of their nationality and language, decentralisation of administrative authorities, and proportional representation in central government.[39]

Brigadier-General Arif Abd ar-Razzaq seen upon arrest after his second coup-attempt in 1966. During his career with the RIrAF and the IrAF, he flew Ansons, Furies, Vampires, Venoms, and Hunters, before serving as the commander of the IrAF, and then as Minister of Agriculture, Minister of Defence and Prime Minister of Iraq. He died in exile in Great Britain on 30 March 2007. (via Ali Tobchi)

RAZZAQ'S SECOND COUP ATTEMPT

The end of the war with the Kurds was welcomed by most of the Iraqi population – and the majority of the armed forces: the entire country was tired of five years of conflict, but also of endless military coups and political struggle, and looking forward to a better future. Just at that point in time, Arif Abd ar-Razzaq and several other exiled Iraqi officers clandestinely entered Iraq via Kuwait – with the intention of toppling the government that has finally brought some peace and stability. Working fast, the plotters established links to numerous of their friends, including the commander of Firnas AB, Major Ahmed Rashid, and the commander of the 4th Division in Mosul, Colonel Younis Atar 'Youssef' Bashi. Expecting widespread support for their action, on 29 June 1966 Razzaq, Rashid and Bashi initiated their coup by taking control of Firnas AB and the 4th Division, and then convincing several crews from Nos. 5 and 8 Squadrons to side with them. Following rushed preparations, at 15:30hrs of 30 June, eight MiG-17s and Il-28s launched in the direction of Baghdad. Attacking in three waves, they rocketed and bombed the Presidential Palace and Washash AB, killing 8 and wounding 15. Half an hour later, Baghdad radio station was secured by officers that sided with the coup plotters, who then broadcasted a call for Arif and Bazzaz to leave their offices and retire. However, the plotters failed to secure Baghdad TV station. Moreover, Arif meanwhile made a call to Mosul and secured help from the commander of the Northern Military District: the latter promptly deployed a commando battalion directly assigned to his headquarters for an assault on Firnas AB: Razzaq, his three aides and about 100 supporters involved in a coup that was staged literally 'at the wrong place and time', were quickly arrested,

SILVER OR LEAD

If there was ever a story making the Iraqi Air Force of the 1960s 'famous' in the West, and tarnishing its image ever since, then it is the one of a – supposed – 'defection' by one of its MiG-21 pilots to Israel on 12 August 1966. Widely publicised ever since, the Israeli version of the story emphasises a 'mistreated Christian pilot', 'ignored by superiors and never promoted', 'disgruntled with his participation in bombing of the Kurds', making his own decision to flee, and then the donation of his aircraft to the USA for studies when the US Air Force needed it the most – at the high point of the Vietnam War. To call all such reports as anything other than propaganda would be an understatement.

Dating back to the late 1950s, all the efforts of the Israeli foreign intelligence service, Mossad ('the Institute') to convince various Egyptian pilots to defect to Israel with one of their 'MiGs' had failed. A new opportunity offered itself in 1965, when, as mentioned above, a group of Iraqi pilots was sent for a staff course at Randolph AFB in the USA. Deploying a group of female agents, Mossad attempted to recruit several of them – all without success: Lieutenant Hamid Dhahee was the first to turn down the Israeli offer. He was murdered in a bar in Lackland, Texas, on 15 June 1965. Seriously concerned about the safety of his students in the USA, Razzaq then recalled them to Iraq. However, several of the Iraqi pilots came back home followed by attractive 'lovers', all Mossad agents. Captain Shaker Mahmoud Yusuf's 'girlfriend' met him in Baghdad on 6 July 1965: when he refused the Israeli offer to defect, he was also murdered. Captain Mohammad Raglob survived only a while longer: he 'fell out' of a high-speed train during a trip to Germany on 11 February 1966. Eventually, the Israelis contacted Captain Munir Habib Jamil Redfa (or 'Ruefa'), now the deputy commander of the re-established No. 11 Squadron. Given the same, 'silver or lead' offer as his colleagues before him, Redfa opted for survival. After the Mossad evacuated 17 of his family members to Iran, he took off from Taqqaddum AB, on 12 August 1966, and flew a MiG-21F-13 to Israel.[43]

The Israeli donation of that MiG to the USA, a few years later, contributed relatively little to the American knowledge about the type. After all, when travelling to Randolph AFB in 1965, the Iraqis had also delivered all the technical and training manuals for the type: an English translation, prepared by the Defence Intelligence Agency (DIA), became available before the end of the same year.[44]

MiG-21F-13 serial number 534, flown by Munir Redfa to Israel on 12 August 1966 and put on display a few weeks later. (IDF)

This is a still from a film showing the ex-Iraqi MiG-21F-13 that became the source of much confusion in the West over the past 50 years. For training purposes, the Israelis applied quasi-Syrian markings on it, supposedly consisting of green, white and black, with three red stars on the white field. Syrian MiG-21s never wore roundels on their fuselages, and from the time that Syria joined the UAR in 1958, Syrian national markings always consisted of red, white, and black fields, initially with three green stars and later with none. (IDF)

As well as the faster and more-modern jets, the IrAF heavily deployed Fury F.Mk 1s of the Firnas-based No. 1 Squadron to fight Barzani's insurgents and for 'air policing' the Kurds in general. This photograph shows serial numbers (from front towards the rear) 249, 247, and 248 in the early 1960s. The unit continued flying Furies until replacing them with Su-7BMKs in 1967. (Albert Grandolini Collection)

Staff Sergeant Rashid Adham Heshan at-Tikriti, who was killed in action on 6 June 1967, during the second Israeli attack on the H-3 airfield. (via Ali Tobchi)

put on two An-12 transports of No. 23 Squadron, and flown into exile in Great Britain: none of them was to see Iraq ever again.[40]

NEW MIGS

With the type being in much demand all around the world at the time, when preparing their delivery in response to Arif's order from April 1966, the Soviets were forced to improvise. Correspondingly, they delivered a total of 22 reconditioned MiG-21F-13s, which originally belonged to the '0 series' of that type. The other 23 aircraft belonged to the MiG-21FL variant, which lacked an internal gun and was armed only with a pair of R-3S missiles. Once again, their deliveries came at an amazing pace: the first batch of MiG-21FLs reached the port of Basra before the end of 1966. The availability of additional MiGs prompted another reorganisation of the IrAF: reinforced by a group of Soviet advisors, No. 17 Squadron began acting as an Operational Conversion Unit (OCU). Its pilots then converted enough of their colleagues to MiG-21s for Nos, 9, 11 and then the newly established No. 14 Squadrons to work on the type. Moreover, in the case of Iraq the Soviets proved ready to make an exception to the rule, and to deliver MiG-21PFMs together with the little-known Kh-66 beam-riding guided missile: although this proved unreliable – and, indeed, very dangerous to deploy by a pilot of a single-seat fighter jet – and thus saw very little operational service with the IrAF, it was the first such weapon deployed in the Middle East.[41]

Deliveries of Su-7BMKs began in spring of 1967, and enabled No. 1 Squadron to finally withdraw from service its remaining Furies and Venoms. However, this big Soviet fighter-bomber proved very sensitive to so-called 'foreign object damage' – caused by ingestion of dirt, stones, and other lose objects from the tarmac and the runway into the engine, and the Soviets were extremely slow with delivering the equipment necessary to clean the runways. Furthermore, while having two wing-root installed NR-30 cannons, it arrived armed only with flimsy S-3K unguided rockets, which tended to literally fall apart when launched, prompting the Iraqis to demand deliveries of a suitable replacement (which arrived in the form of UB-16-57 pods for S-5K unguided rockets, in late 1967). Therefore, conversion process advanced very slowly, and was completed only later the same year.[42]

Overall, by the time Brigadier-General Jassam Mohammed ash-Shaher took over as the commander, in September 1966, and within only three years, the IrAF not only became one of the biggest export customers for the Hunter, and its largest operator in the Middle East, but also the second-largest operator of MiG-21s in that part of the world. Such a rapid expansion provides clear evidence of the far-sightedness of earlier IrAF commanders: regardless how short and turbulent their tenures were, and regardless of what kind of memories various Iraqis might associate with them, by taking care to expand the Air Force College and its equipment, Awaqati, Razzaq, Tikriti and Hilmi had all laid the fundamentals for the future of the force, enabling its further expansion – despite quite severe personnel 'losses' due to successive coups, purges, and – sporadically – combat with the Kurds.

7

JUNE 1967 ARAB-ISRAELI WAR

While the British originally supported the establishment of an Iraqi air force as a tool for maintaining internal security, and the RIrAF/IrAF spent most of 1931-1966 serving precisely that purpose, the thinking of its commanders meanwhile went in an entirely different direction. Since the mid-1930s, their threat-perceptions evolved around a possible confrontation with the arch-enemy of the Arabs in this part of the Middle East: Persia. Dating back to the times of the divide between the Sunni and Shia Muslims of the 7th century, this confrontation was further inflamed during the wars between the Ottomans and the Persians in the 16th, 17th, and 18th centuries, which revolved around boundaries and interference in each other's internal affairs. From the mid-1930s, the Iraqis and their eastern neighbours – who officially renamed their country to Iran (Land of the Aryans) in 1935 – remained at odds with each other not only for their historical animosity, but under the direct influence of Great Britain, because of their respective national interests. In 1948 a new threat emerged in the form of Israel and thus, while all the arms acquisitions of the 1950s and the 1960s described above might appear to be influenced by the necessity of the Iraqi air force to bolster its capabilities in COIN-related disciplines – and some were surely motivated by the Barzani's uprising of 1961 – their actual purpose, at least in the minds of successive commanders of the air force, was that of defence against a) the Iranians and b) the Israelis.[1] Related theories, and resulting planning were to be put to their first test in June 1967, at the time the IrAF was still busy assimilating its latest acquisitions.

UNITED ARAB COMMAND

During the Arab League Summit of 1964, the top Arab leaders decided to organise the United Arab Command (UAC) as a body responsible to first audit their armed forces in respect of their strength and organisation, and then to coordinate and standardise their military strategy, tactics, organisation and weaponry. With President Nasser being widely regarded as 'the Arab leader', and Egypt the 'military powerhouse' of the Arab world in those days, the command of the UAC was initially headquartered in Cairo, and the Egyptian Major-General Ali Ali Amer was appointed as its first commander – although the organisation was largely sponsored by oil-rich states that had only diminutive armed forces of their own and never really joined this pact, like Kuwait and Saudi Arabia. However, disputes between the various governments resulted in the UAC being little more than a token gesture. For all practical purposes, this command was dysfunctional by 1965: the only measure Amer had managed to introduce was for most of the Arab interceptors and fighter-bombers to have large portions of their noses and fins painted in red, for easier visual identification in case they encountered each other in the skies over Israel.

Through all of the 1930s, 1940s, 1950s, and 1960s, not only did successive Iraqi governments – regardless of their ideological orientation – but the whole of the Iraqi armed forces remained loyal to the pan-Arab ideology, and supportive of the Palestinians. This was visible even in the official crests of various IrAF units, nearly all of which contained the Palestinian tricolore, right next to that of Iraq. Contrary to what subsequently happened in Jordan and Syria, in Iraq, such 'signals' were also supported by deeds. Despite all of the political unrest in the country and neighbourhood in the 1950s and the 1960s, and although busy planning campaigns against Barzani's uprising, and being geographically separated from Israel, planners serving with the Chief of the Armed Forces General Staff (at the General Headquarters in Baghdad) all the time kept an eye on Israel. Correspondingly, and UAC or not, they took care to prepare several contingency plans for the deployment of Iraqi armed forces to Jordan and Syria in the event of war. Amongst others, these planned for the deployment of at least one army brigade and three squadrons of fighter-jets to Syria, and an entire army division and three squadrons of fighter-jets to Jordan. Unsurprisingly, it was on 24 March 1967, that the General Headquarters put the IrAF on alert for a possible crisis related to Israel. On 17 May 1967, two days after President Nasser mobilised the Egyptian armed forces – thus 'officially' starting the crisis that led to the June 1967 Arab-Israeli War – Major-General Shaher put his Nos. 6 and 17 Squadrons on alert for deployment to Jordan. However, neither unit received the order to move. Instead, President Arif – whose government always took a strong anti-Israeli line – preferred to bolster Syria with Iraqi units, and thus ordered the 8th Mechanised Infantry Brigade (from the 3rd Armoured Division) to deploy in that direction.[2]

During an exercise shortly before the June 1967 War, two Hunters collided north of Taqqaddum AB. Both aircraft managed to land safely. This photograph shows the damage to one of the two. Note the pair of Tu-16 bombers in the background of the photograph. (Tom Cooper Collection)

On 30 May 1967, King Hussein of Jordan suddenly appeared in Cairo to meet

TABLE 7: IrAF ORDER OF BATTLE, 5 JUNE 1967[5]			
UNIT	BASE	EQUIPMENT	REMARKS
COMMANDER IrAF: MAJ GEN JASSAM MUHAMMAD ASH-SHAHER			
No. 1 Squadron	Hurriyah	Fury F.Mk 1, Venom FB.Mk 50	Undergoing conversion to Su-7BMK
No. 2 Squadron	Firnas	Mi-4	CO unknown
No. 3 Squadron	Rashid	Dove, Heron	CO unknown
No. 4 Squadron	Rashid	Wessex HC.Mk 2	CO Lt Col Hassan Sharif
No. 5 Squadron	-	-	Disbanded in December 1965
No. 6 Squadron	Habbaniya	Hunter F.Mk 59A/B	CO Lt Col Adil Suleimany
No. 7 Squadron	Hurriyah	MiG-17F/PF	CO Lt Col Masroor Bahaedin
No. 8 Squadron	Hurriyah	11 Il-28, two Il-28U	CO Lt Col Mehdi Mahsun as-Sabbah
No. 9 Squadron	-	MiG-21FL/PFM	Working up on MiG-21
No. 10 Squadron	Taqqaddum	Nine Tu-16	CO Capt Farouk al-Tail
No. 11 Squadron	Rashid	11 MiG-21F-13	CO Lt Col Hashem Manhal al-Azawi
No. 14 Squadron	-	MiG-21FL/PFM	Working up on MiG-21
No. 17 Squadron	Taqqaddum	MiG-21FL/PFM	Acting as OCU for Nos. 9, 11 and 14 Squadrons; CO Maj Durhid Ibrahim Muslim
No. 23 Squadron	Rashid	Eight An-2, six An-12BP	CO unknown
No. 29 Squadron		16 Hunter F.Mk 59A/B	CO Lt Col Ismail Wakti
Hunter OCU	Habbaniya	Nine Hunter F.Mk 59 and T.Mk 66	CO 'Capt Crow' (British pilot; real name unknown)
Air Force Academy	Wahda	Chipmunk, Provost, Jet Provost, MiG-15UTI	CO unknown

President Nasser and sign a treaty of military cooperation and offered to put his armed forces under the command of an Egyptian. Interested in increasing the pressure upon Israel, but not provoking a war, Nasser demonstratively agreed and thus the UAC was re-activated, with Major-General Abd el-Moneim Riyadh assuming command.[3] During the same meeting, Nasser and Hussein then made a telephone call to President Arif in Baghdad with a request for the Iraqi armed forces to deploy in Jordan and also be subjected to the UAC. Arif promptly agreed, promising to send one armoured division and three squadrons of fighter-bombers, 'immediately'.[4]

IRAQIS ON THE MOVE

Wasting no time, Major-General Riyadh reached Amman on 1 June: after a quick conference with the Jordanians, he continued to Iraq, where he inspected the IrAF squadrons based at Taqqaddum AB. The same day, the entire 3rd Armoured Division was put on alert and ordered to move all of its elements to Amman with great urgency, while its 8th Brigade underway to Syria was re-routed to Jordan (it crossed the border late on 4 June and early the next day continued for Mafraq AB, with the intention of reaching positions in the Jordan River Valley). In agreement with Riyadh and his Deputy Air Operations, Brigadier-General Shalaby el-Hinnawy (a famous Egyptian veteran of the Palestine War 1948-1949 and the Suez War of 1956), General Shaher then deployed one of his lieutenant-colonels as a liaison officer to the HQ UAC in Amman, while putting Nos. 6, 7, 10, 17, and 29 Squadrons on alert: Hunters and MiG-21s were

Major-General Riyadh shaking hands with Lieutenant-Colonel Hashem Manhal al-Azawi, commander of No. 11 Squadron, in front of one of that unit's MiG-21F-13s at Taqqaddum AB on 1 June 1967. Riyadh's Deputy Air Operations, Brigadier-General Shalaby el-Hinnawy, is visible in the left centre, wearing sunglasses. (Shalaby el-Hinnawy Collection, via Dr David Nicolle)

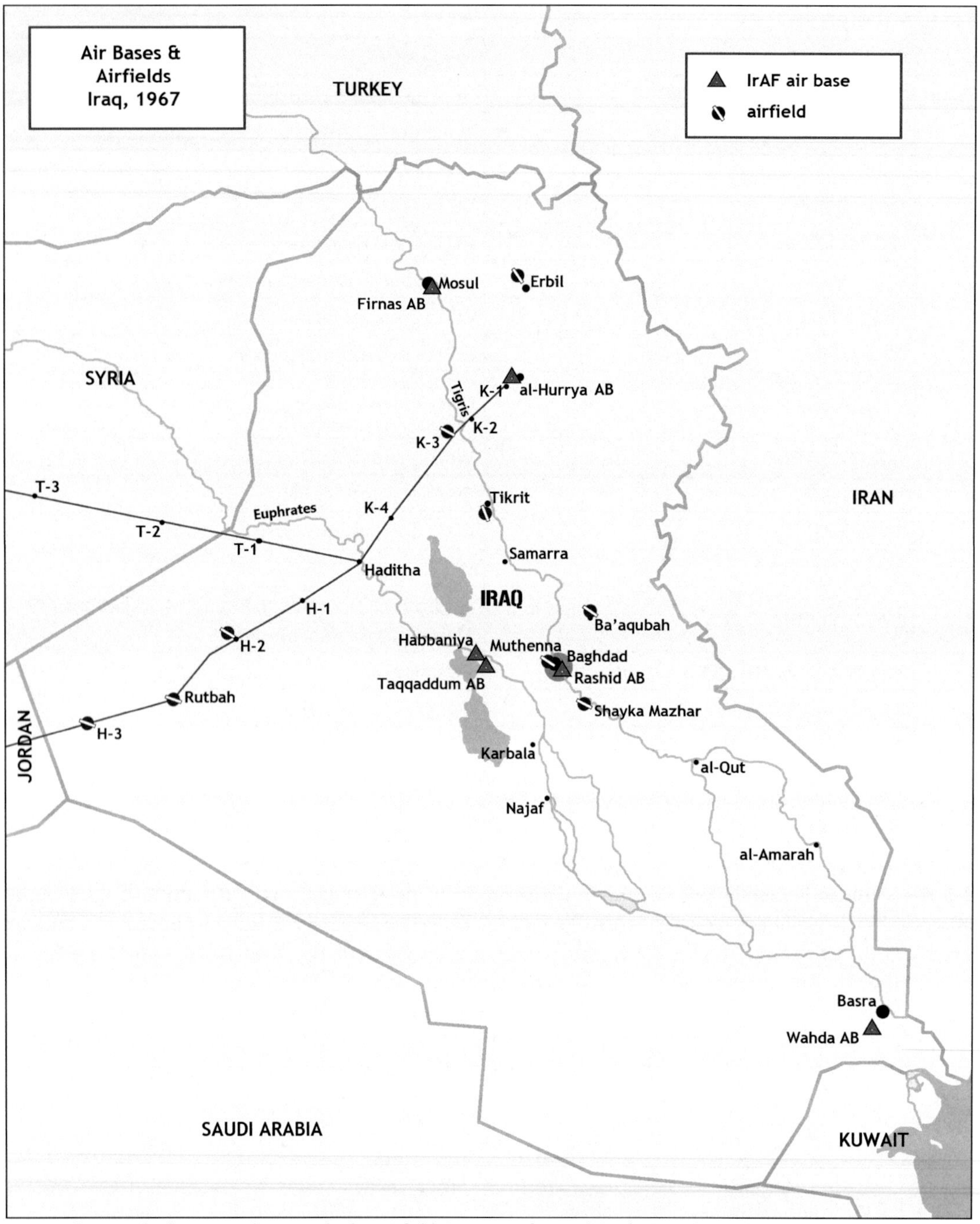

A map of Iraq with all major air bases and other airfields in use as of 1967. (Map by Tom Cooper)

to be deployed to Jordan first; Tu-16s were to fly strikes on Israel from their home-base at Taqqaddum AB, while MiG-17s of No. 7 Squadron were to act as a reserve.[6]

Organising this transfer was easier said than done: Hunters and MiGs could reach Mafraq on their own, but – and despite Iraqi urging – Amman was slow with issuing official permission for them to enter Jordanian airspace. Therefore, the Iraqis decided to stage their aircraft via the H-3 airfield. However, this installation was still essentially the same as when constructed by the IPC for the purpose of supporting the H-3 pipeline in the early 1930s. Due to the failure of the Arab states to build-up the UAC in 1964-1965, the only work undertaken on it was the construction of a 2,000m (6,561ft) long metalled runway. Otherwise, this installation lacked not only a parking area for more than a dozen aircraft, but also all the installations necessary to support operations of even one squadron of combat aircraft – such as weapon and fuel storage sites, and barracks for pilots and crews. Correspondingly, while the pilots of No. 6 Squadron had it easy to transfer their aircraft to H-3, once there they had to wait for their ground crews, ground equipment, weapons and fuel to be brought in by transport aircraft and trucks. Nevertheless, all 19 pilots and 16 Hunters of that unit – reinforced by two from No. 29 Squadron – were at H-3 by 4 June 1967. By the time, the IrAF liaison officer in Amman had managed to obtain the first set of orders for use in the event of war, and to forward these to the commander of No. 6 Squadron at H-3. Correspondingly, late on 4 June, Lieutenant-Colonel Adil Suleimany briefed his crews on what to expect, and about their possible targets in Israel. Indeed, in expectation of receiving permission to continue to Mafraq AB, early the next morning 12 MiG-21FLs from No. 17 Squadron also arrived, followed by an anti-aircraft battery equipped with 100mm guns of Soviet origin.[7]

MISERABLE INTELLIGENCE

Much to their dismay, during the briefing they received on the evening of 4 June, the Iraqi Hunter-pilots at H-3 were first informed that Egypt had decided that Arabs would not initiate hostilities, but wait for the Israelis to do so. Secondly, they were forced into the realisation that the available intelligence on the IDF/AF was 'miserable'. All the maps and intelligence on Israeli airfields were based on information from before 1948. The only useful piece of the briefing was a warning to expect French-made Dassault Mirage III interceptors in the air, and US-made MIM-23 HAWK SAMs on the ground, and thus to approach their targets flying as low as possible.

The failure of the IrAF Intelligence Department (IrAF-ID) to provide any useful intelligence to the pilots going to war with Israel was not an exception, but actually the rule within the Arab armed forces of May-June 1967, and then to a degree where the conclusion that the 'Arabs' were clueless about the IDF/AF's capabilities and intentions can only be described as an understatement. Although the Israeli air force actually operated from only 4-5 major air bases, the Military Intelligence of Egypt (colloquially DM1) – who worked with the help of a small network of local informers – reported dozens of airfields with names including 'al-Naqab', 'Hashur' (probably Hatzor), 'Ibrahim', 'Dimona', 'Matchad', and 'Mashabi Zamon'. Unsurprisingly, President Nasser preferred to listen and to arrive at his decisions on the basis of information provided by

Major-General Riyadh, Shalaby el-Hinnawy, and a group of Iraqi dignitaries watching a trio of IrAF Hunters taking off from Taqqaddum AB on 1 June 1967. (Shalaby el-Hinnawy Collection, via Dr David Nicolle)

Although of poor quality, this interesting photograph shows President Arif (right foreground, with cap), shaking hands with Lieutenant-Colonel Adil Suleimany, commander of No. 6 Squadron, prior to the latter's unit's deployment to Jordan on 31 May 1967. (Ahmad Sadik Collection)

the Soviets.[8] In Iraq, the General Military Intelligence Directorate (GMID), and the IrAF-ID provided at least reasonably good – and sometimes excellent – targeting intelligence on Barzani's forces, but neither had better sources on the IDF/AF than the publicly available literature. As subsequent developments were to show, although bordering on Israel and thus having direct insight into the country, even the Jordanian intelligence was of poor quality. Finally, while the UARAF flew no reconnaissance sorties over Israel since 1960, since 1948 the IrAF had not flown over Israel at all. The overall result was that the only useful piece of information provided by the IrAF-ID was that there was one big base in northern Israel, named Ramat David. For similar reasons, the the IrAF-ID assessed that H-3 was likely to be targeted by the IDF/AF: it knew that Moshe Dayan – Israel's Minister of Defence as of 1967 – had travelled with Habforce to Iraq in 1941, and that in the mid-1950s this airfield was overflown at least once by an Israeli B-17.[9]

CHAOS IN CAIRO AND AMMAN

On 5 June 1967, Israel opened the war by launching a massive air strike on UARAF air bases in Egypt. Cairo was taken by surprise: the General Command in Cairo not only failed to decrypt a coded warning from Amman in time, but was then also slow in keeping the HQ UAC up-to-date on developments. Worse yet, when it finally ordered General Riyadh into action, it began spreading fantasies about the destruction of dozens of Israeli aircraft, a counterattack of the UARAF, and a ground advance into southern Israel. The Royal Jordanian Air Force (RJAF) was put on alert, and the pilots of its sole combat unit – the Hunter-equipped No. 1 Squadron at Mafraq AB – were briefed for an air strike on 'Netanya AB' (which never existed), but not ordered into the air: uncertain about controversial reports from Egypt, Riyadh and his Jordanian colleagues began quarrelling about what to do next. Thus, it was only once the second order from Cairo arrived – around 11:00hrs Amman time (12:00hrs Cairo time) – that the UAC ordered the IrAF and the RJAF into action: even then, the Jordanians did not move before they were certain that the Iraqis would 'do something'.[10]

OPERATION RIYADH

Still at H-3 airfield, pilots of No. 6 Squadron, IrAF were gathered for another briefing at 10:30hrs Baghdad time (08:30hrs in Israel and 09:30hrs in Cairo): Lieutenant-Colonel Suleimany informed them about Operation Riyadh – the code-name for a series of air strikes on Israeli air bases. Next, he selected four of them – Faysal Abdul Mohsen, Hazem Hassan Qasim, Hassan al-Khiher and Fadhil Mustafa – to follow him into an attack on 'Kfar Sirkin AB', which was thought to be a base for Israeli transport aircraft and the home base of the IDF's Paratrooper School. Three other pilots – Mumtazz Abdel Ali as-Saydoon, Najdat an-Naqeeb and Emad Ahmed Ezzat – were to fly an attack on Lod International Airport (IAP). As of that moment in time, there were not enough rockets and fuel at H-3 for No. 6 Squadron to launch all of the available aircraft: each of these eight Hunters was armed with a full load of ammunition for their four 30mm ADEN guns, and carried 24 British-made 3-inch unguided rockets, and two drop tanks. The others were to stay at H-3 and wait for a signal to transfer to Mafraq AB.

Full of enthusiasm, the pilots took off at 12:15hrs (Baghdad time), climbed to an altitude of 7,010m (23,000ft) and took a course for Mafraq. Overflying the latter, they could see RJAF's Hunters still on the ground: subsequently, they descended and penetrated the Israeli airspace at a very low altitude. Only a minute after passing over the Jordan River, the Hunters jinked upwards, flipped upside down and then rolled out, to start their attack. In front of them, the first three pilots sighted multiple aircraft: they quickly aimed and

Hunter F.Mk 59A serial number 668, as seen at Taqqaddum AB, before the June 1967 War. Notable is that the aircraft is parked inside a shallow blast pen covered by camouflage netting – very unusual practice for most Arab air forces at the time. This measure had been introduced by the IrAF in 1963 and was bolstered by influence from Indian experiences during the 1965 War with Pakistan. (Ahmad Sadik Collection)

then unleashed all of their 72 unguided rockets. The rear pair was in the process of following in fashion when one of its pilots saw an Israeli MIM-23 HAWK SAM approaching, and radioed a warning, prompting both pilots to break hard and abort their attack. The formation returned over the Jordan River at low level, and then climbed back to an altitude of 23,000ft for the flight back to H-3. Its pilots claimed the destruction of seven transport aircraft of the IDF/AF. A captured Israeli pilot later told the IrAF-ID that the aircraft hit by Iraqi Hunters at Kfar Sirkin were full of paratroopers preparing an assault on el-Arish, in the Sinai, and the Iraqis convinced themselves that their strike had delivered a particularly painful blow to the IDF. On the contrary, the Israelis admitted the loss of only one (empty) Noratlas transport and one Piper Super Cub light aircraft.

The Jordanians did then launch their air strike on 'Netanya AB': rather unsurprisingly, finding no 'air base', their four Hunters hit a factory hall instead, killing one civilian and injuring seven, before returning safely to Mafraq AB. About half an hour later, not only Mafraq AB, but also Amman IAP, found themselves under a series of highly destructive Israeli air strikes, which destroyed nearly all of the RJAF's Hunters. Surprisingly enough, considering everything that was going on around it, the second Iraqi formation – scheduled to hit the Lod IAP one hour after the strike on Kfar Sirkin – penetrated Israeli airspace undisturbed, but its pilots could not locate their target due to their obsolete maps. Thus, they returned to H-3 with their aircraft each still carrying all 24 unguided rockets.

An Iraqi Hunter pilot gives the thumbs-up to his ground crew prior to a training sortie. Having gathered considerable experience during the fighting against Barzani's insurgents, the Iraqi pilots considered themselves ready for a war with Israel. (Nour Bardai Collection)

An Iraqi Hunter seen passing very low over the Judean Hills while withdrawing towards Jordan following an air strike on Kfar Sirkin airfield on 5 June 1967. The Iraqi attack caught the Israelis by surprise and no Mirages managed to intercept the intruders. (IDF)

THREE-DAY BATTLE

Whatever the Iraqi Hunter-pilots achieved over Israel at noon of 5 June 1967, their two raids left enough of an impression for the IDF/AF to order an attack on the H-3 airfield. Thus began a mini-campaign that was to last for three days, and see some of the fiercest air combats of this war. Launched only minutes after the last pair of Iraqi Hunters left Israeli airspace, the first raid was flown by four French-made SNCASO 450 Vautour fighter-bombers of the Ramat David-based No. 110 Squadron, and was an ad-hoc mission. H-3 was not part of the Israeli war plan and the formation was originally scheduled to attack a target in Syria, before being re-tasked to another target in Syria, and then one in Egypt. Only minutes before the take-off were the pilots briefed to fly to Iraq. Moreover, one of the jets aborted shortly after take-off due to technical problems. Following the H-Pipeline as a navigational aid, the other three jets flew the full width of Jordan unobserved but then experienced problems with finding H-3. As their leader climbed to better orientate, around 16:00hrs Iraqi time, he came under attack by two MiG-21FLs from No. 17 Squadron. The Israeli turned hard to avoid and then descended to very low altitude, thus spoiling the firing solution of the poor R-3S missiles carried by the Iraqi MiGs: indeed, all three

The first An-12BP acquired by Iraq from the USSR in 1962 – serial number 505, seen in this photograph – was one of the examples of this type re-assigned to No. 23 Squadron in 1965. This was probably the An-12 destroyed on the ground during the first Israeli air strike on H-3 airfield, on 5 June 1967. (Albert Grandolini Collection)

The wreckage of this de Havilland Dove (serial number 267) was discovered at the former Habbaniyah AB in March 2006. The aircraft probably wore the same livery as the example destroyed by the Israelis at H-3 on 5 June 1967. The IrAF acquired a total of five Doves, which were operated by No. 3 Squadron. (Tom Cooper Collection)

of the Israelis managed to free themselves sufficiently enough to strafe the aircraft parked on the ground and bomb the single runway. The first to be hit was a single Antonov An-12 transport carrying ammunition and spares for MiG-21s; this was followed by a row of MiG-21FLs from No. 17 Squadron.[11] Finally, one of the Vautours strafed the Hunters that returned from the unsuccessful attack on Lod IAP: Naqeeb barely escaped the explosion of his aircraft. As the Vautours pressed their attack home, the MiG-21FL-pilots finally found targets flying steadily enough to be targeted by R-3S missiles. However, all four that were fired missed: the infra-red seekers were distracted by the heat emitted by the hot desert below. The first air battle over H-3 thus remained inconclusive, but the Israelis claimed the destruction of no less than 12 IrAF aircraft on the ground. Actually, the IrAF wrote off three MiG-21s, one Hunter, one Dove and a single An-12. The runway was damaged, but the ground crews managed to patch it up by the next morning.[12]

IRAQI COUNTERATTACK

Not convinced by the claims of their pilots, the Israeli commanders ordered a new attack for the next morning. However, the Iraqis were quicker. On order from the UAC, six Hunters launched at sunrise from H-3 and then split into two formations: four fighter-bombers were to hit IDF's ground units advancing in the Jenin area of the West Bank, two were to attack Ramat David AB. Due to the lack of 3-inch unguided rockets, this time each aircraft was armed with only eight of these (and a full load of ammunition for their 30mm ADEN guns). Once again, the briefing provided to pilots was very poor: the Iraqi Army still had no FACs deployed in Jordan, and there was still no clarity about the importance of Ramat David AB.

The first formation lost one of its members early: the Hunter in question was forced back to H-3 due to a mechanical problem. Underway at low level, the other three pilots – Mohamed Abdel Wahed Yuzbaki, Faysal Abdul Mohsen. and Abdul Latif Abdul Karem – reached the designated target area near Jenin by around 05:00 Israeli time, completely undisturbed. Failing to find their target where expected, the Iraqis were quick to find an alternative next to the road connecting Nazareth with Haifa: a large group of tanks parked in a semi-circle, and surrounded by support vehicles, obviously in the process of replenishing their ammunition and fuel. This was saturated by a total of 24 unguided rockets. According to a post-war investigation by the IrAF-ID, this attack left five Israelis killed and eight injured, while the extent of damage caused to various tanks and other vehicles remains unknown.[13]

Around the same time, another Iraqi jet appeared over the West Bank, having met as little resistance as the three Hunters that preceded it. This was the first of four Tu-16s from No. 10 Squadron that – each armed with six FAB-500 bombs – were ordered to attack Ramat David AB. Once again, the intelligence provided to the crews involved was very poor. Furthermore, each bomber was to operate as a single-ship, without providing mutual protection with their three defensive barbettes, each of which was equipped with two 23mm cannon, and without any fighter escort. Piloted by Farouk at-Tail (with Majid Turki Abbas al-Jumaily as co-pilot), the first Tu-16 reached Mafraq AB at low altitude before climbing to 25,000ft (7,620m) while crossing the Jordan River and searching for its target.[14] The crew reported to have found Ramat David and released its bombs without any disturbance, around 05:05 local time, and

Photographs of Iraqi Tu-16s are extremely rare; those showing them in the air even more so. This one shows serial number 512 sometime in the mid-1960s. All 10 Tu-16s delivered to Iraq were second-hand aircraft, originally manufactured in the 1950s for the Soviet air force: all of them wore the last four digits of their construction number applied in blue below the cockpit. They went into the June 1967 War against Israel still wearing this livery. (Tom Cooper Collection)

The crash site of the IrAF Tu-16 piloted by Hussein Muhammad Hussein, in a pine forest hiding an Israeli military base outside Afula. (IDF)

Pieces of wreckage of the ill-fated Iraqi Tu-16. (IDF)

then returned to Taqqaddum AB. However, it seems that Tail's report was overoptimistic and his bombs hit an Israeli military installation near Taamach, 10km (6.2 miles) southeast of Afula, where — according to Iraqi intelligence reports — several buildings were demolished, two Israeli soldiers killed and five injured.[15]

The next two Tu-16s were less lucky: their crews were forced to abort due to technical difficulties and return to Taqqaddum AB. The fourth Tupolev was piloted by Hussein Muhammad 'Kaka' Hussein – with co-pilot Faeq Alwan, Sobhi Abdul Karim (navigator), Rashid Adam (weapons operator), and Ghani Yahya (rear-gunner) on board. It missed Ramat David AB and continued climbing over the Mediterranean Sea, whereupon Hussein decided to turn around and try to find another suitable target. Around 08:35 local time, for unexplained reasons and despite a clear order not to attack civilian targets, the crew released its load over the centre of Netanya, hitting the main street and causing a number of civilian casualties.[16] Shortly later, Hussein's bomber was intercepted by two Mirage IIICJs from No. 117 Squadron, IDF/AF. Sabih opened fire with his two 23mm cannons, forcing them to break and reposition while Hussein entered a right turn and began a descent that finally brought him directly over Ramat David — just at the moment that the crews of the four No. 110 Squadron Vautours and two No.117 Squadron Mirage IIICJs were preparing for their second attack on H-3!

Still pursued by the two Mirages, the Tupolev thundered low over the Israeli air base, making a right turn that enabled Sabih and Kargoli to open fire from their barbettes at the aircraft and installations below. Their bomber was then hit by one of two

Squadron Leader H. M. 'Kaka' Hussein was the pilot of the Tu-16 shot down over Israel early on 6 June 1967. (Ahmad Sadik Collection)

Flight-Lieutenant Faeq Alwan was Hussein's co-pilot. (Ahmad Sadik Collection)

The Second Navigator, and responsible for manning one of the 23mm cannon barbettes in the downed Tu-16, was 1st Lieutenant Reashid Adam. (Ahmad Sadik Collection)

The First Navigator and weapons operator ('bombardier') of the downed Tu-16 was Flight-Lieutenant Sobhi Abdul Karim. (Ahmad Sadik Collection)

missiles fired by the Mirages: Hussein reported via radio that the aircraft was still controllable and that he was attempting to escape in an easterly direction. However, while trying to do so, he flew his bomber directly over the IDF barracks near Megiddo airfield, where it was hit again, this time by one of the Mirages and by 40mm Bofors anti-aircraft guns. The big Tupolev crashed into a military storage complex hidden within a pine forest west of Afula, destroying three barracks and two teams of 120mm mortars, and killing its crew and between 11 and 14 Israeli reservist soldiers.[17]

Independently from Hussein's Tu-16, the last two Hunters arrived over the Ramat David area. Flown by Samir Yousif Zainal and Wallid Abdul-Latif as-Samarrai, they reached their target by flying low between hills and above the orchards of the West Bank, without encountering any kind of opposition. The results of their attack remain unknown: available Israeli sources mention an air raid that – supposedly – hit the villages of Nahalal and Migdal Haemek, though without causing any damage or casualties. Curiously enough, these locations are due north and east of the sprawling Ramat David complex, respectively, barely a few kilometres away.[18]

THE SECOND ISRAELI RAID

Shortly after Hussein's Tu-16 was shot down, and after Zainal and Samarrai had left Israeli airspace, the second Israeli attack on H-3 was launched in the form of four Vautours escorted by two Mirages. The aircraft followed the same route as the first Israeli formation that attacked H-3, a day earlier, and the same as that was used by all the Iraqi Hunters. The Israelis arrived over H-3 just as Zainal and Samarrai were about to land, covered by two MiG-21FLs – flown by Khalid Sarah and Mumtazz Abdel Ali as-Saydoon (an ex-Hunter pilot that converted to MiGs in 1966) – and two Hunters, flown by Yuzbaki and Namiq Saadallah. Already airborne and in the process of developing their attack, the Israelis proved quicker off the mark. One Mirage positioned behind Samarrai's Hunter and followed him down towards the runway, while another turned to attack the two MiGs as these were accelerating for take-off. Seeing the threat behind him, Samarrai tucked in his landing gear, broke and then accelerated away, prompting the Israeli to search for another target: the two Hunters rolling down the runway. Under pressure to get airborne, Yuzbaki made the fatal mistake of pulling too hard and too early on his stick: his Hunter stalled, yawed and then struck the main water tank of H-3. The pilot was killed instantly. The Israelis

Flight Lieutenant Abdel Wahed Yuzbaki, veteran of the Kfar Sirkin raid, was killed while scrambling from the H-3 airfield when it came under a second Israeli attack on the morning of 6 June 1967. (Ahmad Sadik Collection)

Flight Lieutenant Galeb al-Hameed al-Qaysee was another veteran of the Kfar Sirkin raid. He was killed when his Hunter was hit by Dror and it crashed into a fuel tank at H-3 during the third Israeli attack. (Ahmad Sadik Collection)

Mumtazz Abdel Ali as-Saydoon, seen earlier during his career, while disembarking from a two-seat Hunter T.Mk 66. During the June 1967 War with Israel he was already an experienced MiG-21 pilot. (Nour Bardai Collection)

missed the three remaining IrAF fighters and these then managed to became airborne and engage the enemy in a confused air battle. Somehow avoiding the debris caused by the crash of Yuzbaki's jet, Saadallah first attacked one Vautour only to be fired upon by a Mirage, the engine of which stalled. Undisturbed, Sadallah opened fire and claimed his target as 'damaged'. In turn, the Israeli claimed to have outmanoeuvred his opponent and then hit him with 30mm cannon fire: supposedly, the Hunter crashed seconds later. Sadallah's Hunter was hit, and the pilot injured, but he managed to land safely at H-3.[19]

Meanwhile, the two MiG-21s made a wide turn around and then accelerated to attack the Israelis that now began to withdraw from H-3. One of the Mirages spoiled Sarah's attempt with R-3Ss, but the Iraqi pressed home his attack – in turn presenting his tail to the other Israeli interceptor: the pilot of the later subsequently claimed that a short burst from his cannon was sufficient to cut off the right wing and cause the Iraqi fighter to crash. In fact, several rounds hit Sarah's MiG-21FL, one causing his braking parachute to pop open, in turn confusing his Israeli opponent. However, a hard turn then caused the parachute to break away and Sarah managed to land safely. The Israeli formation disengaged and disappeared in a westerly direction. Saydoon attempted to pursue one of the Vautours but both of his R-3S missed: he returned to H-3 to bitterly complain about the poor quality of the Soviet-made missiles.[20]

Back at Ramat David AB, the Israeli pilots rather optimistically claimed the destruction of two MiG-21s and six Hunters on the ground, as well as a MiG-21 and a Hunter in air combats. Once again, the IDF leadership was unconvinced: this raid was nothing short of chaotic, with the sole result of one Iraqi Hunter crashing on take-off, and two other IrAF fighters damaged in the air. The IDF/AF thus ordered a third raid on H-3 for the morning of 7 June.

ULTIMATE CLASH

In the meantime, during the night from 5 to 6 June, two groups of RJAF Hunter-pilots travelled by bus to Iraq. At H-3, the commander of the Taqqaddum AB, Colonel Hamid Shaaban at-Tikriti, ordered them to continue for the old Habbaniya AB, because he had meanwhile evacuated of all the remaining aircraft from the exposed airfield. Most of the Jordanians – accompanied by Pakistani Air Force pilot Saif-ul-Azam, who served a tour of duty with the RJAF – reached their destination late in the evening of 6 June. Early the next morning, they were called to the local command centre and then assigned to fly CAPs over the H-3 airfield. The first CAP was launched at 07:00hrs and included a pair of Hunters piloted by the Jordanian pilot Jasser Zayyad and an Iraqi pilot. They flew their

Hamid Sha'ban at-Tikriti served as the commander of Taqqaddum AB and was in overall charge of operations from H-3 during the June 1967 War with Israel. (Ahmad Sadik Collection)

Dror (left) and Glantz-Golan as PoWs in Iraq. (Ahmad Sadik Collection)

Pre-delivery photograph of Hunter F.Mk 59 with serial number 578, showing the handsome lines of this type. According to Iraqi records, Ihsan Shurdom flew this aircraft during his sortie over the H-3 airfield on 7 June 1967. (Albert Grandolini Collection)

mission as ordered, landed at H-3 to refuel, flew another patrol and then returned to Habbaniya AB. At 10:15hrs, a division of four Hunters took off, piloted by the Pakistani pilot Saif-ul-Azam, with Jordanian Ihsan Shurdom as wingman. The rear pair of fighters was piloted by the Iraqis Samir Yousif Zainal and Galeb al-Hameed al-Qaysee. They were to fly a similar mission to the pair before them, including a refuelling stop at H-3.

However, the Israelis came in between: at 10:22hrs, four Vautours escorted by four Mirage IIICJs launched from Ramat David AB for the third Israeli attack. Although approaching at low altitude, this formation was detected by the Iraqis while still about 10km (6.2 miles) from its target, and Shaaban promptly raised Saf-ul-Azam on the radio to advise them to attack.[21] The Pakistani and his Jordanian wingman dove to attack two Vautours as these were bombing the runway, while the Iraqis attacked two Mirages, but, while still in a dive, Azam decided to cross over his formation. Before the Hunters could complete this manoeuvre, the Mirages broke hard, forcing both Iraqis to overshoot: one of the Israelis then hit and shot down the jet flown by Qaysee. Spinning out of control, the aircraft crashed into a fuel tank, instantly killing its pilot. Azam attacked the same Mirage, and claimed it as shot down by the fire from his 30mm ADEN cannons: the Israeli ejected safely and was taken prisoner by Iraqi Army troops only minutes later. Another Mirage attempted to intervene, and claimed another Hunter shot down but actually hit nothing: on the contrary, short on fuel, and trying to disengage, the Israeli formation was now to receive a series of blows. Azam outmanoeuvred one of the Vautours and shot it down with gunfire from such a short range that his Hunter was damaged by the debris. Simultaneously, Zainal attacked another Vautour and fired at it until seeing two ejection seats separating: his target then exploded. Whether shot down by Azam or by Zainal, another Israeli pilot was thus captured only a few hundred meters away from the first. Continuing his attack, Zainal pursued a Vautour and then a Mirage into Jordanian airspace, claiming hits on both before having to break for the lack of fuel. Both Israeli jets were last seen distancing towards the west while trailing smoke. Back over H-3, Saif-ul-Azam decided to return to Habbaniya. He was followed by Shurdom: both returned on their last drops of fuel. Zainal could not manage it back to his base, but landed at H-3 to refuel, despite the damaged runway. He returned to Habbaniya AB slightly over an hour later.

Eventually, Azam, Shurdom, and Zainal each claimed to have shot down two Israelis (for a total of six), and the IrAF officially credited each of them with two aerial victories. The lonesome battery of 100mm anti-aircraft guns was credited with another kill, for a total of seven. The Israelis officially admitted the loss of three of their aircraft and four crewmembers, two of which were captured by the Iraqis, while two were subsequently found dead inside the wreckage of a Vautour that crashed on Saudi territory. Expecting additional Israeli raids, Shaaban continued dispatching further CAPs over H-3 during the afternoon and for the next two days: however, the IDF/AF never came back to bomb this airfield again.[22]

8

SHOPPING SPREE

Although the entire Arab world was stunned by the swiftness and unexpectedness of the Israeli victory in June 1967, the government in Baghdad took good care to keep away the magnitude of the defeat from the people of Iraq. The IrAF prided itself with a major victory over the H-3 airfield and had all involved commanders and pilots – as well as the Pakistani Azam and the Jordanian Shurdom – highly decorated. Instead, after a numbed pause, it was allegations of widespread corruption, followed by mass demonstrations in Baghdad and other major cities that caused the Arif government to lose prestige and popularity. The president reacted by resigning his position as Prime Minister, and appointing Taher Yahya instead, who – aware of the true extent of the defeat, and the fact that the Palestine crisis was far from over – then launched the next massive expansion of the armed forces.

OLD PRACTICES

Theoretically, Yahya's decision was to bring plenty of good news for the IrAF. Just as the Army was authorised to establish six new divisions (including two armoured), the air force was authorised to purchase up to 100 new aircraft. Logically, such a step first required a massive expansion of the Air Force College, in order to enable it to train the necessary pilots and ground crews. Correspondingly, on 18 July 1967, during a visit to Prague by a delegation led by President Arif, a contract was signed for – amongst others – 20 (later increased to 40) Aero L-29 Delfin jet trainers. Partially because Czechoslovakia (which provided most of the armoured vehicles for the two newly-established armoured divisions) was unable to provide tactical combat aircraft, but also because the Soviets offered very favourable payment conditions and quick deliveries, only a few days later Arif signed an order for 20 additional Su-7BMKs in Moscow. Together with the aircraft from the first batch, these big fighter-bombers were used to re-equip No. 1 Squadron (officially declared operational on the Su-7BMKs on 3 December 1967), and then the re-established No. 5 Squadron (declared operational on the type in November 1968). To accelerate the training of additional pilots, in 1968 the IrAF then contracted the Czechoslovaks to convert 20 students fresh from the Air Force College to Su-7BMKs.[1]

Around the same time that Baghdad signed the first order for L-29s, the Iraqi representatives in Paris entered into talks with the French authorities over a possible acquisition of Mirage III fighter-bombers – which, so it appeared to at least a few of the IrAF's officers, had defeated three major Arab air forces during the June 1967 Arab-Israeli War, two of which were entirely equipped with Soviet-made combat aircraft. Unexpectedly, the French proved reluctant and the talks went on for weeks and then months. Therefore, on 25 September 1967, Arif deployed a higher-positioned delegation to Paris with the aim of making a better offer. Even then, it was only in December 1967 that France signalled it preparedness to enter an economic agreement with Iraq and to supply combat aircraft and military equipment: a French military mission then visited Iraq in January 1968, while on 7 February Arif paid an official visit to Paris, followed by an Iraqi military mission. Finally, on 6 April 1968, the French government announced that it had signed a contract for the supply of 54 Dassault Mirage 5s, 46 Sud-Est (later Aerospatiale) SE.316C Alouette III helicopters, and AML-60 and AML-90 armoured cars.[2]

However, the longer the related negotiations lasted, the more opposition to this deal emerged in the French public. Leftist activists launched a public campaign requesting President Charles de Gaulle *not* to supply military material to Iraq 'until the Kurdish problem had been addressed' – to their satisfaction. Already overbooked by a mass of orders for Mirages and other equipment it received from elsewhere after the June 1967 War, the French industry saw little incentive: unsurprisingly, Paris had second thoughts. Moreover the longer the negotiations took, the bigger the opposition to a Mirage-deal became within the IrAF: while an internal study of the air force's High Command concluded that the French fighter-bomber would provide the capability to support ground troops more accurately, carrying heavier bomb loads over longer ranges than any of the available Soviet-made aircraft, and that it could still protect itself against enemy interceptors – an increasing number of officers opposed the idea of having to build-up the necessary support infrastructure. Others declared the Mirage not only 'excessively costly' in comparison to Soviet aircraft (an Iraqi calculation showed that the IrAF could buy three MiG-21s for the price of a single Mirage IIIC), but objected to both the protracted delivery schedules and the long training required for pilots and ground personnel. Furthermore, Soviet representatives in Baghdad did their best to dissuade the government from buying French aircraft. The final nail in the coffin of the Iraqi Mirage deal was delivered by the next two coup d'états in Baghdad that took place in quick succession.

RETURN OF THE BA'ATH PARTY

Through 1967 and early 1968, disaffection with the policies of President Abd ar-Rahman Arif continued to spread: conservative Iraqis were dissatisfied with his support for the leftists, others wanted to improve relations with the West (and the USA in particular), Leftists were deeply disappointed with his failure to address growing economic and social problems, while one of the splinter groups of the ICP launched a low-scale insurgency in southern Iraq. The general impression was that Arif was a 'weak leader' and 'allowing things to drift'. The best-organised political party was meanwhile the Ba'ath, which – although working in deepest secrecy – drawing

Brigadier-General (later Major-General) Jassam Muhammed ash-Shaher commanded the IrAF during the troublesome times of the mid-1960s. Born in 1914, Shaher originally graduated as a technician in 1937 but then re-qualified as a pilot, earning his wings a year later. He underwent staff college in the UK in the 1940s and was the commander of the Royal Flight for much of the 1950s. Although retired early following the 14 Tammuz Revolution, he returned to service in 1963 and served as commander of the IrAF from 22 September 1966 until another early retirement after the coup of 17 July 1968. (Ahmad Sadik Collection)

lessons from experiences of 1963, not only began making links to politicised military officers but, indeed, with some of Arif's closest aides. Thus came into being the circle including not only Major-General Hardan Tikriti, the former commander of the IrAF, but also Major-Generals Ahmed Hassan al-Bakr, Abd el-Aziz al-Uqayli, and Naji Talib (the latter was a Shia from an-Nasiriyah). Convinced they must become a driving force on the Iraqi political scene, they then invited several other parties – including the ICP – to cooperate but were turned down. Instead, they ended up establishing ties to the commanders of the GMID, the Republican Guard, and a newly-established 10th Armoured Brigade, which was subordinated to the Republican Guard. Once their cooperation was secured, the Ba'ath mobilised and armed its members. Although multiple security services had meanwhile warned the president about the growing threat, and Bakr and other officers repeatedly – and publicly – demanded that he initiate changes in his policy, at least to dismiss the Prime Minister Tahir Yahya – Arif failed to react.[3]

Although not assigned to No. 23 Squadron – which was considered akin to a 'flying praetorian guard' for Arif's government during the last two years of its tenure – Freighters continued serving with No. 3 Squadron well into the 1970s. This photograph shows serial number 331 at around the time of the 17 July 1968 'revolution'. (Albert Grandolini Collection)

Almost exactly 10 years after the 14 Tammuz Revolution, at 02:00hrs on 17 July 1968, officers of the GMID seized the Ministry of Defence, elements of the Republican Guards secured the Broadcasting House, while a group of officers led by Bakr and Tikriti, with elements of the 10th Armoured Brigade, surrounded the presidential palace. Guaranteed safe conduct, Arif was then escorted to Baghdad International and placed on an airliner to London. At dawn, the Ba'ath party officers of the 10th Armoured Brigade secured the Abu Ghraib area, while aircraft of the IrAF – now again under the command of Hardan Tikriti – demonstratively overflew Baghdad. Once in control, the Ba'ath party formed the Revolutionary Command Council (RCC) as a government: presided by Major-General Ahmed Hassan al-Bakr, this included Prime Minister Abd ar-Razzaq an-Nayif, several officers involved in the coup, and also civilians, including four Kurds. However, immediately after the coup, it became clear that the RCC was unable to move forward: this time there was a rift between the right and the left wing of the party. To solve the problem, the military wing – still led by Bakr – recalled to service 117 officers retired by Arif's government and arranged a new coup. On 30 July, tanks of the 10th Armoured Brigade entered the capital and occupied all key positions once again. The prime minister was then appointed ambassador to Morocco, seated in an airliner and sent out of the country. Bakr retained the presidency only to unleash the Ba'ath militia – led by his young relative Saddam Hussein at-Tikriti (who was not a military officer) – to purge not only the rest of the party and the military, but indeed to impose itself upon all elements of Iraqi society.[4] In a series of merciless and violent operations, all of which were declared to be 'in the interest of consolidating the Ba'ath' but actually served the purpose of securing his position, Saddam then systematically secured control of the state apparatus.

NEW WAR WITH THE KURDS

On 21 September 1968, Bakr and his aides issued a new, Provisional Constitution: while providing a parliamentary form of government, this entrusted all the legislative and executive powers to the RCC. Simultaneously, and in order to secure the – still fragile – position of the Ba'ath, it included a comprehensive agrarian reform and a proposal for a solution to the Kurdish problems. Considering Iraqi Kurdistan to be an integral part of the Arab world, the Ba'ath insisted that Kurdish self-determination would be impossible, but proposed the same form of cooperation to Mustafa Barzani as it already maintained with Jalal Talabani (who meanwhile crystallised as the leader of the left-wing streams amongst the Kurds). Barzani, who had meanwhile established himself as the representative of the traditional feudal wing of the Kurds, reacted by conditioning his agreement on the RCC ceasing its support for Talabani and, when Bakr refused, he withdrew his representative from Baghdad in disgust.[5]

In an attempt to demonstrate its power, the RCC reacted by deploying 12 brigades (out of a total of 16 that the army had at the time) on the frontlines opposite to the positions of Barzani's insurgents. On 3 January 1969, these launched an offensive with the aim of securing the territory from

A largely forgotten consequence of Iraq joining the Baghdad Pact were the small-scale deliveries of US-made arms during the mid-1950s. These included six Cessna O-1A Bird Dog light observation and liaison aircraft. All were painted black overall and received white serials. This photograph shows serial number 415. They remained in service long enough to serve as FACs during the campaign fought against Barzani's Peshmerga in 1969. (Pit Weinert Collection)

Due to the good combination of range and a payload of up to 3,000kg (6,600lbs) of bombs, Il-28 bombers saw intensive service during all of the Iraqi campaigns against Barzani's insurgents in the 1960s. Even the two Il-28BMs (a little-known target-towing variant, shown here) became involved in combat operations. (Pit Weinert Collection)

Throughout 1968-1969, the ferocity of operations against the Barzani-led insurgency reached such proportions that even MiG-17PF interceptors of No. 7 Squadron were deployed to fly ground attacks. This rare air-to-air photograph (taken from a MiG-15UTI) shows Mig-17PF serial number 460. (via Ali Tobchi)

Ruwanduz in the north to Sulaimyaniyah in the south. Taken by surprise, and shaken by air strikes and artillery barrages, the insurgents fell back: by the time it was forced to stop the operation due to bad weather, three weeks later, the Army had thus secured Penjwin and Kala-Diza, while Talabani took Chwarta and Mahvout. At that point in time, Bakr's government found itself confronted not only by the winter in northern Iraq, but also by the Empire of Iran, where the government of the Shah Reza Pahlavi opposed the Ba'ath's socialist and Arab nationalist rhetoric, and – with US support – sought to establish its regional hegemony. As well as providing arms to Barzani (including artillery pieces), in January 1969 the Shah put forward a claim on Bahrain, and then reopened the question of correcting the border with Iraq, especially along the Shatt al-Arab. In an attempt to avoid the inevitable, the RCC declared its return to the Bazzaz Declaration, but it was too late: on 1 March 1969, Mustafa Barzani's insurgents attacked several oil installations in the Kirkuk area, temporarily paralysing oil production, and then recovered Kala-Diza and Mahvout. The Iraqi Army reacted with a renewal of its offensive, but by the time the weather improved, the ground combatants on both sides were completely exhausted. Therefore, in April the government ordered the IrAF into a new air policing campaign: according to Kurdish reports, over 100 villages were bombed, killing 730 civilians. The operation ended only later the same month, when the GMID reported a concentration of Iranian troops deployed along the border: this forced the General Headquarters in Baghdad to order an end of the offensive against Barzani, and a re-deployment of army units to the southern portions of the border.[6]

By June 1969, the RCC and the Ba'ath found themselves without choice but to renew negotiations with Barzani. Nevertheless, and while the talks were still going on, in August Bakr ordered another offensive, this time with the main objectives being Zakho, Raniay, Kala-Diza, and Mahvout. Although heavily supported by the IrAF, the 30,000 Army troops not only completely failed to reach any of their objectives, but also suffered a major setback when the insurgents attacked and heavily damaged a base outside Dukan, destroying up to 30 tanks in the process. The operation petered out by early October, by when the air force was back to air policing, which – reportedly – destroyed 120 villages and forced 200,000 civilians to take refuge in the mountains.[7]

YET MORE MIGS

Ultimately, through December 1969 and early 1970, the government was forced to reach a new agreement with Barzani: under this, the Kurds of Iraq were not only granted the right to cultivate their nationality, but also to take part in the rule through admission of five of their ministers to the government, and to administer their areas by their own representatives. While thus securing not only their own position vis-à-vis other political parties and movements, and then at least some objectives against Barzani, Bakr and the RCC also went through a major showdown with the restive Shia hierarchy. In response to the Shah's demands, they expelled thousands of

A pre-delivery photograph of three Zlin Z.526Fs manufactured for Iraq – and already decorated with the crest of the IrAF and Iraqi national markings. (via Tom Cooper)

A row of L-29s decorated with the IrAF crest and gaudy red insignia, as common for aircraft assigned to the Air Force College and later the Air Force Academy, seen at Sahra AB shortly after their introduction to service in the early 1970s. (Ahmed Hassan Collection)

Iranian religious students, followed by roughly 20,000 people of – allegedly – Iranian descent, in 1969 and 1970. When the Shia clergy organised days-long mass-demonstrations in Baghdad, Najaf, Karbala and Basra, the RCC and the Ba'ath reacted by deploying the Army to disperse the demonstrators, arrest their leaders, and then proceeded with confiscations of religious endowments in Najaf, and a general ban on religious schools and processions. As soon as the situation quietened down, in September 1970 the RCC abolished the state of emergency, released most of the political prisoners (including several former prime ministers and numerous generals), and lifted censorship.[8]

Simultaneously, Bakr took care to award the armed forces – which had not only suffered due to the purges after the coups of 1968 but were also worn out by renewed fighting with the Kurds – through a renewed attempt at bolstering their capabilities. With lengthy negotiations for French arms ending nowhere, Baghdad turned to Moscow once again: an Iraqi military delegation visited the Soviet Union in September 1968 to request additional aircraft. Still preoccupied with the Czechoslovakia Crisis, Moscow was slow to react, and thus another delegation repeated the exercise in May 1969: this time, the Iraqis were much more successful, and signed a contract for the delivery of 98 MiG-21s, three additional An-12BPs and seven Antonov An-24V medium transports, 10 additional MiG-15UTIs, and four S-125 Pechora (ASCC/NATO-codename 'SA-3 Goa') SAM-systems with 48 missiles. Later the same year, orders for arms from Czechoslovakia were placed, including 25 Zlin Z.526F and 15 Zlin Z.526FI basic trainers, and 10 second-hand MiG-15UTIs. Combined, the two contracts represented the largest arms acquisition in the history of Iraq up to that point.[9]

The Zlins and additional MiG-15UTIs were necessary for the ongoing expansion of the Air Force College into the Air Force Academy, which culminated with the opening of the newly-constructed Sahra AB, outside Tikrit, in the late spring of 1970. The Soviets were slightly slower with deliveries of new aircraft than usual: the reason was that most of these consisted of MiG-21MFs, which entered production only in 1972. Instead, the Soviets promptly delivered the transports, followed – in 1971 – by a batch each of 12 MiG-21UM two-seat conversion trainers and MiG-21R reconnaissance

An extremely rare photograph of one of 12 MiG-21RFs acquired by Iraq through an order placed in May 1969. The jet is recognisable as belonging to this reconnaissance variant from the installation of a reconnaissance pod under the centreline, and was delivered painted in silver-grey overall (see colour section for details). (Ahmad Sadik Collection)

Another rarity is this photograph of MiG-21PFM serial number 863 – one from the second batch of this variant, delivered in 1969-1970. Note the GP-9 pod with the 23mm GSh-23 twin-barrel gun under the centreline. (Ahmad Sadik Collection)

fighters. While the former were used to convert the necessary pilots, the latter entered service with Rashid AB-based No. 70 Squadron, the first-ever dedicated reconnaissance asset of the IrAF. The introduction to service of SA-3s came forward much faster: after the necessary personnel were trained at Krasnovodisk, on the Caspian Sea (in presentday Turkmenistan), all four batteries of these (each was operated by one battalion) entered service with the 125th Air Defence Brigade in late 1971.[10]

SUKHOI CLIQUE

If the Ottoman military education taught the future top brass of the Iraqi armed forces

The relatively small fleet of An-12BPs of No. 23 Squadron provided sterling service during all the campaigns against the Kurds in the 1960s and the early 1970s. In addition to use as a transport, the type was deployed as a makeshift bomber by disgorging loads of Soviet-made FAB-250M-46, FAB-250M-54 and FAB-500M-54 bombs over the rear loading ramp. (Albert Grandolini Collection)

TABLE 8: SERIAL NUMBERS OF IrAF AIRCRAFT, 1958-1970

SERIAL	AIRCRAFT TYPE	NOTES
421-422	Il-28U	delivered in January 1959; c/ns 65009808 and 65009520
423-439	Il-28	delivered in 1959; known c/ns 56605703/425; 56605704/426; 56605717/427; 56606206/430; 56606540/432, and 56606207/434
440-451	MiG-17F	16 delivered early 1959
452-469	MiG-17PF	17 delivered in 1959-1960
470-477	Yak-18	12-16 ordered in 1959, taken up but never pressed into service
478-481	Mi-4	12 ordered in 1958
482-483	Yak-18	
484	Mi-4	delivered in 1959
485-488	An-2	10 delivered from early 1959
489-494	MiG-19S	50 delivered from 1959; only 16 entered service
495	Il-14	1 delivered in 1959
496-497	Mi-4	2 delivered in 1960
498	MiG-19S	
499	Mi-4	1 delivered in 1960
500-504	MiG-19S	
505-507	An-12BP	8 ordered, 3 delivered from 1962
508-517	Tu-16	10 delivered from October 1962
518-521	MiG-19S	
522-537	MiG-21F-13	16 delivered from 1962
538-549	MiG-15UTI	11 delivered from 1962
550-557	Mi-4	
558-559	Tu-16	
560-563	Il-28	possibly acquired from Egypt, 1960-1962
564-565	Il-28BM	ex-Il-28Rs c/n 5901703 and 5901801 delivered 1963
566	Tu-16	
567-569	Hunter T.Mk 66	3 delivered April 1964, serial 567 issued to three different T.Mk. 66/66A/69s over the time
570-587	Hunter F.Mk 59	18 delivered 18 Mar 1964 – 14 Jan 1965
588-599	Wessex HU.Mk 52	12 delivered from 1964
600-619	Jet Provost T.Mk 52	20 delivered from 1964
620-624	unknown	
626-627	Hunter T.Mk 69	2 delivered 17 Jan 1965
628-633	Hunter F.Mk 59A	6 delivered 14 Jan 1965 – Apr 1965
634-635	Tu-124	2 delivered in 1965
636-638	An-12	3 delivered Feb 1966 – Nov 1968
639-656	MiG-21FL	17 delivered Dec 1965 – Jan 1966; designated MiG-21PFM in Soviet documentation
657-661	Hunter F.Mk 59B	5 delivered Dec 1965 – May 1966
662-664	Hunter F.Mk 59B	3 delivered Sep 1965
665-677	Hunter F.Mk 59B	13 delivered 8 Sep 1966 – 13 May 1967
678-680	Mi-4	3 delivered in 1966
681-684	MiG-21FL	4 delivered in 1966
685-686	An-12BP	2 delivered in 1967
687-705	MiG-21FL	36 ordered, 18 delivered in 1966-1967
706-727	MiG-21F-13	22 delivered in 1967-1968
728	MiG-17F	
729-737	MiG-21PFM	10 ordered, 8 delivered in 1967

TABLE 8: SERIAL NUMBERS OF IrAF AIRCRAFT, 1958-1970		
SERIAL	**AIRCRAFT TYPE**	**NOTES**
735-754	L-29	19 delivered in Jan-Feb 1968 (serials overlapping with MiG-21PFMs)
755-774	Su-7BMK	20 delivered in 1967-1968
775-794	L-29	19 delivered Oct-Dec 1968
795-796	unknown	
797-804	An-24V	7 delivered in 1968
805-807	An-12BP	3 delivered in 1968
808-817	Su-7BMK	10 delivered in 1968-1969
818-840?	MiG-21PFM, MiG-21R, MiG-21US	26 ordered, 22 delivered in 1969-1970
845-?	MiG-15UTI	10 second-hand aircraft from Czechoslovakia, delivered 1969
857-869	MiG-21PFM	12 delivered in 1970
870-873	Su-7BMK	4 delivered in 1970
874	MiG-15UTI	probably Czechoslovak-built
875-877	unknown	either L-29, MiG-15UTI or Su-7BMK
878	MiG-15UTI	
879-880	unknown	either L-29, MiG-15UTI and Su-7BMK
881-885	Su-7BMK	14 delivered in 1971
886	L-29	
887-898	Su-7BMK	
899-905	unknown	either L-29 or MiG-15UTI
906-908	MiG-15UTI?	
909	MiG-15UTI	
910-915	unknown	either L-39 or MiG-15UTI
916-940	Z.526F	25 delivered in 1971; 920 and 922 also used on MiG-17Fs
941-955	Z.526AF	15 delivered in 1971
956-957	MiG-21US	delivered in 1971; 956 re-serialled as 21012 in 1989

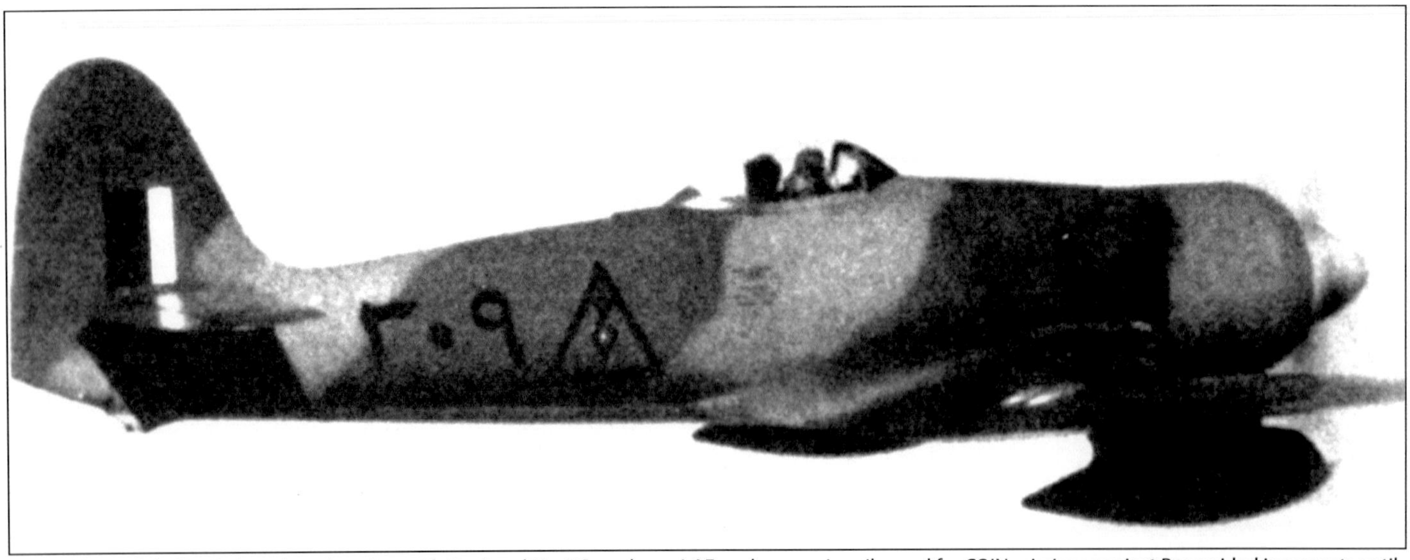

Venerable 'Baghdad Furies' continued serving with No. 1 and No. 7 Squadrons, IrAF, and were primarily used for COIN missions against Barzani-led insurgents until replaced by Su-7BMKs in 1967-1969. (Albert Grandolini Collection)

about the 'advantages' of a strong military-controlled state, and the local military schools indoctrinated them with nationalism and pan-Arabism, decades of British influence taught the IrAF that if it acquired specific types of aircraft and then spent a specific number of hours of training in navigation, aerial gunnery and ground attack, this would be 'enough' to achieve the same level of proficiency as the RAF. The experiences from running air policing operations had largely confirmed some of this. However, the experiences from fighting Israel in 1948 and 1967, and from fighting Barzani's insurgency in 1961-1970, should have brought to the light the fact that merely adopting the British technology and training, and then adopting the Soviet technology to the British training, did not 'automatically' result in a true growth of the IrAF's capabilities.[11] The reasons were complex and primarily evolved around the fact that the CGS in Baghdad was always provided by the Army, that the Army was the sole body in Iraq running serious studies of strategy and tactics, and that the Air Force was thus dominated by the Army. Indoctrinated to ignore lessons from 1941, and lacking understanding of the full flexibility and fire-power of modern air power, Army officers were then lulled into a false sense of security during the fighting against Barzani-led insurgencies because they not only lacked air power, but even serious anti-aircraft defences. Their conclusion was simple: air power was little more than 'flying artillery' or perhaps something like 'extended-range air defence' should the need arise: it was a branch with tactical, rather than operational or even strategic reach. Moreover, experience from fighting Barzani's insurgents taught the Army officers that quantity and the quick acquisition of additional arms would matter more than the quality. The Soviets were providing exactly that, and then at favourable terms, and their aircraft also proved simpler to maintain and operate than those made in the West. Moreover, they earned themselves the reputation of being sturdy and survivable of combat damage. Consequently, during the late 1960s and in the early 1970s the IrAF continued purchasing ever more of the Soviet-made aircraft. The acquisitions were accompanied with the deployment of ever more and ever larger groups of Iraqi students to the USSR and Czechoslovakia for training purposes. Gradually, they completely replaced the British-trained personnel, and then began climbing up the chain of command to influential positions. Thus came into being what was internally known as the 'Sukhoi Clique': a group of well-positioned IrAF officers that insisted on ever further acquisitions of the Soviet-made equipment, regardless of its limited capabilities in regards of payload and endurance, and even though the air forces elsewhere around the globe began to emphasise the acquisition of ever more advanced electronic equipment, which the Soviets proved unable to deliver. The ultimate result was a lack of vision for the future, and the IrAF having its technological development severely curtailed for years in advance. It took painful experiences from two additional wars for this to change and the Sukhoi Clique to lose some of its influence: that story is to be told in Volume 2.[12]

TABLE 9: COMMANDERS OF THE RIrAF AND THE IrAF, 1931-1970

PERIOD	NAME	BACKGROUND & NOTES
1930-1931	Flight-Lieutenant Natiq Muhammad Khalil at-Tayi	pilot, 1st administrator
22 Apr 1931 – 1 Feb 1932	Major Mohammed Ali Jawad	infantry officer (first official commander of the RIrAF)
2 Apr 1932 – 17 Nov 1933	Lieutenant-Colonel Ibrahim Hamdi ar-Rawi	cavalry officer
18 Nov 1933 – 18 Jan 1936	Brigadier-General Ismail Ibrahim Namaq	cavalry officer
19 Jan 1936 – 14 Jun 1936	General Shakir Abdul Wahhab	infantry officer
18 Jun 1936 – 2 Nov 1936	Brigadier-General Khalid al-Zahrawi	infantry officer
2 Nov 1936 – 11 Aug 1937	Colonel Mohammed Ali Jawad	2nd tenure, re-qualified as pilot
12 Aug 1937 – 14 Aug 1937	Colonel Shakir al-Wadi	administrator
15 Aug 1937 – 11 Oct 1937	Lieutenant-colonel Salah ad-Din as-Sabagh	cavalry officer
12 Oct 1937 – 10 Jun 1938	Colonel Akram Mushtak	pilot
11 Jun 1938 – 30 May 1941	Lieutenant-Colonel, then Colonel Mahmoud Salman al-Januby	cavalry officer, re-qualified as pilot
1 Jun 1941 – 2 May 1954	Lieutenant-Colonel, later General Sami Fattah al-Musli	pilot
3 May 1954 – 2 Oct 1954	General Munir Abbass Hilmi Moheidin	Engineer (one of first 16 technicians of the RIrAF)
3 Nov 1954 – 14 Jul 1958	Colonel, later Brigadier-General Abdul Kadhim Abaddi	pilot (last commander of the RIrAF)
14 Jul 1958 – 7 Feb 1963	Colonel, later Brigadier-General Jalal Jaffar al-Awqati	pilot (first commander of the IrAF)
8 Feb 1963 – 1 Mar 1963	Colonel Arif Abd ar-Razzaq	pilot
2 Mar 1963 – 5 Dec 1963	Brigadier-General Hardan Abd el-Rhefal at-Tikriti	pilot
17 Dec 1963 – 6 Sep 1965	Brigadier-General Arif Abd ar-Razzaq	pilot
11 Sep 1965 – 21 Sep 1966	General Munir Abbas Hilmi Moheidin	2nd tenure
22 Sep 1966 – 17 Jul 1968	Brigadier-General Jassam Muhammed ash-Shaher	pilot
17 Jul 1968 – Jul 1970	Major-General Hardan Abd el-Rhefal at-Tikriti	2nd tenure; dismissed and forced into exile in 1970

BIBLIOGRAPHY

PRIMARY DOCUMENTS

Written excerpts and photographs from private documentation of following veteran IrAF pilots were provided by Brigadier-General Ahmad Sadik:

- Mohammad Ahmad
- Fayez Baqir
- Rabee' Dulaymi
- Jameel Salwan
- Mohammad Saaydon ('Pilot Memoir', privately published document from 2005)
- Mohammad Salman
- Major-General Haytham Khattab Omar ('Memoirs of the Commander of the Iraqi Air Force')

Air Ministry (UK), files as listed in endnotes

British Defence Attaché in Iraq (UK), files as listed in endnotes

CIA, *Iraq's Air Force: Improving Capabilities, Ineffective Strategy; An Intelligence Assessment*, October 1987, CIA/FOIA/ERR

DIA, *Electronic Warfare Forces Study – Iraq*, 9 August 1990, National Archives

Foreign Office (UK), files as listed in endnotes

Foreign Technologies Division (USAF), *Fishbed C/E Aerial Tactics* (tactical manual for MiG-21F-13, MiG-21PF, MiG-21FL and MiG-21PFM, obtained from Iraq in 1963 and translated to English by the Foreign Technologies Division USAF, in 1964)

Iraqi Air Force & Air Defence Command, *An Analytical Study on the Causes of Iraqi Aircraft Attrition during the Iran-Iraq War* (in Arabic), (self-published for internal use, May 1991; English transcription provided by Sadik)

Iraqi Air Force & Air Defence Command, *The Role of the Air Force and Air Defence in the Mother of All Battles: After Action Report* (in Arabic), (self-published for internal use, 5 November 1991, captured in 2003 and translated as 'A 1991 Dossier on the Role of the Iraqi Air Force in the Gulf War', by the US Department of Defence-sponsored Conflict Records Research Center (CRRC Record Number SH-AADF-D-000-396) in the course of the 'Project Harmony')

Iraqi Air Force Martyrs Website, 1931-2003, *iraqiairforcememorial.com*

Iraqi Ministry of Foreign Affairs, *Iraqi Air Force Aircraft flown to Iran, in 1991* (in Arabic), (letter to the General Secretary of the UN, September 1991)

IRIAF, *204 KIA and 58 POW pilots of the Sacred Defence* (in Farsi), (self-published for internal use, listing 204 IRIAF pilots and crewmembers that were killed and 58 that were captured during the war with Iraq by their full rank and name, aircraft they flew, date of their death or captivity; date and place of issue unknown; copy provided by Farzin Nadimi)

Ministry of Defence (UK), files as listed in endnotes

Office of Naval Intelligence (USA), files as listed in endnotes

BIBLIOGRAPHY

Alnasrawi, A., *The Economy of Iraq: Oil, Wars, Destruction of Development and Prospects, 1950-2010* (Westport: Greenwood Press, 1994)

Awardi, A al-, *History of the Iraqi Armed Forces, Part 17: Establishment of the Iraqi Air Forces and its Development* (in Arabic) (Baghdad: Ministry of Defence, 1988; translation by Ali Tobchi)

Bergquist, Maj R. E., *The Role of Airpower in the Iran-Iraq War* (Maxwell AFB: Air University Press, 1988)

Boutz, G. M., Williams, K. H., *U. S. Relations with Iraq: From the Mandate to Operation Iraqi Freedom* (Air Force History and Museums Program: Washington D.C., 2015)

Cooper, T. & Salti, P., *Hawker Hunters at War: Iraq and Jordan, 1958-1967* (Solihull: Helion & Co., 2016)

Cooper, T. & Santana, S., *Lebanese Civil War, Volume 1: Palestinian Diaspora, Syrian and Israeli Interventions, 1970-1978* (Warwick: Helion & Co., 2019)

Cooper, T. & Sipos, M., *Iraqi Mirages: The Dassault Mirage Family in Service with the Iraqi Air Force, 1981-1988* (Warwick: Helion & Co., 2019)

Cooper, T., *Hot Skies over Yemen, Volume 1: Aerial Warfare over the Southern Arabian Peninsula, 1962-1994* (Solihull: Helion & Co., 2017)

Cooper, T., *MiG-23 Flogger in the Middle East: Mikoyan I Gurevich MiG-23 in Service in Algeria, Egypt, Iraq, Libya and Syria, 1973-2018* (Warwick: Helion & Co., 2018)

Cooper, T., Sadik, Général de Brigade A., Bishop, F., *La guerre Iran-Irak: Les combat aériens, Hors-Serie Avions No. 22 & No. 23* (Outreau: Éditions LELA PRESSE, 2007)

Cull, B., Nicolle, Dr. D., and Aloni, S., *Spitfires over Israel* (London: Grub Street, 1994)

Dildy, Douglas C., Cooper, T., *F-15C Eagle vs MiG-23/25, Iraq 1991* (Oxford: Osprey Publishing, 2016)

Dupuy, Col T. N. and Blanchard, Col. W., *The Almanac of World Military Power* (2nd Edition), (London: Arthur Barker Ltd, 1972)

Fawzy, Major-General M., *The Three-Years War* (in Arabic), (Beirut: Dar Mustakbal al-Arabi, 1998)

Flintham, V., *Air Wars and Aircraft: A Detailed Record of Air Combat 1945 to the Present* (London: Arms and Armour Press, 1989)

Francona, R., *Ally to Adversary: an eyewitness account of Iraq's fall from Grace* (Annapolis: Naval Institute Press, 1999)

Garello, G., 'Les Ailes Italiennes en Iraq (1937-1941)', *Avions,* No. 183 (September-October 2011)

Green, W., and Frickler, J., *The Air Forces of the World* (London: MacDonald, 1958)

Group of Authors, *The Role of the Iraqi Armed Forces in the October 1973 War* (in Arabic), (Beirut: Establishment for Arab Studies and Publication, 1974)

Harrison, W. A., *de Havilland Vampire* (Warpaint Series No. 27), (Milton Keynes: Hall Park Books Ltd., 2004)

Harrison, W. A., *de Havilland Venom* (Warpaint Series No. 44), (Beds: Warpaint Books Ltd., 2005)

Hiro, D., *The Longest War: The Iran-Iraq Military Conflict* (Routledge: Chapman and Hall Inc., 1991)

Hooton, E. R. & Cooper, T., *Desert Storm, Volume 1: The Iraqi Invasion of Kuwait and Operation Desert Shield, 1990-1991* (Warwick: Helion & Co., 2019)

Hooton, E. R., Cooper, T. & Nadimi, F., *The Iran-Iraq War, Volume 1: The Battle for Khuzestan, September 1980-May 1982* (Revised Edition), (Warwick: Helion & Co., 2019)

Hooton, E. R., Cooper, T. & Nadimi, F., *The Iran-Iraq War, Volume 2: Iran Strikes Back, June 1982 – December 1986* (Revised Edition), (Warwick: Helion & Co. 2019)

Hooton, E. R., Cooper, T., & Nadimi, F., *The Iran-Iraq War, Volume 1: The Battle for Khuzestan, September 1980-May 1982* (Solihull: Helion & Co., 2016)

Hooton, E., R., Cooper, T. & Nadimi, F., *The Iran-Iraq War, Volume 2: Iran Strikes back, June 1982 – December 1986* (Solihull: Helion & Co., 2017)

Hooton, E., R., Cooper, T. & Nadimi, F., *The Iran-Iraq War, Volume 3: Iraq's Triumph* (Solihull: Helion & Co., 2017)

Hooton, E., R., Cooper, T. & Nadimi, F., *The Iran-Iraq War, Volume 4: The Forgotten Fronts* (Solihull: Helion & Co., 2018)

Hoyt, T. D., *Military Industry and Regional Defense Policy; India, Iraq and Israel* (Oxon: Routledge, 2007)

Jawadi, Dr. M. al-, *In Between the Catastrophe: Memoirs of Egyptian Military Commanders from 1967 to 1972* (in Arabic) (Cairo: Dar al-Khiyal, 2001)

Jones, B., *Hawker Hunter* (Ramsbury: The Crowood Press Ltd., 1998)

Khalil, S. al-, *Republic of Fear: the inside story of Saddam's Iraq* (London: Hutchinson Radius, 1989)

Liébert, M. & Buyck, S., *Le Mirage F1 et les Mirage de seconde generation à voilure en flèche, Vol.1* (Outreau: Éditions LELA PRESSE, 2007)

Marashi, I. al- & Salama, S., *Iraq's Armed Forces: An Analytical History* (Abingdon: Routledge Middle Eastern Military Studies, 2008)

Mason F. K., *The Hawker Audax & Hardy* (Profile Publications Number 140) (Leatherhead: Profile Publications Ltd., 1972)

Mason, F. K., *The Hawker Sea Fury* (Profile Publications Number 126) (Leatherhead: Profile Publications Ltd., 1971)

Metz, H. C., *Iraq: A Country Study* (Washington: GPO for the Library of Congress, 1988)

Murray, W & Woods, K. M., *The Iran-Iraq War: A Military and Strategic History* (Cambridge: Cambridge University Press, 2014)

Mustafa, General H., *The June War, 1967, Part II* (in Arabic) (Beirut: Establishment for War Studies, 1970)

Nadimi, F., *The Iranian Oil Industry and The Iran-Iraq War of 1980-88* (PhD thesis, The University of Manchester, 2011)

Namaki, A. R., Afghar, Q., Nowroozi, M., Arevan, M.-R., Monadi, V., Yaghoubi, S., Badi'ee, M.-S., Eshghi-Fakour, A. R., *In the Sky of Babylon, Volume 1: History of Iran-Iraq War in the Air* (in Farsi) (IRIAF Strategic Research and Studies Office, 2005)

Navias, S. & Hooton, E. R., *Tanker Wars: The Assault On Merchant Shipping During The Iran-Iraq Conflict, 1980-1988* (New York: I. B. Tauris & Co Ltd., 1996)

Nicolle, Dr. D. & Gabr, Air Vice Marshal G. A., *Air Power and the Arab World, Volume 2, Military Flying Services in the Arab Countries, 1909-1955* (Warwick: Helion & Co., 2020)

Nicolle, Dr. D., 'Fury over Palestine: Egypt and the Palestine War, 1948-1949, Part 3', *Air Enthusiast*, No. 130, July/August 2007

Nicolle, Dr. D., Gabr, Air Vice Marshal G. A., *Air Power and the Arab World, Volume 1, Military Flying Services in the Arab Countries, 1909-1955* (Warwick: Helion & Co., 2019)

O'Ballance, E., *The Gulf War* (London: Brassey's Defence Publishers, 1988)

O'Ballance, E., *The Kurdish Revolt 1961-1970* (London: Faber and Faber Ltd., 1973)

Ott, G., '1941: Als die Luftwaffe für den Irak flog', *Jet & Prop Historie*, 3/91

Perret, B., *Desert Warfare: From its Roman Origins to the Gulf Conflict* (Northamptonshire: Patrick Stephens Ltd., 1988)

Provence, M., *The Great Syrian Revolt and the Rise of Arab Nationalism* (Austin: University of Texas Press, 2005)

Provence, M., *The Last Ottoman Generation and the Making of the Modern Middle East* (Cambridge: Cambridge University Press, 2017)

Raspletin, Dr. A. A., 'History PVO' (website in Russian: *historykpvo.narod2.ru*), 2013

Riad, M., *The Struggle for Peace in the Middle East* (Consett: Quartet Books, 1981)

Richardson, D., *Techniques and Equipment of Electronic Warfare* (London: Salamander Books Ltd., 1985)

Sadik, Brig Gen A. & Cooper, T., 'Les "Mirage" de Baghdad: les Dassault "Mirage" F1 dans la force aérienne irakienne', *Fana de l'Aviation No.* 434/2006; 'Deuxième partie', *Fana de l'Aviation No.* 435/2006

Sadik, Brig Gen A. & Cooper, T., 'Un Falcon 50 lance-missiles: Avion d'affaires contre navire de guerre', *Fana de l'Aviation No. 470* (2007)

Sadik, Brig Gen A., and Cooper, T. *Iraqi Fighters, 1953–2003: Camouflage & Markings* (Houston: Harpia Publishing, 2008)

Salti, P., *The Royal Jordanian Air Force* (Amman: National Press, 2007)

Shakibania, M. & Bibak, S., *Tomcat Fights* (TV documentary, Iran, 2012)

Shalom, D., *Like a Bolt out of the Blue: 'Moked' Operation in the Six Day War, June 1967* (in Hebrew), (Rishon Le-Zion: BAVIR Aviation Publications, 2002)

Sorby, Jr., K., '1941 British-Iraqi War', *Military History* (in Slovakian), 3 December 2008

Sorby, Jr., K., 'Approach of the Ba'ath Party to the Kurdish question in Iraq After 1968', *Asian and African Studies*, Volume 27, Number 2, 2018

Sorby, Jr., K., 'Iraq 1963: The Short Rule of the Ba'ath', *Asian and African Studies*, Vol. 18, 2009

Sorby, Jr., K., 'Iraq Under the Reign of Faysal II (1953-1958)', *Asian and African Studies*, Vol. 13, 2004

Sorby, Jr., K., 'The 1952 Uprising in Iraq and Regent's Role in its Crushing: Iraq from al-Watba to al-Intifada, 1949-1952', *Asian and African Studies*, Vol. 12, 2003

Sorby, Jr., K., 'The Army's Growing Influence in Iraqi Politics (1937-1939)', *Yearbook of Oriental Studies* (in Slovak), T. LXVIII, Z. i. 2015, 20-36, (Bratislava, 2015)

Sorby, Jr., K., *Iraq Under the Rule of 'Abdassalam 'Arif (1963-1966)*, (Bratislava: Institute of Oriental Studies, Slovak Academy of Sciences, 2010)

Sorby, Jr., K., *Iraq: The Rule of Abdarrahman Arif and Its End (1966-1968)*, (Bratislava: Institute of Oriental Studies, Slovak Academy of Sciences, 2011)

Sorby, Jr., K., *The Two July 1968 Coups in Iraq: the Ba'ath is returning to Power* (Bratislava: Institute of Oriental Studies, Slovak Academy of Sciences, 2012)

Spencer, T., *Gloster Gladiator* (Warpaint Series No. 37), (Luton: Warpaint Books, 2000)

Stafrace, C., *Arab Air Forces* (Carrolton: Squadron/Signal Publications Inc., 1994)

Tripp, C., *A History of Iraq* (Cambridge: Cambridge University Press, 2000)

Woods, K. M., Murray, W., Holaday, T., with Elkhamri, M., *Saddam's War: An Iraqi Military Perspective of the Iran-Iraq War* (Washington D.C.: National Defense University, 2009)

Woods, K. M., Murray, W., Nathan, E. A., Sabara, L., Venegas, A. M., *Saddam's Generals: Perspectives of the Iran-Iraq War* (Alexandria: Institute for Defense Analyses, 2010)

Various volumes of *Armed Forces Magazine* (Egyptian Ministry of Defence, 1950s and 1960s); *El-Djeich* (Algerian Ministry of Defence, 2007-2015); various magazines and journals published by the Iraqi Air Force (Iraqi Ministry of Defence, 1970-1995); *Kanatlar* magazine (Turkey), June 2003.

NOTES

CHAPTER 1

1 The first Arab state to attempt establishing an air force was the ill-fated Sharifian Republic in what at the time was Spanish Morocco of 1921-1927. These attempts failed for the lack of aircraft and related expertise. The second – and the first successful – Arab state to do so was the Kingdom of Nejd and Hejaz: in 1921, they acquired their first aircraft (operated by German and Russian pilots), and constructed the first aerodromes outside Mecca and Taif, in 1921-1924. The third became the Imamate of Yemen, which acquired several aircraft and pilots from Italy, and then from Germany, in 1926-1927.
2 Project al-Hussein was related to stretching the range of the Soviet-made R-17E ballistic missile, better known in the West under the designation given to it by the Air Standardisation Coordinating Committee (ASCC) of the North Atlantic Treaty Organisation (NATO) – as 'SS-1c Scud-B'.
3 Unless stated otherwise, this and the following sub-chapters are based on Provence (2017) & Marashi et al, *Iraqi Armed Forces*.
4 Indeed, Mahmoud Shevket Pasha went on to lead units of the Ottoman Army into Istanbul, in July 1909, to force the abdication of Sultan Abd al-Hamid II.
5 Unless stated otherwise, this sub-chapter is based on Perrett (pp.48-58) and Tripp (pp.30-76).
6 For details on early history of civilian and military flying in Iraq, see Nicolle et al, *Arab World and Air Power, Volumes 1 & 2*.
7 Notably, neither of the top military leaders of this campaign – German General von der Goltz and the British General Frederick S. Maude – survived the war: Von der Goltz died of Typhus near Baghdad in April 1916, while Maude died of Cholera, in November 1917.
8 Unless stated otherwise, the rest of this chapter is based on Provence (2017); Marashi et al, *Iraqi Armed Forces;* Barr, *A Line in the Sand* & Nicolle et al, *Air Power & Arab World Vol.2*.
9 Named after the British diplomat Mark Sykes and the French Francois George-Picot, and originally concluded in secrecy in Paris, the Sykes-Picot Treaty was revealed in public by the Bolshevik government of Russia in late 1917. Until today, much of the map of the Middle East still resembles what was drawn by Sykes and Picot.
10 Quote from Article 22 of the Paris Peace Conference of 1919.
11 Due to the multiple blockades by the British and French governments, the findings of the commission led by US diplomats Henry King and Charles Crane were published only three years later, by when the British and the French were firmly entrenched in the Middle East, and their control over former Ottoman provinces had been officially sanctioned by the League of Nations.
12 This is not to say that the future of the Middle East would have been any better without the British and the French, or that the area would have developed into some sort of paradise. On the contrary, there is no doubt that much of the subsequent unrest in this area was common for a situation in which a huge power vacuum emerged following the collapse of an empire, or when non-industrialised nations are in the process of industrialising. However, there is no doubt that the powers deciding about the future of the Middle East from around 1918 until at least the late 1940s were the British and the French. It is impossible to say what the history might look like 'if', and indeed, discussing 'what ifs' is *de-facto* pointless.
13 For details on the French invasion of Syria, see Provence, *The Great Arab Revolt*.
14 Marashi et al, p.17 & Nicolle (2020).

CHAPTER 2

1 Unless stated otherwise, this chapter is based on Provence (2017).
2 Marashi et al, p.20.
3 Notably, as repeatedly stressed by Provence (in *The Last Ottoman Generation*), and contrary to countless reports since (including those by Marashi and Salama), not one of the Arab officers that subsequently served with the Iraqi Army had defected from the Ottoman Army during the First World War. The mass of the Sharifian officers had been captured during the Palestine Campaign in 1917-1918, and then convinced to join Faysal's Arab Uprising while interned in prisoner of war camps. All the others joined Faysal only after the Mudros Armistice.
4 O'Ballance, p.23 & 'Chronological History of the Iraq Levies', *AssyrianLevies.com*, 24 April 2009. Notably, in 1928, the administrative responsibility for the Iraq Levies was transferred from the Colonial Office to the Air Ministry in London, and the headquarters of the unit moved to RAF Hinaidi in Baghdad.
5 Awardi, pp.45 & Marashi et al, pp.20-21.
6 Marashi et al, pp.21-22 & 28. Notably, the Officer School in Iraq – which was open to all students regardless of their ethnic or religious backgrounds – was the first institution in the modern-day Arab world to start translating modern military terminology to Arabic language, and thus replacing the Ottoman terminology.
7 Marashi et al, pp.21-22 & 26.
8 O'Ballance, p.21 & Awardi, p.45. Notably, right from the beginning of all the military training activities in the Mandate of Mesopotamia and then in Iraq, the British authorities developed a 'strong predilection' for praising Assyrians and Armenians for their discipline and loyalty, and Kurds for their diverse skills, while severely – and at every opportunity – criticising 'Arabs'. These were essentially the same officers and other ranks that defeated them at Gallipoli and al-Qut while fighting with the Ottoman Army. Indeed, it was during this period that the 'tradition' of Western patronising of all the 'Arab' armed forces developed that was to give birth to such theories as that of the 'Arab culture of military incompetence', nowadays dominant in all the related reporting in the English language.
9 O'Ballance, pp.21-22 & Marashi et al, p.22. Overall, during the 1920s and the 1930s, the RAF became involved in more than 120 'air policing' operations in Iraq (Marashi et al, p.35).
10 Marashi et al, p.23.
11 Permitted to return to Iraq only a year before, Hashimi was appointed the governor of the desert province of Muntafiq, with the capital in an-Nasiriyah – an area rife with anti-British sentiment – where he exploited the opportunity to establish good relations with the local (predominantly Shia) population and grew immensely rich: famed for his successful service with the Ottoman Army and in the Arab Kingdom of Syria, he established himself as a highly respected and dominant figure on the political scene, exercising strong influence not only in Iraq, but in all of what were now the mandates of Syria, Transjordan and Palestine.
12 Provence, (2017) & Tripp, pp.59-87.
13 Awardi, pp.47-48
14 Awardi, pp.47-48.
15 Awardi, p.50. The first 16 Iraqis qualified as aircraft technicians were Abdullah Mahmoud Shihab, Hatim Hussein, Sayed Mohammed Abbas, Mohammed Abbas, Michel Faihallah, Saeed George, Abbas Ahmed, Abdul Wahab Ali, Sahib ad-Deen Khadhum, Mustafa Hussein, Kamel Khairi, Jassem Mohammed, Sabri Mohammed, Jassem Mohammad ash-Shaher (who went on to serve as the commander of the IrAF, later on), and Yassin an-Nimaa.
16 Awardi, pp.49-51. As an example of this first generation of native Iraqi officers and pilots: Mohammed Ali Jawad was born in Baghdad in 1902, finished a teacher's course in primary school, and then joined the Army. He graduated from the Military School in 1924 and was then sent to the RAF Cranwell Air College on 9 May 1927, from which he graduated on 1 August 1929.
17 Awardi, pp.51-53.
18 According to O'Ballance (p.25), the RAF alone destroyed 1,365 homes during this operation.
19 Awardi, pp.51-53, 120 & O'Ballance, p.24.
20 Provence (2017), pp.209-211 & Awardi, p.48. Notably, Christians, Jews and Kurds were never exempted from general conscription, and thus they served in the Iraqi armed forces exactly as members of all other ethnic and religious groups have served in the Ottoman Army under the constitution of 1908.
21 Born in Kirkuk of 1890, and of Kurdish origin, Siqki belonged to the last generation of Ottoman Army officers that graduated from the General Staff College in 1914. After the Great War, he served in the Army of the Arab Kingdom of Syria, before joining the Iraqi Army in 1921. Favoured by the British, he underwent advanced military education in India and then at Sandhurst, Great Britain, before returning to Iraq in 1932, to receive promotion to the rank of Brigadier-General. Ironically, the British authorities continued praising him as the 'most efficient commander' in the Iraqi Army and were happy to look the other way when he became involved in multiple massacres of Assyrians and Yazidis in 1933-1935. This earned him both a fearful and controversial reputation in Iraq: he was praised as a national hero, but also suspected of favouring promotion of Kurdish officers in the Army and plotting to establish an independent Kurdish state in northern Iraq. For details, see Provence (2017), p.210, and O'Ballance, p.25
22 Originally, Iraq ordered eight DH.80As, but since one was written off in an accident before delivery, a ninth example was acquired as a replacement.
23 Awardi, pp.46-48.
24 Marashi et al, pp.28-29.
25 Established in 1932, the Flying School was initially commanded by Captain Moussa Ali and based at RAF Hinaidi.
26 Arawi, pp.48-50 & 127.
27 Awardi, pp.141-143 & Mason (1972), p.9. Notably, during the mid-1930s, Hawker developed a line of highly adaptable biplanes, including the Fury I single-seat fighter, the two-seat Demon fighter, the two-seat Audax scout bomber, the two-seat Hart trainer, the two-seat Hardy close air support bomber, and the two-seat Hind light bomber. Powered by different versions of the Rolls Royce Kestrel engine, they were sold to several air arms throughout Europe and the Middle East. The variant manufactured for Iraq was named Nisr (Eagle in Arabic): in Great Britain it was also known as the 'Iraqi Audax'.
28 Provence (2017), pp.216-217.
29 Awardi, pp.134-135 & Tripp, pp.83-84.
30 'The Turkish Petroleum Company', U.S. Library of Congress (*countrystudies.us*).

31 Provence (2017), pp.217-218.
32 Provence (2017), pp.241-242.
33 Provence (2017), p.244; Marashi et al, p.48 & Sorby (2015), pp.21-23. Contrary to what is still frequently reported, Hashimi was never supported by the British: the coup against him was launched with at least verbal British support and to prevent him from introducing further reforms rather than in order to prevent him from toppling the king and establishing a dictatorship (any such steps would be perfectly fine with the British as long as they remained in overall control – and certainly preferable to what Sidqi did subsequently). Although the crucial figure and well aware of his key role in putting down the uprisings of 1933-1935, Bakr Sidqi was not the mastermind of the coup: this role was reserved for Himkat Suleiman, who was actually a leftist, yet opposed Hashimi's idea of establishing a republican system of governance and the distribution of state lands.
34 Awardi, p.120 & Marashi et al, p.35.
35 Awardi, pp.64, 66-67.
36 Awardi, pp.141. According to Cull et al (p.23), their original RAF serial numbers were K6140, K6141, K6147, K8005, K8006, K8007, K8011, and N5827. According to Awardi (p.141), the two Gladiators lost in 1940 were piloted by Lieutenant Abdul Razzak an-Naqash, who crashed in bad weather outside Fallujah on 18 February 1940; and by Lieutenant Fakhri Ahmed al-Jabouri, who crashed outside Kirkuk in September 1940. A third Gladiator was written off in early 1941 when Lieutenant Najeeb Naji crashed on take-off from al-Hurriyah AB.
37 Awardi, pp.66-67 & Sadik et al, p.156.
38 Contrary to what is reported almost without exception – both in Great Britain and in Iraq – Madfaai did not 'defect' from the Ottoman Army to join Faysal's Great Arab Uprising during the Great War: he was captured by the British and then joined Faysal after interment in a prisoner of war camp in Egypt. For details, see Provence (2017), pp.57, 94, 105 & 217.
39 Awardi, pp.64, 66-67.
40 Awardi, pp.64, pp.66-69. The Northrop 8A-4D – or A-17 – was an export variant of the Douglas DB-8A, powered by the Right R-1820-G103 engine, and manufactured for Argentina, France, Peru and Great Britain. Eventually, the design was developed into the famous Douglas SBD Dauntless bomber operated in huge numbers by the US Navy during the Second World War. The 8A-4D was armed with four .30 (7.62mm) machine guns installed in the wing, and a single .30 in the rear cockpit. It was capable of carrying a bomb load of up to 600kg (1,200lbs) but, contrary to its legendary successor, it was not equipped for dive-bombing.

CHAPTER 3

1 Notably, even the Mufti of Jerusalem Hajj Amin al-Husayni, was not only a religious figure, but a former Ottoman Army officer: during the First World War he served with Mahmoud Salman at Izmir (see Marashi et al, p.59).
2 Sorby (2015), pp.29-30 & Marashi et al, p.52. All members of the Golden Square were Sunni Arabs, and former Ottoman Army officers that joined Faysal after he assumed power in Damascus. For example, during the First World War, Sabbagh fought in Macedonia and Palestine.
3 Sorby (2015), pp.32-34.
4 Sorby Jr., 'Iraq on the Eve of the Second World War', *Asian and African Studies*, Vol.17, pp.258-259 & Tripp, pp.100-101.
5 Sorby (2008), p.88.
6 Sorby, p.87 & Tripp, pp.101-102
7 Sorby (2008), pp.87-89 & Tripp, pp.102-103
8 When the Iraqis demanded that all flying at Shaibah stop, the British commander replied that any interference with 'routine training' would be considered a 'hostile act'. See Sorby (2008), p.88.
9 Without doubt, and as London knew from intercepting Italian diplomatic communications, Khaylani had contacted Berlin and Rome and requested arms and military support several times through April 1941. However, the response from the Axis powers was lukewarm. German Foreign Minister Joachim von Ribbentrop informed Adolf Hitler about the developments in Iraq and announced his expectation that the British would react with a military intervention. Correspondingly, he recommended that Germany support Khaylani's government with arms and the aircraft of the Luftwaffe. Moreover, on 8 April 1941 he wrote a letter to Khaylani convincing him that Germany was guaranteeing its support in the case of 'any war undertaken by the Arabs against the British…'. It is indisputable that Khaylani then requested air support in a message to Berlin on 17 April, and then not only weapons (preferably British-made, captured in France), but German troops on 24 April (and even more so on 28 and 29 April). However, obsessed with preparations for his megalomaniac invasion of the USSR, Hitler reacted in his usual fashion: hesitantly. He requested additional information regarding the capability of the Iraqi armed forces to resist a British military intervention. By the time von Ribbentrop eventually managed to convince him to send the Luftwaffe to Iraq, it was already too late, and then only a token force was deployed. On the contrary, there is no trace of evidence that Khaylani's policy as of April-May 1941 was motivated by anything other than pan-Arab nationalism; no trace of evidence that he staged a 'pro-Axis coup'; and no evidence of the Iraqi government planning military action against the British in Iraq. For details, see Sorby (2008), pp.87-104.
10 Sorby (2015), pp.30-31.
11 Awardi, p.64.
12 Awardi, pp.66, 151, 158.
13 Sorby (2008), p.103-104.
14 Sorby (2008), p.104; Bell, pp.39-40; Awardi, p.66.
15 Sorby (2008), p.104; Awardi, pp.140-141; Bell, p.41 & Cull et al, pp.42-43.
16 Sorby (2008), p.104.
17 Sorby (2008), p.104; Bell, p.41 & Cull et al, p.43.
18 Awardi, pp.66, 140-141 & Cull et al, p.43.
19 Awardi, pp.120 & 157. This was to remain the only confirmed loss of an Iraqi SM.79 during this war.
20 Bell, p.42 & Cull et al, p.43. Notably, losses of RAF units, elements of which were rushed to help the STFS during this battle were never recorded.
21 Sorby (2008), p.104 & Bell, p.41.
22 Awardi, p.135; Sorby (2008), p.104 & Bell, p.42.
23 Bell, p.42 & Awardi, p.141.
24 Cull et al, p.44.
25 Sorby (2008), p.104; Bell, p.43 & Cull et al, p.44.
26 Awardi, pp.141-142. Notably, Awardi stressed that Nos. 1, 2 and 3 Squadrons RIrAF did not fly any combat sorties during the war.
27 Ott, p.24. While his unit was designated Sonderkommando Junck in order to help cover-up its task, Junck received the official title Flyer Commander Iraq (*Fliegerführer Irak*): as such, he received the authority comparable to that of a divisional commander of the ground forces, even if actually commanding only a squadron-worth of aircraft and personnel.
28 Ott, p.23.
29 Ott, p.24. Convinced that they had encountered the first Messerschmitt over Iraq on 11 May, two days later the British launched a series of air strikes on Palmyra, deploying for this purpose Curtiss Tomahawks (the export variant of the US-made Curtiss P-40) and Blenheims from H-4 airfield in Transjordan. They claimed the destruction of two aircraft on the ground: both were over-laden He.111s, which the Germans were forced to abandon there after their tail-wheels were damaged on landing. Palmyra was attacked twice more on the morning of 15 May, when post-strike reconnaissance brought back photographs showing a burned-out He.111, and four other damaged aircraft (including one Ju.52). For details, see Bell, p.43.
30 Ott, pp.23-24; Sorby (2008), p.104; Bell, p.43.
31 Bell, p.43 & Ott, pp.25-26.
32 Ott, pp.25-26.
33 Cull et al, p.44 & Ott, p.26. The Bf.110 forced to land outside Fallujah was subsequently recovered by the RAF, repaired and test flown.
34 Sorby (2008), p.104; Bell, p.44; Ott, p.26.
35 Ott, p.26 & Cull et al, p.46. Additional information on the Italian involvement kindly provided by Hakan Gustavsson, May 2010. Once back in Greece, Junck desperately attempted to convince his superiors to reinforce his unit and send him back to Iraq. On 28 May, the decision was taken to use Ju.53/3ms of the K.Gr.z.b.V 104 to deploy a battalion of the Regiment for Special Purposes 800 Brandenburg (*Regiment z. b. V. 800 Brandenburg*), supported by three He.111s and five Bf.110s back to Iraq. In preparation for the new deployment, a single He.111 was sent to Mosul (via Aleppo) on 1 June: however, on arrival there the crew was nearly arrested by the new authorities, and managed to escape only at the last moment. When reports of this reached Berlin, the Luftwaffe's adventures in Iraq were over: instead of an entire battalion (supposed to wear Iraqi Army uniforms), only four of the Brandenburgers reached Iraq, and they were quickly withdrawn. (Ott, p.26).
36 According to Awardi (p.90), the commander RIrAF during the Anglo-Iraq War of 1941, Colonel Januby, fled with Khaylani to Persia, but returned to Iraq: he was arrested, court-martialled and shot by a firing squad on 5 May 1942.

CHAPTER 4

1 Awardi, p.67. According to the same source (p.90), Musli was born in Mosul in 1905, graduated from the Military School in Baghdad in 1925, and from Sandhurst in 1928. He underwent a pilot course at RAF Cranwell from 1930 until 1931, and then a staff course at the Military School in Baghdad a year later. After a few years in an operational unit, Musli served as a staff officer before being appointed as the commander of the RIrAF. After his career with the air force, Musli served as the Deputy Chief of Staff and then a Director at the Ministry of Defence in 1952-1953. Following his official retirement from the armed forces, he served as Minister of Social Affairs in 1954-1955. The three Gladiator Mk Is taken away by the British in 1943 were K6140, K6141, and K6147: the first and the third of these are known to have served with the No. 1412 and No. 1415 Meteorological Flights of the RAF during the mid-1940s.
2 Awardi, p.142.
3 Awardi, pp.69-70. Amongst the Gladiators known to have been sold to Iraq starting in 1942, were K7907, K7929, and K7989 (delivered in December 1942), N5780, N5825 (delivered in 1943 and 1944), and N5828, N5830, and N5857 (delivered in March 1944).

4 Awardi, p.121.
5 Tripp, pp.118-119.
6 Mason (1971), p.9.
7 Awardi, p.72; Cull et al, p.179 & Nicolle, p.58.
8 Cull et al, p.120-121.
9 Awardi, p.72 & Cull, pp.120-121.
10 Awardi, p.141 & Nicolle, p.58. Unless stated otherwise, the following data on RIrAF operations during the Palestine War of 1948 are based on interviews with Major-General Arif Abd ar-Razzaq (retired), 04/2002. Notably, Razzaq was one of the first entirely British-trained Iraqi pilots. He joined Class 20 of the Army College in Baghdad in 1941, graduated three years later and then joined the RIrAF, to graduate as a pilot on Course No. 9 (the first post-1941 course by the Flying School, RIrAF) in 1947. He was assigned to No. 1 Squadron and converted to Ansons during the same year. As of May 1948, he was undergoing conversion to Furies, when sent to fly Ansons in Transjordan: he completed that course only in September of the same year. After the Palestine War, Razzaq underwent multiple conversion, advanced flight, and navigational courses in Great Britain, before being assigned as a pilot to the Royal Flight in 1951 (Razzaq, interview, 04/2002 & Awardi, pp.93-94). Finally, according to Awardi (p.141), the RIrAF concluded that Abdullah was probably 'eaten by wolves'.
11 According to Israeli publications, no B-17s (or any other aircraft) of the nascent Israel Defence Force/Air Force were destroyed during Iraqi air strikes on Ein Shemer, Megiddo and Ramat David in 1948.

CHAPTER 5

1 Sorby (2003), pp.167-173.
2 Awardi, p.73 & Mason, p.9.
3 Sorby (2003), pp.174-194.
4 Razzaq, interview, 04/2002; Sorby (2004), pp.3-4; Awardi, p.74; Harrison (2004), p.58.
5 Razzaq, interview, 04/2002; Awardi, p.74 & Harrison (2005), p.19.
6 The Baghdad Pact (1955) and the Central Treaty Organisation (CENTO), *U. S. Department of State* (online release), 20 January 2001; Sorby (2004), pp.15-17 & Ovendale, pp.139-140.
7 Awardi, p.75 & Ministry of Defence of the Republic of Lebanon, 'History of Lebanese Armed Forces', 26 February 2010 (*lebarmy.gov.lb*). This short service of the T-6 Texan in the RIrAF – from 1951 until 1956 – is the principal reason why that type's presence in Iraq remains next to unknown and is not mentioned in any related Western publications and why no photographs of T-6s in Iraqi markings are available.
8 According to Awardi (p.92), Abadi was born in ash-Shamiya in 1913. He graduated from the Military School in 1934, joined the RIrAF and received his pilot wings in 1939. Following a staff course in Great Britain, he served as the Commander Flying School and then the Commander Nos. 5 and 7 Squadrons, before being appointed the Commander RIrAF in 1954, and the Commander of Arab Union Air Force (the short-lived union of Iraq and Jordan) in February 1958.
9 Unless stated otherwise, all details related to the operational service of Hawker Hunter in Iraq, and associated negotiations with London and Washington in the 1955-1958 period in this and the following sub-chapter, are based on Cooper et al, *Hawker Hunters at War*.
10 According to British researcher Andy Marden, reports according to which one of the first six Hunters made for Iraq crashed during a pre-delivery training flight on 10 November 1956, are wrong. Certainly enough, Iraqi pilot Gharib Mahmmoud, was forced to eject over the English Channel on that day, and, sadly, died of hypothermia after being thrown out of his dinghy in the heavy swell and then remaining too long in the cold water. However, Mahmmdoud flew a Hunter F.Mk 1 coded WT587, from No. 229 Operational Conversion Unit of the RAF on that occasion.
11 Ministry of Defence, P.S. to S. of S., 'U.S./U.K. Arms Supplies for Iraq', from 17 January 1958. Notably, it remains unclear if the 'Austers' mentioned in that report were actually British-made Auster Aircraft (or any of their sub-variants), or US-made O-1As.
12 Sadik, interview, 03/2005.
13 The 14 Tammuz Revolution was named after the date on which it took place: Tammuz was a Babylonian God of Fertility, after whom a month in the calendar was named. Subsequently, the name Tammuz was adopted to refer to a month in the summer season by many other calendar systems, including the modern-day Arab world, where it corresponds with July.
14 Sadik and Awardi, pp.120-121, 127-128, 134-135, 141-143, 150-152, 158-159, 165-167, 172, 179-180.

CHAPTER 6

1 Sorby (2007), pp.206-209 & Tripp, p.151.
2 Awqati was a particularly interesting officer. According to Awardi (p.94), he was born in Baghdad in 1915, and belonged to the first generation of native Iraqi officers. After graduating from the Military School in 1935 (with Class 12), he joined the RIrAF and graduated as a pilot on Course No. 5 in 1936, and then underwent a staff course in Great Britain. After a tour as staff officer at the RIrAF headquarters, he served as an instructor-pilot and then the Deputy Commander of the Flying School before converting to Furies and serving a tour of duty in Palestine in 1948. Back to Iraq, he was appointed the Commander Air Force College, but then sent into early retirement with the rank of Lieutenant-Colonel, for unknown reasons, in 1952. He was re-activated on Qasim's personal wish, advanced in rank to Colonel (and then to Brigadier-General in 1959) and appointed the Commander of the IrAF from 15 July 1958 until 8 February 1963. (Awardi, pp.93-94).
3 Sorby (2007), pp.208-209.
4 For details, see Cooper et al, *Hawker Hunters at War*.
5 Sorby (2007), pp.144-147 & Awardi, pp.76, 179-180.
6 Sorby (2007), pp.144-147; O'Ballance, p.67; Awardi, p.121 & Sadik, interview, 03/2005.
7 Razzaq, interview, 04/2002; Sadik, interviews, 03/2005 & 07-10/2007; Tobchi, interview 9/2019 & Awardi, pp.77-80.
8 Awardi, pp.175-176; Razzaq, interview, 04/2002 & Sadik, interviews, 03/2005 & 07-10/2007.
9 Sorby (2007), pp.144-147 & O'Ballance, pp.68-69.
10 Razzaq, interview, 04/2002; Sadik, interview, 03/2005 & O'Ballance, pp.72-73.
11 O'Ballance, pp.76-78 & Flintham, p.179.
12 For details on the Kuwait Crisis and the British military intervention of 1961, see Hooton et al, *Desert Storm, Volume 1*. The IrAF is not known to have been involved in any of the related operations by the Iraqi armed forces, which were actually limited to planning by the General Headquarters in Baghdad, and re-deployment of a single brigade from Baghdad in the direction of Basra.
13 Sadiq, interview, 03/2005.
14 O'Ballance, pp.80-89, 93 & Awardi, pp.179-180.
15 O'Ballance, pp.96-97 & Sorby (2009), pp.16-18.
16 Razzaq, interview, 04/2002; Sadik, interview, 03/2005; O'Ballance, pp.96-97 & Sorby (2009), pp.16-18. Notably, Munthir al-Windawy was not directly related to Jamal al-Windawy, but they both belonged to the same clan.
17 Razzaq, interview, 04/2002; Sadik, interview, 03/2005; Awardi, p.77-80 & Sorby (2009), p.20. One of the IrAF officers that fled to Jordan after the coup of February 1963 was Aboud Salem. He joined the Royal Jordanian Air Force and pursued a highly successful career, peaking with his tenure as the commander of that service, in period 1973-1976.
18 Razzaq, interview, 04/2002 & Sadiq, interview, 03/2005. Regarding Hardan Tikriti, and according to Awardi (p.94), he was born in Tikrit in 1925, graduated from the Air Force College with Course No. 10 in 1952, then underwent a staff course and commanded No. 3 Squadron before serving as the Deputy Commander Hurriyah AB in the early 1960s.
19 Cooper et al, *Hawker Hunters at War*, p.20 & Confidential Telegram No. 552, from the British Embassy in Baghdad to the Foreign Office in London, 21 May 1963, Air Ministry Files.
20 Confidential Telegram from the British Embassy to Baghdad to the Foreign Office in London, 30 May 1963, Air Ministry Files.
21 For further details, see Cooper et al, *Hawker Hunters at War*.
22 O'Ballance, p.106.
23 O'Ballance, & Sadik, interview, 03/2007.
24 Sorby (2009), pp.35-36, Sadik, interview, 03/2005; Saydoon, *Memoirs*. From what is known about his career, al-Windawy graduated from the Air Force College in the mid-1950s, and then converted to Hunters at RAF Chivenor with the second group of Iraqi pilots to do so, in 1957. Following his involvement in the revolution of 8 February 1963, he was advanced in rank to Lieutenant-Colonel and, as noted above, appointed as the commander of the Ba'ath's National Guard. After fleeing in November 1963, Windawy remained in Syria for the next four years: in 1967, all charges against him were dropped, and he was invited to return, which he did a year later. However, following the coup of 17 July 1968 (for details see below), and although remaining loyal to the Ba'ath Party, Windawy – the proverbial 'Maverick of the IrAF' – was de-facto exiled through appointment as Military Attaché to Iraq's Embassy in Bucharest, Romania. Deeply dissatisfied, he quit service and moved to Beirut in Lebanon. In 1973, Saddam Hussein asked him to return to Iraq once again. Windawy then joined the Iraqi diplomatic corps, from which he retired only in 1991. Subsequently, he moved to Marbella in Spain, and launched a tourism and trade business. Munthir al-Windawy was never to see Iraq again: he died in 2015 of heart complications – like so many Iraqis forced into exile.
25 Sadik, interview, 03/2007 & Awardi, pp.79-80.
26 Sorby (2010), pp.94-101 & Sadik, interview, 03/2005. In the UARAF, ex-Iraqi MiG-19S's were grouped with examples originally acquired by the UARAF in 1960-1961 to form the No. 20 Squadron. Instead of serials, they received the names of major Arab cities applied in white on their forward fuselages. While often serving ceremonial purposes, this unit also made a combat tour during the Yemen Civil War in 1966 (for details, see Cooper, *Hot Skies over Yemen, Volume 1*). Nearly all of the aircraft in question were destroyed and No. 20 Squadron disbanded during and after the June 1967 Arab-Israeli War, respectively. A detailed reconstruction of related affairs is to follow in a future volume of the Middle East@War series.

27 Sadik, interviews, 03/2005, 03/2006, 03/2007, 7-10/2007; Razzaq, interview, 04/2002; Awardi, pp.77-80 & Jones, p.133.
28 Sadik, interviews, 03/2005, 07-10/2007 & Jones, p.133
29 Air Marshal S Raghavendran, 'The Day I (Almost) Missed going to Iraq', 29 March 2015, *bharat-rakshak.com*
30 Sorby (2010), pp.94-95 & 100-103.
31 Sadik, interview, 03/2005.
32 Sadik, interviews, 03/2005 & 07-10/2007; Sorby (2010), pp.104-105.
33 O'Ballance, pp.108-111, 116-118, 123.
34 O'Ballance, p.126-129.
35 O'Ballance, pp.130-131 & Sadik, interview, 03/2006.
36 Sadik, interview, 03/2005 & Awardi, p.92.
37 O'Ballance, pp.133-135 & Sadik, interview, 03/2006.
38 O'Ballance, p.135 & Sadik, interview, 03/2006.
39 O'Ballance, pp.138-140 & Sorby (2018), p.218.
40 Sadik, interview, 03/2005 & Sorby (2011), pp.6-7.
41 Awardi, pp.175-176, 179-180 & Sadik, interview, 03/2005. For comparison, unofficial Russian sources quote the delivery of 'only' 18 MiG-21FLs to Iraq – but on basis of a Decree No. 1068-420 of the Soviet Council of Ministers from 19 January 1965. Obviously, subsequent negotiations between Baghdad and Moscow brought about changes in the Soviet planning. Particularly noteworthy is that this order included six reconditioned MiG-21F-13s from the 0-series: they are known to have remained in service as advanced trainers well into the mid-1980s. On the other hand, the Kh-66 remained such a secret, that it never received an ASCC/NATO-codename: together with the stock of K-5M missiles delivered with MiG-19Ps, but never used, all were rebuilt into unguided rockets in the late 1980s.
42 Awardi, pp.77-80.
43 Saydoon, *Pilot Memoir* & Sadik, interviews, 03/2006 & 03/2007.
44 See *Fishbed C/E Aerial Tactics*, Foreign Technologies Division, USAF (details in Bibliography).

CHAPTER 7

1 Sadik, interview, 03/2007 & 07-10/2007.
2 Sadik, interview, 03/2007 & 07-10/2007.
3 As far as is known, Major-General Riyadh was the best-educated, most professional, non-political officer in the Arab world of 1967, and probably also the greatest expert in regards of modern air defence operations. However, he was an outspoken critic of Field Marshal Abdel Hakim Amer, the Egyptian Minister of War and Commander-in-Chief of Armed Forces in 1952-1967. Therefore, Amer 'put him on ice' in 1965, while assigning him the post of the Air Defence advisor to the General Staff. Left with little else to do, Riyadh underwent further education and travelled around the Middle East, visiting multiple Arab armed forces, including the IrAF. By 1966, he became convinced – and began demanding – the establishment of an integrated air defence system for Egypt, Lebanon, Syria, Jordan, and Iraq, which would be capable of controlling and coordinating operations of all the local air forces. Understanding that the 'Arabs' were unlikely to obtain the best equipment available for such purposes, he expected that such a system would enable them to conduct a centralised offensive against the IDF/AF, thus making the expected Israeli mission – that of knocking out Arab air forces right at the start of the war – at least more difficult. Alternatively, such an integrated air defence system was to grant freedom of movement to the Arab ground forces. Amer turned down all his requests, and only granted permission for the establishment of an Air Defence Command as a separate branch of the Egyptian armed forces. Indeed, Amer was more than happy to remove this 'thorn in his side' by sending Riyadh 'into exile' in Amman, on 30 May 1967. In turn, Riyadh was bitterly disappointed by his new assignment and, upon arrival in Amman requested that the Jordanians relieve him, so he could return to Egypt to organise air defences there. King Hussein turned this request down. For details, see Jawadi, Chapter 2 and Fawzy, Chapter 8.
4 Mutawi, *Jordan in the 1967 War*, pp.108-109 & Sadik, interviews, 03/2007 & 07-10/2007.
5 Based on *History of the Iraqi Armed Forces, Part 17* (various chapters).
6 Sadik, interview, 03/2006 & 03/2007.
7 M. S. (retired IrAF Hunter- and MiG-21-pilot), interview (provided on condition of anonymity), 03/2007. Unless stated otherwise, all further details on Hunter and MiG-21 operations from H-3 during the June 1967 Arab-Israeli War are based on the transcription of the same interview, kindly provided by Sadik, 03/2007.
8 Jawadi, Chapter 2 & Fawzy, Chapter 8.
9 M. S., interview, 03/2007 & Sadik, interviews, 03/2006, 03/2007 & 07-10/2007.
10 For an extensive discussion of related affairs, see Cooper et al, *Hawker Hunters at War.*
11 Sadik (interview, 03/2007) recalled the serial number of the An-12BP in question as '508'. However, this serial number was worn by the first IrAF Tu-16. Most likely, the An-12BP destroyed by the Israelis at H-3 on 5 June was 505, which was never seen after 1967.
12 Sadik, interview, 03/2007.
13 Sadik, interview, 03/2007.
14 Sadik, interview, 03/2006. Majid at-Turki continued a successful career with the IrAF for two years longer. Sadly, he was executed on order of Saddam Hussein at-Tikriti in 1969, under the pretext of 'conspiracy against the state'.
15 Sadik, interview, 03/2007. According to Sadik, the IrAF-ID report in question was apparently drawing upon at least some of Israeli media reports, and various printed publications. The best available example of media reports is 'Killed in Explosion of Bomb they were Guarding', Jerusalem Post (English edition), from 8 June 1967.
16 'Woman Killed, 21 wounded in Netanya Bombing', *Jerusalem Post* (English edition), 7 June 1967.
17 Sadik, interview, 03/2007. According to Sadik (who based his recollection on an IrAF-ID report), Hussein's Tu-16 was first hit by a Matra R.530 missile that proximity fused and caused some damage to one of the engines. Eventually, so the Iraqis concluded, it was shot down by a HAWK SAM-site protecting Ramat David AB. The same report concluded that the Israelis credited this Tu-16 to the crews of their Bofors cannon because so many of these were killed in the crash of the bomber on their military base.
18 M. S. interview, 03/2007; Sadik, interviews, 03/2006, 03/2007 & 07-10/2007 & 'As the News Broke', *Jerusalem Post* (English edition), 8 June 1967.
19 Namiq Saadallah continued a successful career with the IrAF and flew MiG-21s during the October 1973 War with Israel, when he claimed one 'Mirage III' as shot down over Syria, at an unknown date. Samarrai continued flying Hunters and served as deputy squadron commander when shot down and killed by Israeli Mirages over the Sinai, on 8 October 1973.
20 Sadik, interview, 03/2007.
21 Due to their training in Great Britain, all Iraqi and Jordanian pilots – and thus also the Pakistani pilot assigned to No. 1 Squadron, RJAF – used English for their radio communications.
22 The Israelis never attacked the H-3 airfield again. However, late on 8 June, a lonesome Noratlas and three of their Aerospatiale SA.321 Super Frelon helicopters were dispatched in that direction to search for the downed crews. This group was forced to withdraw after the Noratlas came under attack from a Syrian MiG-21. Moreover, according to Sadik (interview, 03/2007), the Saudi and Iraqi troops actually found a total of three bodies, and the Israelis then demanded the return of five of their crewmembers (including the two captured alive). These were exchanged on 27 June 1967, on the River Jordan, before the Iraqis were able to identify the third Israeli that had been killed in the air combat over the H-3 airfield on 7 June 1967. Provided this report would be ever confirmed, it would mean that the IDF/AF actually lost four, not three aircraft over the H-3 on that day.

CHAPTER 8

1 Based on documentation kindly provided by Martin Smisek (including OMNIPOL Contract 117-0012, from 18 July 1968, acquired from the Military History Archive, Prague). Notably, the reason for such a quick conclusion of this deal was that the Iraqis first expressed their interest in Czechoslovak-manufactured aircraft in 1964, when Moscow – which was supportive of Barzani – was (still) reluctant to deliver additional arms to Baghdad. After three years of related talks, the conclusion of the Contract 117-0012 advanced extremely quickly. A conversion course for the first three Iraqi L-29-pilots – Sabah Saleh, Usmet Shawkat Khaffaf, and Waffiq Abdullah, all of whom were rated as 'excellent' by the Czechoslovaks – and 21 ground personnel ('Course 262') was organised and run by the Czechoslovak arms-exporting consortium OMNIPOL, between 1 September and 11 November 1967 of the same year: it took place in Czechoslovakia and was run in English.
2 Unless stated otherwise, the rest of this sub-chapter is based on Sadik, interview, 03/2005; O'Ballance, *The Kurdish Revolt*, pp.144-147; Styan, pp.88-89 & Trip, pp.188-189.
3 Sorby (2012), pp.297-306.
4 Sorby (2012), pp.309-314.
5 Sorby (2018), pp.218-220 & Tripp, pp.199-201.
6 Sorby (2018), pp.220-221; Tripp, pp.201 & O'Ballance, pp.151-152.
7 O'Ballance, p.156.
8 Sorby (2018), pp.221-222 & Tripp, pp 204-205.
9 Sadik, interviews, 03/2007 & 07-10/2007. Details on Iraqi orders for Zlins as provided by Martin Smisek.
10 Sadik, interviews, 07-10/2007 & Raspletin, 'History PVO'.
11 Contrary to widespread supposition in the West, all the officers of the Iraqi Air Force interviewed over time are insistent that they found diverse Soviet training manuals to be 'useless', and thus never used them. Instead, they all used 'British and US books'. Moreover, there is no evidence for the Soviets ever providing any kind of tactical training to any Iraqi fighter-interceptor, fighter-bomber or bomber-crews: if at all, something at least similar to tactical training was provided by the Czechoslovaks (Sadik, interviews 03/2005, 03/2006, 03/2007, 07-10/2007; M. S. interview, 03/2007 & Tobchi, multiple interviews, 2012-2019).
12 Sadik, interviews, 03/2005, 02/2006, 03/2007 & 07-10/2007.

ABOUT THE AUTHORS

TOM COOPER

Tom Cooper is an Austrian aerial warfare analyst and historian. Following a career in the worldwide transportation business – during which he established a network of contacts in the Middle East and Africa – he moved into narrow-focus analysis and writing on small, little-known air forces and conflicts, about which he has collected extensive archives. This has resulted in specialisation in such Middle Eastern air forces as of those of Egypt, Iran, Iraq, and Syria, and various African and Asian air forces. In addition to authoring and co-authoring more than 50 books – including an in-depth analysis of major Arab air forces during the wars with Israel in 1955-1973 – and over 1,000 articles, Cooper is a regular correspondent for multiple defence-related publications.

MILOS SIPOS

Milos Sipos is a Slovakian military historian. While pursuing a career in law he has collected extensive documentation on interconnected political, industrial, human resources and military-related affair in Iran, Iraq, and Syria. His core interest is a systematic approach to studies of their deep impacts upon combat efficiency and the general performance of local militaries. After more than 10 years of related work on the ACIG.info forum, he co-authored the much-acclaimed book 'Iraqi Mirages: The Dassault Mirage Family in Service with the Iraqi Air Force'. This is his second instalment for Helion.